Creating the
Congruent Workplace

Creating the Congruent Workplace

Challenges for People and Their Organizations

LLOYD C. WILLIAMS

Q

QUORUM BOOKS
Westport, Connecticut • London

Library of Congress Cataloging-in-Publication Data

Williams, Lloyd C.
   Creating the congruent workplace : challenges for people and their organizations /
Lloyd C. Williams.
      p.   cm.
   Includes bibliographical references.
   ISBN 1–56720–422–8 (alk. paper)
   1. Organizational effectiveness.   2. Work environment.   I. Title.
   HD58.9.W55   2002
   658.4'063—dc21   2001049185

British Library Cataloguing in Publication Data is available.

Library of Congress Catalog Card Number: 2001049185
ISBN: 1–56720–422–8

First published in 2002

Quorum Books, 88 Post Road West, Westport, CT 06881
An imprint of Greenwood Publishing Group, Inc.
www.quorumbooks.com

Printed in the United States of America

The paper used in this book complies with the
Permanent Paper Standard issued by the National
Information Standards Organization (Z39.48–1984).

10 9 8 7 6 5 4 3 2 1

This book is dedicated to all those who seek to
create newness in people, business, and groups
through a better understanding of balance.

*   *   *

To my partner, Anthony Edward Abbott Williams:
May your growth, integrity, honesty, and belief in
all people continue to propel me.

To business leaders and consultants everywhere:
Truly risk being congruent with who you are
in the work that you do!

Contents

Tables and Figures

Preface

I have focused on the issue of congruence for much of my professional career as a professor, writer, therapist, researcher, and consultant. In my book, *The Congruence of People and Organizations* (Quorum Books, 1993), the initial focus was on the issues of connectivity between people and systems. To address that connectivity, the issue was approached through the underlying values and belief systems that are created within organizations and societal systems. My book, *Organizational Violence: Creating a Prescription for Change* (Quorum Books, 1994), presented a strategy to address the actions and thinking of organizations that create separation among employees. The premise of the book was that the inconsistency of thought and action of organizational leaders creates a subparadigm of systemic violence impeding the ability of employees to act, thus reducing the effectiveness of the organization as a whole. My book, *Business Decisions, Human Choices: Restoring the Partnership Between People and Their Organizations* (Quorum Books, 1996), focused on the integration of people and system issues to create an effective pathway for change and development. The book introduced the Trinity System (the connection of people, business systems, and congruence characteristics) and focused on the integration of context, content, and process as behavioral strategies for change.

What has grown out of my twenty-seven years of consulting practice and research and publication efforts is the belief that incongruity occurs between people and organizations and among people within organizations. *When inconsistency between role prescription and role behavior prevails in the organizational setting, both the organization and the person become disconnected, disjointed, and dysfunctional. Such inconsistencies create historical and systemic dysfunction in organizations.* To test this belief, a Congruence Development

Model was developed and published in *Business Decisions, Human Choices* (Quorum Books) in 1996.

The model is a dual-process paradigm that requires the utilization of business and human characteristics to create effective alignment of thought and action in organizations, its leaders and managers. The model consists of six characteristics in each of two paradigms that create opportunity and capacity for people to sense completeness in their decisions and the implementations of those decisions. The two paradigms in the Williams Congruence Model are referred to as the Business Process Paradigm and the Human Process Paradigm. The purpose of the paradigms is to establish connection points for thought and action in business and human behavior, which will create the emotional and systemic tensions necessary for change. The more connectivity between thought and action, the more congruence between human behavior and organizational performance.

Each time one creates a new theory for embracing people and organizations, the challenges embedded in the process can either propel one to new heights or suppress one into moroseness. This book has had the former effect. I thank with all my heart my partner, Anthony Edward Abbott Williams. Without his support, cajoling, and humor, this book might not have been completed. For his help in getting this book to press, I will be eternally thankful. To my clients, their willingness to risk challenging their own congruity has helped me enormously in thinking and rethinking the theory and practice of this work. To my life mentors—Jack Gibb and Paulo Freire—their tutelage and vision have been and continue to be inspirations for me. To my publisher and friend, Eric Valentine, I can only say a most heartfelt thanks and appreciation for his willingness to press forward with writings that challenge the current paradigms of business and its relationship to humanity. He remains an inspiration to me, demonstrating that there are people of congruence out there in the business world making a difference. Finally, I thank all of my students at the John F. Kennedy School of Management, especially Patty Stokke and Curt Mandell, for their willingness to allow me to use two of their papers, and to my students at Clark Atlanta University.

Asante!

Introduction: Getting the Picture

A BEGINNING

The last half of the twentieth century saw massive mergers and acquisitions by means of attempts by which organizations sought to achieve growth by controlling other firms within their industry. Each time a merger and acquisition occurred, one resource within the organization was forgotten: the people. As the paradigm of business took control of organizational and societal decision making, an imbalance developed between the four capitals of congruent development within organizations and society: human, resource, political, and community capital. These capitals must be balanced if an organization, government, culture, or society values creating sustainability as the desired outcome of any effort it takes. The challenge looms even larger when one thinks of the global nature of organizations. Consider Microsoft, Phelps Dodge, Case Corporation, Andersen Consulting, Deloitte and Touche, and approximately one thousand other organizations that are focused on expanding market share. Each of these organizations has intervened in the lives of companies to expand their sense of business. Yet statistically, more than 50% of mergers and acquisitions fail within one year; 86% fail within two years; and almost 40% never get off the ground in a congruent manner, costing over $250 billion annually because of the failure rates in this process.

Unfortunately, current educational processes in master's of business programs see sustainability as only one strategy for organizational growth. Yet the process requires that sustainability not achieve the highest profits. To that end, many leaders of organizations have tried to grow and meet stockholder expectations by singular focused strategies on money and profit. The primary result has been mergers and acquisitions without regard to the less important partner in the process. A secondary result has been the recent departure of corporate executives from secure positions. In their departure, they have stated that the strategies currently employed are nonsensical and dysfunctional. There has been little to no balance of the other capitals in the actions of organizations other than resource gain. People, communities, and systemic approaches to networking have been the big losers.

This explicit dysfunction continues minute by minute. More and more of the new millionaires from corporations like Microsoft are leaving corporate America to delve into the third world of nonprofit ventures. When asked about their choices, they report that they needed to create a better balance in their lives and that remaining in corporate America would only destroy them, not enable them. One could say that the analytical process of due diligence and corporate growth was somehow flawed; yet that answer is too simplistic to frame the issues embedded in a doomed strategy for growth, change, and development. The larger issue becomes a challenge to the thinking paradigms that have driven the current decision processes of organizations. So what does help us understand the current events of organizations, and what helps us "jump start healthy change within organizations" to create sustainability in the future?

The Changing Paradigm of Thought and Action

The process of creating sustainable change, both personally and organizationally, is about the understanding and creation of reasoned balance (an equality in thought and action within the person) and alignment (a matching of organizational strategy to people success), a strategy that may be termed *congruence building*. This process explicitly focuses on creating a metanoic shift—a change in thinking—that establishes different outcomes for the work, growth, and change within organizations *and* among people. The Society of Human Resource Management states that employees spend more than 70% of their year at work. If that claim is true, then organizations and their leaders are challenged to create a more balanced life that is aligned with the long-term, sustainable needs of the employees, the community in which they reside, and the networks essential to healthy communal living, as well as attending to the critical issues of organizational success and sustainability. What blocks that movement are often the thinking and practice paradigms of organizations, leaders, and stockholders. What would the shift look like? How would one shift their thinking? Where could one explore honoring self and others? Where would one develop a sense of culture and society? What is the key to understanding these issues? *The key is congruence building—a new approach to personal, organizational, and business systems development.*

We continually believe that we can separate what we do at work from who we are in our lives at home. Instead we (1) lack *clarity* about who we are and what we do, (2) are unable to effectively *collaborate* with one another because the rewards of individuation outweigh the nuances and enlightenments of joint or collaborative efforts and ventures, (3) lack an awareness of the *complements* in our lives that create effective anchors for risking the development of change, (4) retreat from *creativity* and change, (5) abdicate personal and professional *choice* that creates codependency and systemic moroseness and the desire to simplify life and work, and (6) are unable to understand and embrace *complexity* which enriches and challenges us to go beyond the known and conscious to the unknown and unconscious to bridge the past, present, and future to be fully present in our personal and professional lives. Organizations have lost their direction, their connectivity to the entrepreneurship that created them and to their responsibility to their partners—the people. What we have lost and need to create is *congruence* in our personal and professional lives, which we may consider *the seventh thought paradigm.*

What is the significance of paradigmic thinking? Most fundamentally, paradigmatic thinking is critical to business and people development. Whether *classical* (no chaos, tight boundaries, company person), *scientific dynamic* (cause and effect driven, blame and shame—"not my fault" type of person), *communication cybernetic* (data driven to the point of no decision—"give me more information to get it right" type of person), *field* (test processes for decision making—"prove it to me/show me" type of person), *evolutionary* (change for change sake—change now—change every day type of person), or *process thought driven* (a balance and alignment in thought and action to the outcomes necessary—if it works and if it moves me and others type of person), the underlying thought process impacts, empowers, influences, and directs the actions of organizations. When that thinking is compartmentalized and controlled and when it is designed to protect and limit rather than understand and grow, then the process of imbalance, misalignment, and incongruence sets in, with people, and organizations the ultimate losers.

*Congruity and the process of becoming congruent may be defined as the creation and embracing of balance, alignment, integration, and transformation as the key anchors in understanding and reframing who we are, how we think, when we act, and what **context** drives our personal and professional development—our being if you will—versus the compartmentalized **contents** and soundbite **processes** that drive American living and corporate survival.* When we are asked daily to narrow our approach, provide our professional history in one page, give our managers all information in "bullets because they will not read," think only as the team will think, dress only as the organization perceives appropriate dress, look as European Americans look in order not to offend or threaten, we are continually participating in strategies that dishonor the uniqueness and the congruence of each individual for the sake of an ideal or belief that has little place in a world of global diversity and global differences. We are asked to create more imbalance and misalignment in our lives, and the cost is the loss of the critical congruence essential to the fluidity and flexibility essential to organizational and business growth and development.

This book, therefore, looks at the components of congruence and challenges people to embrace congruity through a paradigm and experiential shift. Although numerous approaches are available to create the shift, this book will look at one approach that was tested and validated in a recent research study.

THE NEED FOR CHANGE

Every day organizational leaders report difficulties in their efforts to create strategies that work without increasing dysfunction among their employees (National Bureau of Professional Management Consultants [NBPMC] 1999 Annual Report). A number of factors contribute to the manifold problems and barriers that haunt organizational leaders:

- Managers' failure to understand organizational strategies, thus affecting the comfort levels of the employees charged with implementing those strategies.
- Development of strategies that focus on one part of the organization without recognition of their impact on other areas of the company, creating problems that formerly did not exist.
- Continuation of unresolved issues, or one-way decisions, that only favor the organization, creating areas of mistrust and discomfort that prevent managers from effectively planning or developing strategies to resolve organizational and human resource issues.
- Differing mindsets between executive managers and descending levels of accountability within the organization, creating tangents in strategies that veer off track from the leaders' plans.
- Unclear or unsafe strategies that set employees up to fail, creating strategies for protecting employees rather than promoting the success of a product or service (NBPMC 1999 Annual Report).

Each of these issues seems to influence the health and sustainable development of organizational strategies. In addition, numerous theoretical concerns dating back to Karl Marx, Max Weber, and Emile Durkheim regarding the role of the distribution of labor versus the needs of organizations impact the successful development of balance strategies within organizations. Western society's initial understanding of how and why the division of labor should exist emerged from their writings, setting both the stage and the standards for modern-day thinking. However, there has been a continual division between people and organizational systems that continues even as this book is being written.

What is the real issue before us? What makes it difficult for employees, managers, and chief executives to work together to create strategies for success and sustainability? Somehow none of them—not even theorists—recognize that a *connectivity must exist between the actions and thinking of people and between the strategies and structures of systems, if congruence is to be accomplished for all*. That is the underlying premise of this book.

This book therefore explores the concept of congruence by framing the issues of thought and action. Thinking is the basis for real personal and organizational

Table I.1
Creating Congruence in the Workplace

CONGRUENCE PHASES	THOUGHT MOVEMENTS	BEHAVIOR MOVEMENTS		PROCESS TECHNOLOGIES
		Paradigms		
		Business	Human	
Analysis	Clarity Collaboration Complements	Empowerment Reciprocity Representation	Discord Emergence Disclosure	• Belief Systems • Four Capital Analyses • Ways of Knowing • Intrapsychic Structure • Paradigm Thinking Systems
Planning	Creativity Choice	Equality	Acknowledgment	• World Perspective • Strategic Planning • Detailed Work Breakdown Structure • Thematic Analysis
Intervention	Complexity	Interpretation Commitment	Self-Indulgence Reemergence	• System Connection Strategy (Theoretical Perspective) • Process Connection Strategy (Psychological Development)
Sustainability	Congruence	Wholeness	Congruence	• Historical Auditing (Thought Sustainability) • Process Paradigms (Behavior Sustainability)

movement to congruence. We are so trapped in our sound-bite society that we have lost sight of the real challenge that we face as people and systems. The loss discussed in this book is that of a society becoming dissociative—that is, a society unable to create effective bonds, relationships, and connections with one another and with the world—and afraid to risk becoming fully human. Table I.1 identifies the total structure of the congruence process that will be discussed in this book. As will become evident, many components go into an understanding of congruence for people and organizations. What is really important is recognizing that all components should be accomplished if congruence is to truly be an outcome of your organizational development.

Chapter 1 begins with a discussion of congruence, a definition of terms, and a perspective on personal and organizational movement. Chapter 2 explores the concept of thinking and describes six paradigms of thought that currently govern the thinking processes of people and organizational systems in our society. Chapter 3 explores the theoretical history and framework for thinking about congruence as C^6. Congruence is looked upon as an exponential development. The more one understands, the more the concepts expand, thus creating growth through thinking and acting that enhance personal and systemic development. Chapter 3 also presents a comprehensive history of congruence and examines the connections of congruence to anthropologic and ethic alignments.

Chapters 4, 5, and 6 focus on the issues of discovery and analysis. Clarity—creating comprehensive understanding; collaboration—creating effective partnerships and team approaches to human and organizational performance; and complements—understanding and developing the anchors that can ensure personal and organizational success around the work—are the components of analysis. Historically, the analysis of organizational performance centers on the behavioral outputs that either succeed or fail based on an established plan. These chapters show how thinking impacts the success of organizations and what needs to be explored if the success strategies are to work.

Chapters 7 and 8 explore the movement necessary for congruence thinking based on the discovery process. Chapter 7 looks at the area of creativity and challenges conventional notions of innovation and renovation—prevalent actions and thought processes of families and business. Chapter 8 then discusses choice and its ability to empower or disempower us in life and work.

Chapter 9 focuses on the intervention strategy—moving to complexity. This chapter takes an andragogical, respectful approach to change and development rather than a banking educational—pedagogical approach that has not always served people and business well.

Chapter 10 puts it all together, with the focus extending from the behavioral issues embedded in *Business Decisions, Human Choices* from 1996 to the thought issues of this book. Chapter 11 discusses implementation of this strategy through a medical complex. Chapter 12 brings the reader full circle with a discussion of differing strategies for use of the system.

Hopefully, what you read here will mark the beginning of an exploration that will put you on the path to becoming a more fully cognizant and balanced human being.

Creating the
Congruent Workplace

Chapter 1

The Destruction of Balance in Our Personal and Professional Lives and the Need for a Change

STATEMENT OF THE PROBLEM

The lived experiences of employees within organizations are seldom considered valid expressions of meaningful information that leaders of organizations can use to create change, movement, and direction. Executive decisions are most often based on quantitative data provided by departments on past performance and on narrow (variance avoidance) research within organizations. However, other sources of information are available to organizations as they prepare strategies for change and development. These sources include e-mails, memos, reports, retreats, focused discussions, and other records of interactions within an organization. Organizations historically rely less, if at all, on these records to provide some understanding about what happens within the organization. As a result, valuable qualitative data generated from the lived experiences of managers and executives often take a back seat to more traditional quantitative data.

Every employee has a number of sources for data collection. These sources—conversations, coffee breaks, rumors, family experiences, and dialogues—inform and shape their thinking while impacting the actions they take in both work and play. These informal, nonscientific data sets often influence the direction and actions of people more than the quantitative information that is available. Consider the number of times you have said—*"they can make numbers say anything—I don't trust their data—they didn't ask me, so they don't consider what I have to say as important."* In those statements is embedded the influence of phenomenological inquiry—lived experiences—that is seldom used in an organization's decision making.

Within every organization are phenomenological (lived experiences and appearances) and hermeneutic (biased interpretive) data that can impact the *think-*

ing and actions of managers. Often discounted is the utilization of these data to enrich and streamline the actions of organizational leaders. These data were often suspect, and therefore, were considered anecdotal—not for business consumption. Generally, safety was the norm, and quantitative information was the answer to data required for decision-making, structure development, environmental happiness, or manager/employee satisfaction.

Most organizations continually face struggles in developing approaches needed to achieve the outcomes defined by organizational leaders and stakeholders *without* destroying the employees and managers charged with accomplishing those outcomes. Research (Burke, 1997; Jennings, 1998; Maier, 1997; Mallinger, 1997) suggests that some strategies may create disruptions in the behavior and thoughts of employees and managers, thereby reducing the effectiveness of an organization. Burke's research focused on ethical issues; Jennings' on gender and employee performance; Maier's on organizational transformation and its challenges in corporate strategy; and Mallinger's on decision making. Each researcher stated that there was a *central core missing* in creating organizational effectiveness.

Senge, Covey, Burke, Bennis, Sommerville, Goldsmith, and numerous other researchers have posed many questions regarding the causes of organizational failure. These questions center on development of a core understanding of what creates organizational and employee success. Each speaks to the need to align people with organizational outcomes; *yet none states what that sense of alignment or balance must look like.* As this discussion among theorists continues to evolve, it is believed that focusing on the concept of balance and alignment will generate the necessary framework for the strategies managers and organizations can use to provide a better path to organizational and managerial success. Years of consulting have demonstrated that the lived experiences, stories, and accounts of employees are an important vehicle for discovery. Even with that belief, however, developing a perspective to identify or describe the issues without numbers is difficult.

The challenge in such an application is determined by the definition of terms used to frame the issues for exploration and discovery. *The challenge in this book was to explore a concept of congruence as applied to the development of more effective managerial and organizational performance, through the use of a thematic analysis methodology.* The challenge was predicated on the assumption of a gap between organizational and people development as postulated by Daniel Goleman in his book *Emotional Intelligence* (1995: xiii–xiv) where he said,

If there is a remedy (to the dysfunctions of people), I feel it must lie in how we prepare for life. At present we leave the emotional education of our children to chance, with ever more disastrous results . . . I can foresee a day when education will routinely include inculcating essential human competencies such as self awareness, self control, empathy, the art of listening, resolving conflicts and cooperation.

In the *Nicomachean Ethics* (a philosophical inquiry into virtue, character, and the good life), Aristotle's challenge is to manage our emotional life with intelligence.

Our passions when well exercised, have wisdom; they guide our thinking, our values, our actions, and our survival. The question of appropriate emotion is essential to effective being in the workplace, in society, and in our own lives. Somehow we have lost that connection, and in that loss, we have removed from our thinking and acting the necessity of emotion in our decisions and in our practice.

Goleman's research and statements were explicitly directed at the actions of individuals; however, organizational leaders and managers are also confronted with the issues of human emotion, competencies, group and team awarenesses, team and individual control, and the resolution of conflict. Whereas Goleman speaks of the actions of the individual, the present volume explores the same concerns through use of five determinants of managerial success: decision making, structure, people behavior, organizational environment, and satisfaction.

Goleman's statement addresses the relationship between the structure and functioning of the human brain and human emotions and, thus, the consequences of this relationship for human behavior and development as individuals and as groups. By implication (throughout the entire book), Goleman asserts that we do not have an understanding of this relationship and its impact on human learning and behavior. Furthermore, Goleman asserts that our lack of understanding of the brain/emotion relationship and its consequences for group and individual development and behavior is the missing piece in our definition of human intelligence, thus causing a deficit in the education of the young. It seems fitting, therefore, to use Goleman's analogy to support the direction of this study. If there is a connection between the human brain and emotion, can there be effectiveness in organizations without congruence—as an analogy to Goleman's perspective? Can there be movement in the world of business through compartmental actions–disconnected actions, or does real movement require some understanding of both the concept of congruence and congruent actions in the creation of strategies for change and development? Can congruence occur within organizations if only the needs of the organization are met? If the needs of employees are also essential to the success of the organization, how might the organization ensure the balance and alignment of the employees and the organization? Can an analysis of lived experiences yield the necessary information that governs the future of organizational change and development?

Similarly, can individuals achieve personal congruence where they sense that their sustainability in the workplace is based on acting like everyone else in the workplace when they don't perceive themselves as being themselves? What happens to personal/individual contributions in the workplace when one must operate through a personal façade? If your family operates on the basis of a communal value set, and yet the workplace focuses on individuation, what will happen to your ability to contribute?

A study conducted by the American Society for Training and Development in 2000 examined the average annual training expenditures of more than 500 U.S.-based publicly traded firms. The study concluded that firms in the top half of the group (i.e., firms that spent the most on training) had a total stockholder return that was 86% higher than that of firms in the bottom half and 46% higher than the market average. Studies such as this one reveal that the right kind of investment in people will generate exponential returns. Yet, what happens each time the stock market hiccups? Look at any paper from any city and you will discover massive layoffs from corporations and increases in compensation for executives who do the laying off.

DEFINITION OF TERMS

The following are key terms essential in developing a common language for use by readers. Throughout this book, these terms will help elucidate various aspects of congruence.

Congruence

Congruence is the state or quality of being in agreement, correspondence, or harmony with one's self in a personal environment or with one's role in an organizational environment. Congruence in the context of organizational action is the consistency and continuity of organizational policies and strategies that (1) create an effective roadmap for managers and employees to understand the content areas and (2) will drive their organizational thinking and individual performance to ensure the success of the organization (Williams, 1996). As an example, congruence can be seen in an employee changing and growing through training programs offered by an organization. Over time, she recognizes that the changes are without alignment because she lacks the formal education to support her changes. She proceeds and completes a bachelor's degree to round out her experience in her job. Ultimately, the change creates opportunity and a more satisfying alignment in the work world.

Alignment

Alignment is bringing together the components of a whole, as prescribed by organizations or individuals, into close cooperation (Williams, 1994). This coalescence determines the healthy or unhealthy relationships that frame decision making, people behavior, environmental changes, and structural directions of organizational and people actions. An example is the process of team building whereby actions are based on ensuring completeness with some structure, decision, or people behavior required by the organization. It can focus on development of a project management schedule that blends people time and resources with organizational timelines and resources.

Congruence Theory

Congruence Theory (Rogers, 1956; Williams, 1993, 1994, 1995, 1996) is an identification of components that establish boundaries or frameworks for achieving alignment and harmony among people and systems. An example is an organization's decision to include its customer base in the strategic planning process as well as its employee and shareholder base. If all pieces of the system are not considered, the system is incomplete; therefore, any analysis performed on the system will be incomplete.

Phenomenology

Phenomenology is the study of appearances in both people and organizations that establish definitions and descriptions for (1) people's work behavior and (2) people's organizational social behavior (Denzin, 1989). An example is the disparity of perspectives on the verdict in the O. J. Simpson trial. There was a perception that African Americans were happy about the acquittal, and that European Americans were enraged by the same acquittal. Appearances differed for the two groups, therefore creating differing perspectives regarding the validity and importance of the trial's outcomes. This process of lived experiences gives rise to the utilization of phenomenological inquiry. Phenomenological inquiry can help explain disparities. Phenomenological inquiry, therefore, looks at how people experience themes that emerge from appearances and establish generalizations.

Decision Making

Decision making is the act of choosing among alternative courses of action utilizing a set of facts within a rational frame (validation of data) to settle a dispute or to create a set of outcomes (Williams, 1994, 1995, 1996). From families to organizational systems, facts and the framework that drive one's thinking can alter the decision-making act or the process and procedures that form the actions. This process (valid or invalid) looks at how decisions are created, implemented, and evaluated and at their impact on the facts developed.

Horizonalization

Horizonalization (Horizonal) is a phenomenological reduction technique. Horizonal (lived) experiences make conscious the experiences of individuals and create perceptions of experiences that will remain forever, even though the contents of conscious life appear and disappear. Moustakas believes that we experience things that exist in the world from the vantage point of self-awareness, self-reflection, and self-knowledge. The phenomenological reduction makes it possible for the mind to discover its own nature (Moustakas, 1994: 95).

People Behavior

People behavior is the manner in which people conform to or rebel against the prevailing standards of decorum, and it implies the direction or guidance of one's actions in a specific way (Argyris, 1983, 1985; Gibb, 1973, 1982, 1986). An example is the differences in gender, age, and sexual orientation that create behavioral actions different from the norm expected in a family or organization. This action traditionally generates a reaction that is designed to control and insulate behavior in order to ensure the comfort of the larger society, not the individual. Policy and job design are additional examples. People behave according to what they believe organizational policies require, and they work within the framework of a job design or job description. However, actions outside of prescribed roles or actions within the prescribed roles determine the behavior analyzed by the organization and the peers of the individual.

Structure

Structure is the arrangement and interrelation of all parts of a whole that establishes the boundary of organizational functioning (Gibb, 1978). One example is an organizational design that establishes hierarchy in a tiered fashion, slowing down the decision-making process when the nature of the work needs a horizonal structure for quicker decision making.

Environment

Environment is the interface between people and organizations and between organizations and the community (Williams, 1996). An example is the importance of Apple Computers choosing to pull out of Texas because its environment was too different from the environment in California. Apple determined that the impact on its employees and its organizational culture would be too great.

Employee Satisfaction

Employee satisfaction is the recognition that one's expressed needs, expectations, and desires have been met through the organization's structure, environment, people behavior, and decision making (Williams, 1994). An example can be employees believing that the more an organization promotes, compensates, and increases an employee's status, the more they will be satisfied with the organization.

Manager Satisfaction

Manager satisfaction is the recognition that one's expressed needs, expectations, and desires have been met through the organization's structure, environment, people behavior, and decision making, and further, that the structure, policies, and procedures of the organization provide a rational framework by which managers can direct the activity of employees such that employee satisfaction is achieved in the accomplishment of organizational outcomes (Williams, 1994). For example, managers believe that the organization's decisions and rules help create effective pathways for them to direct employee action in their approach to work.

Equality

Equality is the state of creating sameness in quantity, class, group, or society. It is the state of creating impartiality and tranquility of mind or mood by creating identical values (*Webster's Dictionary*, 7th ed., 1997). Equality in the decisions and actions we take focuses on the ability of the individual or organization to strategically balance effective work actions, strategies, policies, or procedures *with concern for the skills of the people, the cultures driving people's thoughts and beliefs, and the limitations of the organization based on policies and procedures encountered in doing the work.*

Reciprocity

Reciprocity is the process of creating mutual dependence, action, or influence, or of creating mutual or equivalent exchange. Reciprocity focuses on ensuring proportional return for work done by the organization and the team, individual, or manager. Praise, money, job retention, and promotion are all based on reciprocity. If you do not take care of my organizational and personal needs within the organization, then there is no need to take care of your personal or organizational needs (Hammer and Organ, 1978).

Empowerment

Empowerment is the process of trusting individual creativity to accomplish planned outcomes of work. In the workplace, empowerment involves increasing organizational flexibility in policies and strategies to frame the boundaries of the work to be accomplished. Empowerment can cause a reduction of fear-based strategies within the organization, creating capacity for expanding the role of employee influence and innovation to meet long-term organizational needs.

Representation

Representation is the act of participation to ensure the inclusion of one's thoughts, feelings, or actions in the outcomes and opinions that can affect a change in one's current state of being or work. Representation is the companion of equality and reciprocity where the inclusion of everyone impacted by the decision is considered prior to any decision, action or policy (Williams, 1996).

Interpretation

Interpretation is the act of explaining or translating the meaning of beliefs, judgments, or circumstances that influence one's factual experiences. The interpretation of any organizational or managerial action focuses on the ability of the decision to meet and balance organizational and employee need. As interpretation usually focuses on the organization's need to meet a cost/profit or service outcome, the organizational need will usually be considered first. However, the decision will be inappropriate if employee needs are not balanced by the decision (Williams, 1996).

Commitment

Commitment is the consistent determination to stay focused on all parts of the decision process to ensure maximum "buy-in." Without buy-in, commitment begins to dissipate and create problems in understanding personal and organizational rationales.

Discord

Discord is the lack of agreement or harmony (as between persons, things, or ideas). Discord represents the extent to which one is uncomfortable with emerging perspectives and change. In the workplace, discomfort may be caused by exclusion, disregard, being discounted, or unresolved issues that suggest an individual is not valued. The more one responds to being valued, the more difficult one becomes regarding perceived exclusions.

Emergence

Emergence is the development, as a natural and logical consequence—or evolution—of biological, emotional, or philosophical theories involving the appearance of new characters and qualities (as life and consciousness) at more complex levels of organization that cannot be predicted solely from the study of less complex levels. As we develop, we change. Yet it is often hard to change when we have a history that speaks to each of us, governing how we function.

The challenge is to honor our changing process and have the integrity to acknowledge what is happening within us (Williams, 1996).

Acknowledgment

Acknowledgment is the recognition of a new thought, feeling, belief, or action that impacts both personal and organizational understanding. Acknowledgment is also the inclusion of others in the changes developing in the recognition of beliefs or actions in the person within a group. In the context of the Williams Congruence Development Model, acknowledgment is recognizing that as we become more comfortable with our changes internally, it is important that we share these changes with others. This is to ensure that they understand who we are, what we value, how we are changing, and what impact it has on our interactions with one another.

Disclosure

Disclosure is the stating of our values and beliefs in our work and our play. Too often, people focus on what they sense the organization or the family requires rather than on what actually exists. Disclosure is openness in expressing one's true values, beliefs, feelings, and attitudes.

Self-Indulgence

Self-indulgence is the focus and development of one's own views to the exclusion of another view. It is the unfortunate perspective that "I am the only one who is right and you are wrong" to the extent that I harm, destroy, or manipulate others to prove a point. Arrogance is the actualization of self-indulgence, and dishonesty is the hallmark of this state of being.

Reemergence

Reemergence is a reawakening of values and beliefs that cause people to rethink their positions and to challenge their own behaviors in their development of people congruence. Some call such behavior a move to integrity and fairness; others may call it the reawakening of spiritual values; and still others say it is understanding humanity. It is the aligning of who one is to what one does.

Dual-Process Paradigms

Dual-process paradigms are connecting frames for viewing the world in the actions of businesses and the processes of people. The paradigms, as world views, focus on the integration of multiple anchor points that are required to achieve a comprehensive whole for business and people action. In the case of materials for this study and the Williams Congruence Development Model, dual-process paradigms are the integrating and intersecting frames of business holism and human holism that influence personal and organizational thinking. These two frames are the lenses through which managers and executives assess their ability to make decisions and achieve performance outcomes within an organization.

PERSONAL AND ORGANIZATIONAL MOVEMENT

So where do we begin the discussion of change? For the past fifty years, *behavioral strategies* have been employed to create change. Whether in employee groups within organizations, in families raising children, or in leaders determining strategies, behavior has driven the process of change. The existing database, however, suggests that behavior has not made the difference.

When you look at the 1929, 1987, 2000, and 2001 downturns in the stock market, organizational strategies have all employed the same behavioral strategies—to reduce the organizational size. *Business Week* (March 1, 1999), citing the 1999 Emerging Workforce Study, estimates the average cost of losing a worker at $50,000. The same study also reports that 41% of employees who rate their company's training offerings as poor plan to leave their company within a year. The study suggests that continual downturns are a result of the strategy employed and that workforce concerns are based on the inability of companies to divert resources to the development of their workers. To that end, the study suggests that a 1,000-worker company with ineffective training stands to lose $14.5 million a year.

Similarly, the existing research on mergers and acquisitions by *The Economist* (July 22, 2000) cites global research from KPMG International where they reported that half of all global mergers and acquisitions destroy shareholder value because of miscommunication, inefficiency, mistrust of employees, deliberate discount of employees, and cultural conflict.

Consider the plight of marriages, of developing children, and of employees in the workforce. Daily data and current research show that valuing the person occurs only when the person acts outside of the expected norms of the society. When a child shoots another, when a person commits rape, when an employee brings a gun to the workplace or threatens a manager, when a spouse is involved in domestic violence—when any person acts outside the norm—then and only then is there a concern for the person.

Economic development is valued more than human development, and political power is valued more than human power. Money has become the supreme god of all, and as a result all of us have lost.

How can one begin to shift the paradigms of organizational and personal misalignment? What does one employ to right the balance? *We start with our thinking, not our behavior!*

Chapter 2

The Challenge to Think Differently: Explorations into Our Organizational Thinking and Its Impact on Our Lives

Thinking differently is a critical component of becoming congruent. When thinking about this book, the first issue that came to my head was how the change process occurs within people and systems. Over the past twenty-five years, focus on the behaviors that block successful movement has been the preferred strategy of theorists, consultants, educators, and business leaders. This movement has challenged the actions of employees, managers, and leaders in the business sector as well as families in their development of children and each other in their quest to build character and conformity in this society. Yet in this quest to ensure a level of conformity in business and family development, both people and systems have lost the essential creativity that drives both individuation and collaboration.

Instead, society has been treated to uncontrolled competition among people and groups and to unbridled conformity that condemns any form of difference or diversity. From the clothes that people must wear to the hairstyles deemed appropriate and reactions to differing perspectives, business and families have become less willing to tolerate any challenge to common perspectives or standards. The insistence on conformity has diminished the complexity and diversity of life and work. We therefore find ourselves struggling to respond, rather than react, to differences that were not part of our original strategies. Children don't understand how to deal with bullying, managers don't manage conflict effectively, leaders can't lead, and families can't raise children. All have lost because the focus on behaviors has left out a critical ingredient—*thinking*.

With regard to thinking, Freud spoke of a perceptual, memory, and consciousness system in his *Interpretation of Dreams*. Freud stated that the perceptual system must be organized in a manner permitting the restoration of one's thoughts, beliefs, and values to a resting state. In contrast, his memory system process must be capable of undergoing permanent modification. Freud believed that memory was between one's perception and one's consciousness. Consciousness was Freud's explanation for receiving input from both perception and memory, and it represented the special qualities of psychic "ahas" in the lives of individuals. Thus, the use of Freud's perspective might suggest that when people get ahas, they begin to think differently and to raise their level of consciousness for action or motor trends in his words. If this perspective is true, then the more consciousness arises in the lives of people and organizations, the more the ahas and the greater the possibility that one's thinking might unleash a more rational way of being and becoming in the world.

When we look at current organizational and personal action, we are told that if you change your behavior, it will change your thinking. The psychological process, however, suggests that to truly change your behavior, you must change your thinking first. Most business consultants, leaders, and managers (and most fathers, mothers, siblings, and friends, too) suggest that if you just change your behavior, everything will fall into place. This is not true. Change your thinking and your behavior has a chance for newness, growth, opportunity, and success. If you change your thinking about families, then you can see the possibilities of alternative structures (single parents, gay and lesbian parents, etc.). If you can change your thinking about work and success, then it is possible to see and experience the value of being yourself at work rather than a facade that you perceive will allow you to be successful. If you can change the paradigm for who is the client, then you can broaden the sense of client to include human and community capital—not just money and politics. Thinking sets the stage for newness, regeneration, change, and development; action alone does not.

Figure 2.1 represents a systems thinking paradigm chart created to explore the issues of thinking within organizations and people. You will notice that the top of the figure describes a classical thinking paradigm for looking at the world. In this classical thinking frame, no chaos or lack of chaos, tight boundaries for what is allowable, clear hierarchical authority, and Cartesian-compartmentalized thinking are valued as essential to the world view. This mode of thinking is that used by approximately 84% of the world's corporations and business structures, even when the policies of those organizations differ.

The second thinking paradigm, scientific dynamic thinking, represents the compartment theory thinking of Newton by which he proposed that cause and effect always exist in the actions of people and systems. The premise for this paradigm was that elements of a system are connected, and when one works or tweaks one aspect of the system, all other aspects will be automatically corrected. Unfortunately, this cause and effect system of thinking has not panned out either in the work world or in family life. Thus, the system created a blame and shame focus on thinking. Although the society has operated predominantly from classical thinking, the secondary or stress mode in the classical model has been the scientific dynamic thinking of blame and shame. Think of the times in your organization when people stated that they were not at fault for an error,

Figure 2.1
Williams's Paradigms of Thought and Action

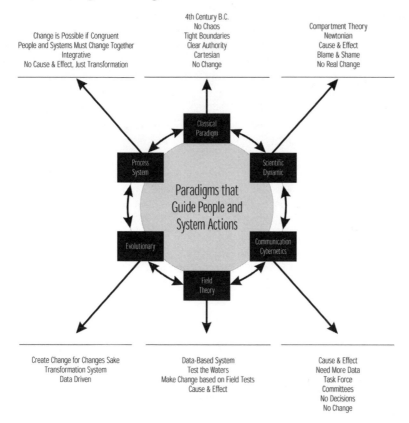

4th Century B.C.
No Chaos
Tight Boundaries
Clear Authority
Cartesian
No Change

Change is Possible if Congruent
People and Systems Must Change Together
Integrative
No Cause & Effect, Just Transformation

Compartment Theory
Newtonian
Cause & Effect
Blame & Shame
No Real Change

Classical Paradigm

Process System

Scientific Dynamic

Paradigms that Guide People and System Actions

Evolutionary

Communication Cybernetics

Field Theory

Create Change for Changes Sake
Transformation System
Data Driven

Data-Based System
Test the Waters
Make Change based on Field Tests
Cause & Effect

Cause & Effect
Need More Data
Task Force
Committees
No Decisions
No Change

that someone else had done it. Society generally does not reward anyone for honesty or for making mistakes. The normal mode of our society has instead been to blame someone and punish. Consider the supervisor in the Los Alamos fire and employees in an organization who risk being penalized when a new strategy doesn't work. Consider your own family history. Remember when you tried something new and got punished when it did not work or when your actions existed outside of the norm of the family. *In these two thinking styles, risking, changing, growing, and becoming are anathema to the values of the thinking system.* Finding something new, trying something new, becoming someone different are not valued. Almost 94% of all businesses operate from this thinking mode.

The third paradigm in the figure is the communication cybernetic paradigm. This has been called the government paradigm because it is required for more data. The process of thinking for this paradigm is as follows. The organization needs an answer on a strategic planning problem. To ensure that it gets the best information, a task force is created. The task force takes four months to complete its work and produce the needed data. The manager says, "This is great—however, we need to get the perspective of some key players, so let's create a focus group committee." Now the organization shifts to the focus group, and two months later it reports the results. The manager again says "great job" but adds that community hearings must be held to ensure that the data are correct. Now the process shifts to community meetings, and the materials are presented three months later, with the manager stating that now the politicians need to give their input. However, they can't meet for another four months, and so on and so on. We are now stuck with the nondecision-thinking paradigm. This paradigm is characterized by an inability to make a decision, accept responsibility, or be accountable for one's actions. Consider your own experiences. When you have experienced the blame and shame paradigm, you often become gun shy and are unwilling to risk being accountable or out in front on any decision. Therefore, you make no decision (which in itself is really a decision).

The next paradigm of thinking is the field theory paradigm, or what I call the Missouri paradigm. It is governed by the concept of the "show me—prove it" thinking process. In this paradigm, movement from the historical stance of the organization occurs only when the movement has been "field tested," providing assurances that it works and that it integrates effectively with other aspects of the organization. It is, however, a cause and effect system like the scientific dynamic system. Blame and shame become underlying paradigmic concerns in this thinking process.

With these four systems of thinking, we have now covered approximately 98% of all organizational entities—profit, nonprofit, and government—in the society. Sadly, all four paradigms have as a critical ingredient of the thinking process the idea of *no change!* No change is the bottom line of all four paradigms and motivates the actions of organizations and organizational leaders in these thinking processes. When you work for a classically thinking organization, any effort to create change will be thwarted. When you work in a scientific dynamic thinking organization, all effort to create real change will result in no change, as well as blame and shame for your efforts. When you work for a communication cybernetic organization, all effort to speed up the process or create change in the processes of the organization will be met with resistance to the extent that one becomes frustrated with the slowness of the process, and no change again is the outcome. When one works for a field theory thinking organization, the field testing process is usually so cumbersome that change again is thwarted. We all have worked for these types of organizations. Often the result is that who we are, what we believed, and how we operate to survive are confounded by the thinking processes of the organization, and so the incongruence grows in us and in the organization.

As we return home to our families, significant others, and friends after work, the frustrations of the day are repeated in the actions of our personal lives. John Gedo and Arnold Goldberg (1973: 72) state that

Table 2.1
Thought Paradigms

Thought Paradigm	Personal Value in Thought Paradigm
Classical	Status Quo—Keeper of the Flame
Scientific/dynamic	Political Skill and Aptitude
Communication/cybernetic	Caution and Safety
Field	Credibility
Evolutionary	Change
Process	Transformation

a model always illustrates a principle of construction or operation, it is a symbolic projection of an object which need not resemble it in appearance at all, but must permit one to match the factors of the model with respective factors of the object, according to some convention. The convention governs the selectiveness of the model and thus governs the actions and behaviors within the model.

In effect, the thinking models of organizations and of individuals are the explanatory maps for analytical data. Whether one talks of psychoanalytic theory, organizational theory, business modeling, or interrelational grouping, the model of operation sets the stage for analysis and action. The thoughts that govern and bind are the thoughts that heal or create rifts. In the unfortunate case before us in organizational and personal development, the governing thoughts revolve around the destruction of the person, the family, the group, and the organization. As long as we continue on this path of destruction, congruence never becomes a picture in one's mind, heart, or being—congruence becomes a nonword, nonthought, nonaction, and everyone loses for failing to attain congruence.

There has been a monumental shift in the workplace and the family over the last generation. The primary change has been the inability to look at both change and balance. When the primary paradigm of organizational life is no change, the impact in the mental model is the person's inability to embrace change. So when change is presented as an option, either for personal advancement or organizational development, there appears to be an all-out attempt to destroy the concept of change.

Even though there is a thought process for the entire paradigm, in both their work and personal lives persons with this thought frame find themselves focusing on key underlying values for their interfacing with the world. In effect, if you are classical in your personal thinking, you want things to remain the same (see Table 2.1). If you are scientific dynamic, you believe that your political skill and aptitude will guide your thinking. If you are communication cybernetic in your thought process, caution and a safety value guide your behavior and thinking in the workplace and in your interactions with persons at work or home.

If field theory characterizes your thinking, credibility for yourself and the work is the answer. Interestingly in personal relationships, commitment is difficult because the burden of credibility is on the individual and trusting someone else to be equally credible is difficult. As an evolutionary thinker, change for change sake is the watchword value, and for the process thinker, transformation for self, others, and the work is the highest value. The thinking paradigms of evolutionary and process thinking are discussed later as a way of looking at the creation of personal and systemic change in the thinking process.

So at what juncture are we in our exploration of thought as a critical dynamic of change and congruence? Our first concern is that *companies are not always congruent in their thinking paradigm to the product or service that they provide.* Consider a utility corporation that states that it values its employees, desiring creativity, cleverness, continuity in the work, and diversity in its thinking. Yet when one works in the corporation's environment, one experiences a tiered, hierarchical, authoritarian leadership and decision style. Employees become angry for feeling shut down in their process of creativity, and managers feel the employees are overstepping their bounds. In actuality, the organization's product or service is highly regulated, and leaders fear mistakes that can cost them in fines and sanctions. They traditionally operate from a classical thinking frame of mind, and the condition of no chaos, tight boundaries, and clear authority as essential to the organizational success. For them, hiring critical thinkers, visionaries, change agents, and the like is anathema to their success.

The policies are not real for persons who think differently. A classical thinker may see the rules as sufficient in terms of tightness and rigid structure. In contrast, a process thinker will feel trapped, blocked, penalized, and depressed. The type of thinking paradigm should govern the type of employee to ensure that what is needed in the organization works for the employee as well. Similarly, marrying a classical thinker when one is a process thinker will lead to frustrations, fights, misunderstandings, and often divorce. So you can begin to see that *how* you think is essential to *where* you work and *whom* you select as a significant other. The combinations become endless. Let's look again at the thinking styles.

THINKING STYLES

Classical Thinking

The classical thinker believes that lack of chaos, clarity in roles and assignments, and adherence to the rules and to an organization's policies are critical to organizational success. *Thinking is about structure, order, boundaries, and the status quo.* For this person change is difficult, if not impossible. Change is perceived as the realization that the structure, strategies, and processes currently employed by an organization are wrong. The classical thinker states that what exists is best; it may just not be understood as fully as it needs to be, but change is not a part of the equation. In the workplace, this individual will accomplish all assignments that fit within the craftsman or experts role, for the individual sees himself or herself as having control, power and authority over the skills and products that must be produced. This person is a "keeper of the flame" and avoids conflicts, looking for ways to retain the calm in the organization that he or she is used to enjoying. This style focuses on the *what and why* of the thinking. This philosophical thinking style was created by Descartes and focuses on the attainment of calm and clarity.

Scientific Thinking

The individual who adopts this thinking style seeks to escape blame and shame while ensuring that blame is placed on others. *This thinking is about safety, the status quo, anonymity, and control.* But its focus is not on harming the other person; rather, it is on avoiding cause and effect, blame, and shame. The strategies behind scientific thinking are the same as those used in classical thinking, however. Cause and effect rules the scientific system: Everything has a cause, and every cause has a reaction or effect. It is the beginning of the accountability system for employees regarding assigned work. Persons with this profile believe that the plan is right and that deviations are the fault of one or more parties. Rather than expert skills as in the classical model, political skills and aptitude are key tools for advancement in this model. Data is the critical factor here, enabling employees to identify right and wrong, clear versus obscure, and establishing accountability. This thinking style focuses on the **who and when** of the thinking process. This thinking style, the creation of Isaac Newton, focuses on the development of compartments as a strategy for identifying all the work and all the people of an organization. When achieved, there is no change outside of the compartments.

Communication Thinking

The individual with the communication thinking style avoids all contact with the classical and scientific thinker, believing that change should occur when necessary in an organization. However, bruised by the actions of the classical and scientific thinker, this individual is ruled by caution and safety in his actions and thoughts. *Communication thinking is about controlled responses to disruptions to the norm and the need for comprehensive information.* Since there never seems to be enough data to make a decision that will create safety, continual review, task forces, focus groups, and team processes become the thinking outcomes for this person. Generally, no decision is made until safety has been achieved. This person believes that only knowledge is important to create change. Where knowledge is obscure, no change should occur and no new decision is required. This style focuses on the *when* of the thinking process.

Like scientific thinking, communication thinking is also influenced by compartments. Change can occur only if the information and data are sufficient to make a decision different from the present. Therefore, cause and effect rules the decision process.

Field Thinking

The field thinker is a "Missouri" person—a "Show me! Prove it!" person who believes that change should occur only when it has been field tested. *The thinking frame therefore focuses on the ability of the organization to prove the success of a change or to prove that a tangible understanding of the issue is possible.* Persons with this thinking style believe that change is inevitable but not without proof. These persons often become evaluators and process managers in organizations, yet slow down the work or add in significant steps to ensure the credibility of the work product. The field thinker looks for the meaning in the work and how that meaning is informed by data and knowledge. This style focuses on the **how** of the thinking process. Field thinking is also driven by cause and effect, thus, the testing process is a strategy for change.

These four thinking styles avoid change as a realistic option for organizational action. Maintaining the current organizational processes and strategies is critical to their status quo.

Evolutionary Thinking

The evolutionary thinker provides the greatest challenge to the first four styles of thinkers. This individual believes that change is always with us and that we should learn to embrace it as a challenge. *Evolutionary thinking focuses on the ability to rapidly and fluidly move from one place in history to another based on facts, feelings, impressions, or new information.* In the workplace, this individual takes on all new challenges, upsets the status quo, and views teams and other actions as strategies for work performance. However, the individual would be happier as a sole contributor. Change is the watchword for this style. Project management, crisis management, and special assignments are creative opportunities for this thinker and allow the thinker to shine before the organization. This person focuses on the continual development of meaning for actions of the organization or the person. The evolutionary style focuses on the **what and how** of the change more than the **why**. Although this person values change, credibility is based on the collection of data that supports the change.

All five of these thinking styles address external influences as the primary influence on style.

Process Thinking

The process thinking style supports a balance and alignment between the communication, evolutionary, and classical thinking styles. Change needs to occur, but it is not change for change's sake. It is balanced change based on recognizing organizational need and personal style. Key here are meaning, wisdom, and a philosophical direction or system rather than data, information, and knowledge. *Thinking in this style focuses on creating harmony with one's values and beliefs, as well as with one's sense of calm and peace within the organization.* This thinking style also supports diversity of thinking. It is concerned not with blame and shame, or cause and effect, but just with the recognition that all things are possible. The strategy in process thinking is to understand the **why** more than the **what, how, who, and when**.

Process thinkers focus on issues of congruence in their lives where external thinking is balanced by congruence with internal values, beliefs, and experiences. The goal of this thinking is integration and transformation, by which a person moves consistently and congruently to new ways of viewing life, issues, strategies, and aspirations. *Process thinking is the primary thinking style that comes from one's own understanding of self. The influences for this thinking style are internal influences.*

Although all forms of thinking are critical in an organization, one type of thinking may be more effective in one organizational role than in another. The challenge for the leader of the organization is to match the thinking style with the work to be performed. One style of thinking does not have more value than another; rather, congruence for each individual and for the organization can be enhanced through a more creative and effective balance of people to the system based on thinking styles.

The second concern we have in our exploration of thought as a critical dynamic of change and congruence is that *families and individuals are unwilling to embrace their value set as equal to the value sets imposed by a society or a workplace*. This becomes important in the challenge to think. Thinking is about courage. When one thinks, one accepts responsibility for the actions that result from the process of thinking. When families reject their gay children because of what other family members, neighbors, and friends might think, one wonders what would occur if the family stood its ground and declared, "This is my child and I love him as he is, not as you would want him to be!" The emotional intelligence of Goleman would rise exponentially.

THINKING APPLICATIONS

We will now look at how thinking impacts our decision making and problem solving. Research has shown that certain factors traditionally impact the decision-making and problem-solving process in organizations and individuals. Thought is valued because it directly influences problem solving, decision making, model development, technology utilization, and historical auditing—whether one speaks of the organization or the person. We each look to our perspectives of fear of reprisal, history, and unresolved conflicts as guides to our response or reaction to change and newness. For organizations, change occurs when they seek less regulation, better integration of business practices, higher return on investments, reduced risks and uncertainty, greater compatibility, competitive advantage, increased innovation, customer assurance of management, enhanced self-image and market share, improved cost control, decreased liability, improved efficiency, improved communications, reduced complexity, improved interpersonal relationships, and improved industry / government relations. For individuals, change occurs when they seek improved interpersonal relationships, increased communication, improved relational understanding, enhanced influence in personal and systemic relations, greater understanding of self, reduced stress, and increased satisfaction.

Change is usually managed inappropriately and is therefore based on fear of consequences, inability to make effective decisions, vindictiveness and politics, changing priorities without substance, interpersonal conflicts, and discounting of the value of the positions affected by the change. However, the ability to think effectively allows the inappropriate to become more appropriate. In effect, when thoughtful change occurs, change is either revolutionary or evolutionary.

Revolutionary change is designed to upset the structure, process, and character of the people within the organization in order to allow them to achieve a given outcome. The process is based on challenging the existing–incremental–one-step-at-a-time aproach that usually exists within organizations. Therefore, the purpose of revolutionary change is to abruptly and sharply alter the existing realities of the organization and its people.

Evolutionary change permits a smooth transition based on the changing values and beliefs of the people and the organization. Evolving from one space to another is the focus of the change, and it can be both revolutionary and incremental. The key to the change is that inclusion of all affected is the underlying value of the evolution. Everyone involved recognizes that it is coming, and they all want to participate in its end results.

Therefore, the process of thinking is designed to enhance transformation— the process mode—in six ways: (1) to transform the design of the organization and its members; (2) to transform by accident through external and internal intrusions; (3) to transform through restructuring of the organization or one's life; (4) to transform by empowerment of people in the thinking process; (5) to transform through community creativeness and a groundswell of support; and to transform through construction of a new agenda.

These six methods are important as the decision process of old is based on past performance, fear, and unresolved conflictual issues: action gets people in trouble and creates dysfunction rather than wellness. So if the paradigm of thought can take precedence over the paradigm of action, then organizations and people will have the opportunity to expand their capacity for the present and the future.

Figure 2.2 represents a strategy for using thinking as the baseline for creating understanding and change. The premise in the decision and implementation process is that thinking through critical data is essential to the issues of organ-

Figure 2.2
A Systems Approach to Change

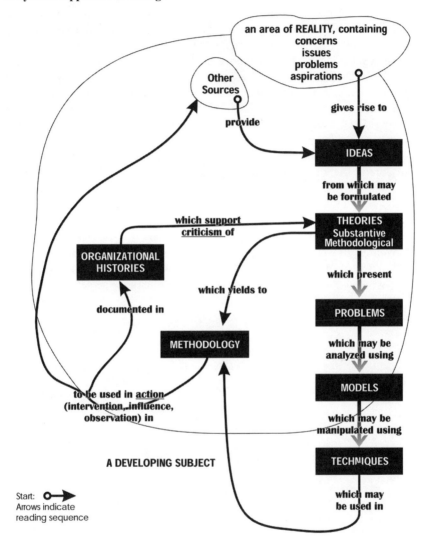

izational and personal resolution. Looking at the concerns, issues, problems, and aspirations, one is expected to have the full level of data—quantitative, qualitative, prescriptive, and phenomenological. In effect, one has a full disclosure of information essential to thinking through the strategies that respond to all of the concerns, issues, problems, and aspirations. One must develop a theoretical response before behavioral action can be taken, thereby ensuring that the theory or theories will allow for resolution or response to all factors. Only then does one look at action, and action is tempered by assessment of the theory that drives it.

Rarely do organizational leaders or family patriarchs and matriarchs consider the theory that drives. History, that is, how it has been done before, seems to drive the action. When action resembles history or is a reaction to fear, we begin to sense what is lost in the congruence of situations. Our challenge is to decide on the basis of thinking rather than action. Our challenge is to allow thinking to give us a framework for understanding the factors impacting us, not action which often incrementally or inappropriately drives us in a counterproductive direction. The challenge for each of us is the path that we choose. Thinking gives greater credence to success.

So where are we in the scheme of things? We understand that thinking is more appropriate than action when problem resolution and decision making occur. We recognize that each of us operates with a thinking style that has underlying values—each framing how we look at the world and how we operate when challenged to be different from what is our norm. We understand that consciousness is the key ingredient to achieve ahas; it is essential to personal and systemic growth. What we don't know is this concept of congruence. What is it? Where does it come from? Why is it so essential? What level of importance should we give it, and how can we use it to help us both personally and systemically?

Chapter 3

Exploring the Concept of Congruence: The Makings of C⁶

PSYCHOLOGICAL IMPACT ON ORGANIZATIONAL ACTIONS

Understanding the issues of congruence and lived experiences is a challenge to any theoretical exploration of organizational psychology, social-cultural anthropology, and business ethics. Chapter 1 discussed the needed ingredient in organizational practices that seek to balance people and systems issues. Students of organizational psychological theory, anthropologists, and management—individuals seeking knowledge of their own psychological balance that drives their thinking and action—can begin that exploration only when they consider the historical and transformation theories that guide the thinking in these fields. This chapter creates a continuum of congruence by discussing the impact of and void in organizational psychology, social-cultural anthropology, and ethics. The chapter also identifies the theoretical impact on government and areas where governments need to enrich their thoughts and actions.

BUSINESS PERFORMANCE THEORIES

Historically, the scientific study of society was a critical dynamic in the creation of a psychological approach to the study of business. When ideas are promulgated over a period of time, a cumulative enterprise is created that frames a picture of a society, or at least a portion of that society. Such is the case with business development. The great thinkers of our age created an intellectual pond for an understanding of business that can be central to understanding this research. An examination of the issue of psychological influence in the study of business logically begins with a study of Karl Marx.

Karl Marx

Karl Marx believe that the individual inventor or the individual entrepreneur was just a cog in a larger, more complex machine. For Marx, the individual was not more valuable than the larger society. Marx was the first to describe a hierarchy in society, especially business, in which the society (the organization) was held to be more important than the individual. Marx stated,

In the social production which men carry on, they enter into definite relations that are indispensable and independent of their will; these relations of production correspond to a definite stage of development of their material powers of production. The sum total of these relations of production constitutes the economic structure of society—the real foundation on which rise legal and political superstructures and to which correspond definite forms of social consciousness. The mode of production in material life determines the general character of the social, political and spiritual processes of life. It is not the consciousness of man that determines their existence, but on the contrary, their social existence that determines their consciousness. (Marx, 1859: 24)

Central to Marx's analysis of history is the concept of alienation, a psychological principle of personal and organizational development. Alienation or dehumanization occurs when the producer (corporation, leader, manager) is divorced from the means of production and when dead labor (capital) dominates living labor (the worker). The individual therefore becomes a commodity rather than a human being. This concept becomes critical as one assesses the efficacy of the relationship between the corporation and the employee. Suffice it to say, if employees become commodities, the psychological focus on employees becomes another product for the corporation to manage. According to Marx, the Industrial Revolution institutionalized alienation as the prevailing human condition. Marx's influence was essential to the concepts of change postulated by Gibb in his book, *Trust* (1978).

Emile Durkheim

Emile Durkheim was directly concerned with the antecedents and consequences of the Industrial Revolution, and focused on the differentiation and cohesion of society. Unlike Marx whom Durkheim saw as an ardent critic of an unjust system that needed changing through revolutionary means, Durkheim strongly supported the idea of an evolving society based on mutual interdependence. Man, he believed, could not survive solely through his own devices. Rather, collaboration with others was critical to the long-term success of the individual and of society. For Durkheim, the movement to urban areas was destroying the concept of community and began to create the higher value of companies over people and community. Companies created the cities, increased human interaction, and augmented population growth through technology.

Durkheim believed that differentiation had the additional effect of changing the structure of social interaction. Because of increased moral density and because people engaged in different but mutually interdependent tasks, the basis of social interaction had become more explicit and circumscribed, creating a new structural arrangement in order for society to function effectively. According to Durkheim, society had lost its potential for bonding. Society had now become a means whereby humanity was defined by work, not by who one was. Durkheim noted that the functional importance of the economic sector to modern society was critical and that the division of labor was most pronounced in the working roles of society. He proposed that all occupational groups and associations be so instituted that they would provide a moral power capable of containing and controlling individual egos, and create a common solidarity and spirit within the consciousness of all workers. Durkheim believed that the community of interests (corporations) had replaced the community of blood (family) in preserving the overall ethical and moral principles of society. Durkheim effectively helped set the stage for applying psychological knowledge in business. His work, together with that of Marx, provided perspectives for evaluating human behavior in organizations and its consequences for organizational health, profitability, and survival.

Into Marx and Durkheim's perspectives came the classical and scientific dynamic thinking processes that often guide today's corporate thinking, bringing the underlying belief that corporate identity and needs take precedence over personal and community needs. The prevailing issues of organizational violence (Williams, 1994) are predicated on this misplaced belief that has driven organizational life for so many years. Training people in traditional business programs or psychology programs that focus on compartments perpetuates the detachment and alienation that have existed in society since the 1800s.

Max Weber

Max Weber expanded on the works of Marx and Durkheim. He explained the worker's predicament in his book *The Protestant Ethic and the Spirit of Capitalism*, published in 1904. Weber stated that Protestant sects had a common ethical approach to life which had been developed through an adherence to attitudinal and behavioral characteristics that created capitalism. Ideals of hard work, self-denial, and unwavering devotion to God and legitimate (political and organizational leadership) authority were the hallmarks of capitalism; yet they created potential dysfunction in people and disconnections between the actions of individuals and the practices of organizational systems, unless one was a Protestant. For Weber, the Protestant Ethic was the necessary ingredient in a capitalist society. To ensure its success, he created a bureaucratic structure that would ensure that commonality and homogeneity were the rule of the hour, day, week, month, or year.

This structural process resulted in a system that was rationally designed to protect individual freedom. Unfortunately, the structural system diminished individuality and, thereby, freedom. Durkheim's rational system of production and consumption, created on the basis of ethical standards and principles, remains the underlying standard for business and organizational structures.

The psychological directions of business thinking and action were influenced directly by Weber's perspective on business, and the employee's values in the workplace directly influenced the psychological directions of business thinking and action. In turn, Weber influenced the following theorists important in the thinking of organizational and business change.

Adam Smith

Adam Smith (1776) was an economist responsible for the "division of labor" theory which stated that productivity within corporations rises with rises in the worker's skill level. This perspective gave theoretical direction to the field of training and development. Heretofore, training, or skill enhancement, was not perceived as critical to the division of labor. Smith believed that without training, an organization's attempt to be more flexible and adaptive to market and product changes would result in greater cost.

Robert Owen

Robert Owen (1789) created the processes for caring and concern for the worker by assessing how the Native Americans worked. Owen's theoretical approach set the stage for regulated workdays, child labor laws, public education, and business involvement in the community as a way of life. His concept of community involvement suggested the focus governments should adopt in the development of their work strategies.

Charles Babbar

Charles Babbar (1832) was a mathematics professor who expanded Smith's theories by creating processes to reduce the time needed for job learning, as well as to attain advanced skills and to match skills to physical abilities. Babbar's work ultimately became the framework for introducing self-paced learning modules, computer-induced training, and training on the Internet.

Frederick Taylor

Frederick Taylor (1930) created the scientific management process which defined the best way to get a job done. He is known as the father of scientific management and industrial engineering, and his perspectives have framed how organizations structure not only the boundaries of the organization, but also the work of the organization.

Henri Fayol

Henri Fayol (1930) developed a process to define the universal functions of good managers and the principles of good management—the fourteen-principle theory. Fayol's fourteen principles were based on a concept of trust in managers. Sometimes his model was in conflict with Taylor and his work.

Mary Parker Follett and Chester Barnard

Mary Parker Follett and Chester Barnard (1930) created a framework for describing group and individual process strategies to assess individual and group behavior within organizations. They looked at the process of group ethics and the impact of behavior on motivation, leadership, power, and authority. They expanded the concept of social systems through the "social man theory," which stated that social systems are reflections of man's development.

Hugo Munsterberg

Hugo Munsterberg (1930) began the study of industrial psychology, the scientific study of human behavior, and the development of the first psychological test for selection. His premise was that all people are alike, and that "sameness," would enable one to pick the best person for the position to be filled.

Hawthorne Studies

Hawthorne Studies (1930) demonstrated that productivity has nothing to do with the individual and that only group standards impact worker output. A strong impact on organizational behavior moved organizations away from the values and perceptions of Weber, Marx, and Durkheim.

Dale Carnegie

Dale Carnegie (1950) believed that success is created by influencing and winning the cooperation of others. He looked at the value of appreciation, first impressions, sympathy, and face-saving. Carnegie began to reintroduce into management thinking the idea that the value of one is equal to the value of many.

Douglas McGregor

Douglas McGregor (1930–1950) is remembered as the Theory X–Theory Y guru. McGregor believed that the worker could not be trusted to perform without the close guidance of the manager or the organization. He called this Theory X. He stated that Theory Y focused on managing from the framework of trusting the employee. His later writings suggested that Theory Y was only a strategy that would explain those actions and behaviors that did not follow the Theory X paradigm.

Jacob Moreno

Jacob Moreno (1950) conducted critical research on the analytical techniques of sociometry in which the study of group interactions was first developed. He created sociograms of interactions and determined the importance of the relationship of people within the work.

B. F. Skinner

B. F. Skinner (1950) developed the theory of behavior modification and the importance of stimuli in the actions and predictability of employees in the workplace. His research and theories also diminished the importance of thinking and feeling by human beings as a factor of comprehensive change in people.

Fred Fiedler

Fred Fiedler (1960) studied the issues of leadership, situational leadership, and leadership behavior. He reintroduced the concept of individuation and originated the concept of individuation in organizational outcomes.

Frederick Herzberg

Frederick Herzberg (1960) investigated what people wanted from their jobs and expanded the concepts of achievement, responsibility, and growth. His work was critical in the development of satisfaction parameters in organizational actions.

Jack Gibb

Jack Gibb (1960 and beyond) was considered the first major theorist in the field of organizational development and organizational psychology. He was the key theorist on T-Groups, organizational behavior, organizational process, organizational transformation, and business consultation and established the importance of trust in the innovation, growth, and transformational change.

These theorists and many others, such as Peter Senge, Margaret Wheatley, and Diane Beaky, have greatly expanded our understanding of past psychological theoretical influences on corporations today.

HUMANISTIC PSYCHOLOGY: IMPACT ON CONGRUENCE THEORY AND THINKING

Carl Rogers

Prior to 1955, there was a continuing disparity between the valuing of business concerns and human needs. The writings of Marx, Durkheim, and Weber had set the standards for a psychological approach to business. In 1955, however, Carl Rogers (p. 59) stated, "I used to wonder who I am, I am not sure I want anyone to know the real me, but it feels good to let myself go and just be me." Rogers believed that the ideal self is the self that a person most values and desires to be. It is the self-concept that the individual would most like to possess, on which he places the highest value for himself (Rogers, 1955: 100). Therefore, successfully pursuing the ideal self was a major precondition for feelings of worth and value. One's self-concept may be more or less in agreement with experiences related to the self.

Rogers believed that a person valuing what business believed or felt about the human being, the worker, impacted the balance necessary for human development. His writings began a course correction by workers about values and self-development. He called his concept of development the search for congruence. When a person is in a state of *congruence*, his or her self-concept and experiences related to self are consistent. The actualizing tendency is then relatively whole and unified, and the person shows maturity as well as psychological adjustment. By contrast, *incongruence* reflects an inconsistency between self-concept and experiences relating to self. Self-perception may be inaccurate because of beliefs that are rigid, distorted, unrealistic, or overgeneralized (Rogers, 1959: 101–103). Inaccuracies result from denial and distortions. Denial involves the inability to recognize or accept the existence of an experience that has occurred. Distortion involves a reinterpretation of an experience so as to make it consistent with how one wants things to be. Rogers' comments set the stage for a study of congruence as a requirement for human development and human sustainability. At the same time, they established the framework for examining the same concepts in relationship to organizational behavior, organizational development, management performance, and leadership.

Rogers believed that the concepts of unconditional positive regard and accurate empathy were essential to the concepts of congruence. To Rogers, when a person was able to accurately perceive another's internal world in a nonevaluative manner, that person was able to see the inner feelings, values, attitudes, meaning, and motives of that person in relation to the world and all its experiences. To do so is to understand the congruence of the situation. Therefore, if congruence is to occur beyond the individual, then congruence is based on that individual's willingness and courage to fully show him or herself and be genuine toward another. When the two feel the same level of comfort or emotional involvement—when there is communion with one another—then congruence exists.

Humanistic psychology emphasizes the present experience of the whole person. Historically, it has had close ties to existential psychology. The linkage is based on a concept that the person is the center of humanistic psychology. People are viewed in a positive light and are capable of solving their own problem; thus, they have an inherent generalizing tendency that is organismic, active, directional, and selective. The process of self-actualizing is a life-long process of realizing one's potentialities that involve openness to experience, awareness, living existentially, and trust in one's organismic functions. Congruence, therefore, occurs when our self-concepts are in agreement with the selves we actually experience. External factors, particularly interpersonal ones, often determine whether personal growth can occur. According to Rogers, unconditional positive regard, accurate empathy, and congruence are the essential ingredients for growth and development. Rogers and the humanists was asked whether people can ever experience the congruence, empathy, and positive regard required to grow, or whether experiences will get in the way of the development of self-awareness and growth.

Abraham Maslow

Abraham Maslow expanded on Rogers' work when he spoke and wrote of the gestalt and existential influence on developmental processes. Gestalt psychology, initially concerned only with the concept of perceptions, held that simple perceptions were "wholes" made up of integrated and connected parts (Matilin and Foley, 1997). One could consider the parts or the whole but not *both at once*. This notion was important because Gestalt theory was largely composed of "laws of organization." These laws explained how parts are formed into wholes. The rules stated that one should (1) group similar objects together to form a whole, (2) group proximal objects, and (3) adopt the law of closure, that is, incomplete objects—such as a circle with a section missing—are completed by the mind's eye. The idea of wholeness and of parts that are inextricably tied to the whole was fundamental to Maslow's thinking. To Maslow, the individual was an integrated, organized whole.

Existentially, Maslow believed that the "meaning of being" movement of the 1960s and 1970s was critical because the external world—the corporations, organizations, and governments—had lost all sense of values and worth. Existentially, Maslow believed that only a focus on the individual could save the world. Maslow believed that the "congruence in life" could only be found in the person, not in an organization or a corporation. Maslow also believed that as people transcended themselves, they became more members of their species and less members of their particular cultures. As one ascends toward self-actualization, one transcends culture and becomes a little more a member of one's species and less a member of a local group. As managers become more congruent, do they become less members of the organization and more members of a manager profile or group? As an organization becomes more congruent, will it become the epitome of effective organizations and less aligned with other organizational cultures?

THE CULTURE SHIFT

Between the 1960s and 1970s, numerous theoretical perspectives were developed to address an emerging body of knowledge focusing on the origins, actions, and thoughts of organizational life (Ott, 1989). Organizations are part of society and the culture in which they are situated. Human behavior, thus organizational behavior, is heavily influenced by culturally rooted beliefs, values, assumptions, and behavioral norms affecting all aspects of organizational life (Ott, 1989). For this reason, a society's way of thinking about behavior in organizations does not develop in a vacuum. Society continually reflects on the changing paradigms in the contemporary world of work and play. Contributions to the field of organizational behavior, organizational psychology, and organizational development vary by what happens—when and where—and in different cultures and subcultures. The advent of World War II, the American POWs who defected following the Korean conflict, the flower child/anti-establishment/self-development era of the 1960s, and the computer/information society of the 1970s—all substantially influenced the evolution of our subsequent thinking, theories, and research about people in organizations. To fully understand the issues of organizational psychology and the field of organizational development, one must appreciate the historical context and the cultural milieus of this body of knowledge (Ott, 1989). Theories critical to this body of knowledge include the Hawthorne experiments (1927), the theory of human motivation by Maslow (1933), the human side of enterprise by McGregor (1957), Festinger's motivating effect of cognitive dissonance (1960), the achievement models of McClelland (1942), Herzberg's motivational theories (1952), and Campbell's expectancy theories in the areas of motivation (1962).

The theorists relevant in group and intergroup behavior include

- Asch in the area of judgment distortion (1964).
- Job satisfaction and informal interaction by Roy (1963).
- Group dynamics by Cartwright (1969).
- Interdepartmental conflict by Walton (1970).
- Group and intergroup relations by Schein (1984).
- Groupthink by Janus (1986).
- Coalitions by Pfeffer (1988).

Their works have heavily influenced the field of organizational behavior and have directed the theoretical and praxis work prevalent in today's academic programs on group work.

Issues of leadership have been delineated by:

• Follett and Barnard (1962) in the areas of executive functions.
• McGregor in the areas of leadership analysis (1960).
• Kahn and Katz in the areas of leadership practices related to productivity (1969).
• Fielder in the creation of the contingency model theory (1970).
• Sergiovanni in the area of leadership (1972) as cultural expression.
• Ulrich in the area of leader transformation (1986).

Although the theoretical issues impact long-term development, a theoretical understanding of the context of organizational life is essential to the overall understanding of this continually changing field.

• Merton (1952) was critical to the understanding of bureaucratic structure and personality.
• Trist (1964) was critical to our understanding of the social and psychological consequences of system and people behavior.
• Whyte (1964) was critical to the issues of the organizational man.
• Thayer (1983), like the others, was critical to the issues of democracy as hierarchy and alienation (1983).

In addition, numerous theorists have written on the issues of power and influence.

• Cartwright's treatise on power and social psychology (1973) helped shape an organizational understanding of power and influence.
• French (1974) wrote consistently on the issue of social power.
• Haire (1977) adapted French's writings to focus more completely on the concepts of power and of man (1977).
• Kotter (1978) focused on power, dependence, and effective management.
• Yates (1966) examined power and influence as frameworks for political resources.

To the aforementioned we add the issues of change and development. The following theorists shaped change development theories.

• Coch (1981) writes on the issues of overcoming resistance to change.
• Lewin (1978) developed the first theories on group decision and social change.
• Leavitt (1969) maximized Lewin's initial writings to focus on structural, technological, and humanistic approaches to change development.

- Bennis (1966) wrote on the value and strategy employed in applying behavioral science to organizational change.
- Argyris and his son (1963) wrote on intervention theory and methods.
- Kelman (1978) created the framework for assessing the ethics of social intervention.
- Moss Kanter (1966, 1972, 1984, 1990) developed an architecture of culture and strategy change.

Each theorist helped frame the issues of organizational behavior, which can be defined as the study of human behavior in organizational contexts. It examines the manner in which people cope with the problems and opportunities of organizational life. This field is the product of many complex interactions that occur daily between humans, groups of humans, and the organizational environment. Organizational behavior is the actual behavior of individuals and groups around purposeful organizations (Schein, 1992). It involves the application of theories, methods, and research findings of the behavioral sciences—particularly of psychology, social psychology, sociology, cultural anthropology, and, to a much lesser degree, economics (Schein, 1984). An understanding of organizational psychology and the concept of congruence in organizations and among its leaders, therefore, comes from some knowledge of these fields. The larger issue is the application of the knowledge, understandings, and techniques from the behavioral sciences to effectively intervene in the lives of organizations in order to create a more healthy whole.

Organizations are not interchangeable, however. Over the past fifty years the separation between private industry and government has continued to grow. Private industry has not equally valued the issues of psychology, social psychology, cultural anthropology, and ethics. Business schools and consulting groups are increasingly discovering that the primary focus on economics has commonly taken the lead in the literature and actions of private organizations. The results have included an increase in mergers and acquisitions and a decrease in such inclusive strategies as discussed by Edgar Schein (1992). Conversely, government continues to be perceived as the bastion of integration of these disciplines, without economics as the driver of thinking and actions. Governments continue to resist the temptation to "function under the principles of corporate America" because the desired outcome of corporations is assumed to be money, while the required outcome of government is assumed to be the increased quality of life of the citizenry of the community being served.

A level of cognitive dissonance occurs in developing an understanding of organizational psychology/organizational behavior. Differing lenses govern one's ability to embrace the developmental thoughts and strategies embedded in the field of study. Sociology, psychology, social psychology, sociology, and cultural anthropology each have an underlying paradigm that guides human thinking and acting. *Thus, the analysis and research that drives creative change gets skewed by the lens of inquiry.* Into that venue, therefore, comes the challenge to the history of organizational psychology/organizational behavior. History is critical for contextual understanding, content is based on one's disciplinary approach, and process becomes the strategy for creating the future of the field.

A chronology of theoretical developments in organizational behavior and organizational psychology (Ott, 1989) is shown in Table 3.1. Through short, this chronology frames the issues that set the stage for understanding the influence of organizations over humans. The challenge has been the extent to which organizations have *replaced* humans in the dynamic of being and the misalignment and imbalances have grown. This issue of replacement has been the critical complaint about private industry; human beings have been replaced by a valuing of numbers and strategies. Although government continually struggles to *maintain* the influence of human beings on organizational decision making, the retention of the human equation remains a difficult choice in the face of economic control in the society.

Richard Hall's *Organizations: Structure, Processes and Outcomes* (1996) gives rational reasons for the study of organizations. He postulates that organizations are the dominant component of contemporary society and that the great transformations within society have been organizationally driven an based. Therefore, studying organizations provides one further reason rise to study and understand societies and cultures. From a psychological perspective, debate over the fate of the individual continues. One could wonder whether the fate of humanity is based on organizational systemic thinking or is predicated on the maintenance of personal power. The question itself sets the stage for the study of organizational psychology.

Can there be a realistic balance between the issues of being human and the issues of being systemic? Can man and organization be the same? Is there humanity within organizations? Is there a system among men? Can there be a perspective of wholeness that permeates the divide that seems to have developed since the times before Christ?

Additional issues must be considered. If Hall (1996) and Ott (1989) are correct in their assessments of the value of organization, then the ultimate question revolves around the value of the human being and the human condition. And into that question enters the issues of ethics and cultural anthropology.

THE IMPACT OF ETHICS ON THE ISSUES OF ORGANIZATIONAL CONGRUENCE

In the field of ethics, one is faced with the root development of personal ethics, organizational or systems ethics, and impacts on the decision-making process. This issue is often a critical one for managers when they are responding to directives regarding work, and it can impact the ability of managers to perform with congruence. The challenge of ethics is to achieve a balance between personal ethics and organizational/systemic ethics on the choices made by or-

Table 3.1
Theoretical Influences on Organizational Psychology

2100 B.C.   Hammurabi, King of Babylon, establishes a written code of 282 laws which control every aspect of Babylonian life, including individual behavior, interpersonal relations, and other societal matters. The first employee handbook.

1750 B.C.   Ancient Egyptians assign ten workers to each supervisor while building the pyramids. The first span of control concept.

1491 B.C.   During the Exodus from Egypt, Jethro, Moses' father-in-law, urges him to delegate authority over the tribes of Israel along hierarchical lines. The first organizational structural change.

525 B.C.   Confucius writes that obedience to the organization (government) is the most respectable goal of citizenship. The basic justification for authority systems.

425 B.C.   Socrates suggests that organizations as entities are basically alike, though their purposes and functions might vary. The beginning of generic management principles.

370 B.C.   In his description of an ancient Greek factory, Xenophon explains the benefits of division of labor. Specialization of services is identified.

350 B.C.   In *Politics*, Aristotle develops the foundations for many modern management concepts, including specialization of labor, delegation of authority, departmentalization, and leadership selection.

1200 A.D.   Medieval European guilds function as quality circles to ensure fine craftsmanship.

1490 A.D.   Religious reformer John Calvin promotes the merit system by promising a "reward for your work." The Puritans also discussed time management.

1527 A.D.   Machiavelli's perspective of man sets the stage for authoritarian structures.

1651 A.D.   Thomas Hobbes, in *Leviathan*, advocates for strong centralized leadership as a means of bringing order to the chaos created by man.

1762 A.D.   Jean-Jacques Rousseau, in *The Social Contract*, postulates that governments work best when they are chosen and controlled by the governed.

1832 A.D.   In the first managerial textbooks, *The Carding and Spinning of Master's Assistant* and *The Cotton Spinner's Manual*, Ole Montgomery promotes the control functions of management: Managers must be just and impartial, firm and decisive, and always alert to prevent rather than check employee faults.

1883 A.D.   Frederick Taylor begins the study of scientific management.

1902 A.D.   Vilfredo Pareto becomes the father of the concept of social systems; Mayo applied the concepts in the organizational context.

1909 A.D.   Hugo Munsterberg, the father of organizational psychology, writes *The Market and Psychology,* in which he cautions managers to be concerned with "all questions of the mind" such as fatigue, monotony, interest, learning, work satisfaction, and rewards. He is the first to encourage government-funded research in industrial/organizational psychology.

1911 A.D.   The first application of the principles of psychology to business is Walter Scott's "The Psychology of Business."

Table 3.1 (continued)

1913 A.D. Psychology is applied to personnel selection, equipment design, product packaging and other concerns to balance the best man with the best work.

1939 A.D. Kurt Lewin, Ronald Lippert, and Ralph White's article, "Patterns of Aggressive Behavior in Experimentally Created Social Climates," is the first empirical study of various leadership styles. It becomes the basis for participatory management.

1943 A.D. Abraham Maslow's *Hierarchy of Needs* is published.

1948 A.D. Coch begins the human relations movement.

1950 A.D. Stogdill predicates the issues of the leader's role in goal attainment.

1951 A.D. Organizational effectiveness is based on sound information as postulated by Barrett.

1954 A.D. Drucker writes *The Practice of Management*; creation of the MBO process.

Bass's *Leaderless Group* is published.

Leader assessment centers begin.

Flanagan's development of the "Critical Incident Technique."

---

ganizations and its leaders. It is an issue adjunct to this research because the field of ethics, driven by theological inquiry, often sets the boundaries for individual and organizational action as an outside factor of development; it is not an internal perspective that is conscious in the minds of leaders within organizations.

The history of ethics reveals a widely shared conviction that ethics can and should be rooted in the so-called moral point of view. For many, the moral point of view is understood in religious terms, a perspective that reflects God's will for humanity. For others, it is understood in secular terms and is not dependent for its authority on religious faith. Setting aside differences about its ultimate source, a significant consensus has been reached regarding the general character of ethics. The moral point of view is a mental and emotional standpoint from which all persons are seen as having a special dignity or worth. The Golden Rule gets its force from the moral point of view, from which words like "ought, duty, and virtue" derive meaning. It is the principal guide for action.

Two basic features of action are critical to one's understanding of how people and organizations make ethical decisions. Each and every action has an *aretaic aspect* that highlights the expressive nature of our choices. When a person acts, he or she is revealing and reinforcing certain traits or habits of the heart which are called *virtues* (and/or vices). The same may be true of groups of persons in organizations. Sometimes the traits and habits are referred to as the culture, mindset, or value system of the organization. The key to the aretaic aspect of action is its attention to actions as manifestations of an inner look, character, set of values, or priorities. Four classical virtues that have often been the focus of ethical analysis and reflection in the past are (1) prudence, (2) justice, (3) temperance, and (4) courage. Others include honesty, compassion, fidelity to promises, and dedication to community (the common good). The vices of individuals or groups may include greed, cruelty, indifference, and cowardice.

People's actions also have a *deontic aspect* highlighting the effective nature of one's choices; in this aspect one's actions influence relationships with others and change the world around oneself. When viewed from this perspective, actions have stakeholders and consequences because they are transactions that affect the freedom and well-being of others. The deontic stakeholder of actions relates to effects on the world, in particular effects on living creatures whose interests or rights might be at stake. Management and the Board of Directors are legally and ethically bound to a fiduciary role in relation to the shareholders of the enterprise or organization. But they must also be attentive to other stakeholders. This kind of extended moral awareness, despite the ambitions of some of the great thinkers of the past, is no more reducible to a mechanical decision procedure than is balanced judgment in education, art, politics, or even sports. Ethics need not be unscientific, but it is not a science (which becomes difficult in government where ethics is often perceived as the scientific application of policies and rules). Ethics is more like staying healthy. Acknowledging one's limitations (such as the dissertation writing) regarding knowledge and certainty in ethics is not the same as embracing the motto, "There's no disputing tastes!" Sometimes, the stakeholder's interests and rights, as well as the needs of the larger community, are in tension with one another, making ethical judgments very difficult for individuals and managers.

This bifocal perspective on action signals a duality in what one can refer to as the moral point of view. Through one set of lenses, moral judgment concentrates on the expressive meaning of actions and policies—what one believes who initiates them. Through another set of lenses, the focus shifts to the transactional significance of what one does. *If one's inquiry concentrates on an individual's or organization's habits or culture (content, genesis, need for maintenance or change), it is aretaic. If the focus is on the interests and rights of stakeholders of personal or organizational decisions, it is deontic.*

Figure 3.1 demonstrates the moral point of view in business between virtue-based thinking and stakeholder-based thinking and suggests that there is a significant difference between personal action and organizational action and Figure 3.2 displays all four avenues of ethical analysis.

Ethical thinking can influence, if not change, the decision process of leaders and managers. This review of one's thinking, however, may provide avenues for thinking about ethical analysis in the sense that discussion of cases or pending decisions by managers often can be illuminated and even resolved by ethical inquiry. The challenge in this review is to identify the ethical issues as a component of congruence development. When individuals or organizations review ethical choice as a factor in organizational and personal decisions, the creation

Figure 3.1
Two Units of Analysis and Two Aspects of Action

The Moral Point of View in Business

	Aretaic, "Virtue-Based" Thinking	Deontic, "Stakeholder-Based" Thinking
Personal Action in a Business Setting	Personal virtues/vices; habits, conscience	Personal principles or beliefs
Organizational Action in a Societal Setting	Corporate culture	Corporate ethics policy or code of conduct

---

of a state of harmony essential for congruence becomes a component of the ethical analysis.

Three of these avenues fall under the heading of stakeholder-based thinking.

SHAREHOLDER-BASED ETHICAL THINKING

Shareholder ethical thinking is the most highly developed approach to ethical analysis, and it displays three distinctive logics or avenues: *interest based, rights based*, and *duty based*.

Interest-Based Avenues of Ethical Thinking

One of the influential avenues of ethical analysis is interest-based thinking. The fundamental idea is that the moral assessment of actions and policies depends solely on consequences, and the only consequences that really matter are the interests of the parties affected. In this view, ethics is about the respective harms and benefits to identifiable parties. Moral common sense is thus disciplined by a single dominant objective: maximizing net expectable utility (happiness, satisfaction, well-being, and pleasure). In this view, ethical thinking or analysis amounts to testing one's ethical instincts and rule-of-thumb judgment against the yardstick of social costs and benefits.

Interest-based analyses vary, depending on the relevant beneficiary class. For some (so-called egoists), the class is the actor alone. Therefore, the focus is on the short- and long-term interests of the self. For others, it is some favored group—Greek or English or American—where others are ignored or discounted in the ethical calculations of interests. For example, Caucasians during the 1950s, 1960s, and beyond consistently believed that the interests of white Americans were more valid than the interests of black Americans or Native Americans. The most common variation enlarges the universe of moral consideration to include all human beings, if not all sentient beings.

In business management, interest-based reasoning is often manifest as a com-

Figure 3.2
The Moral Point of View and Four Avenues of Ethical Analysis

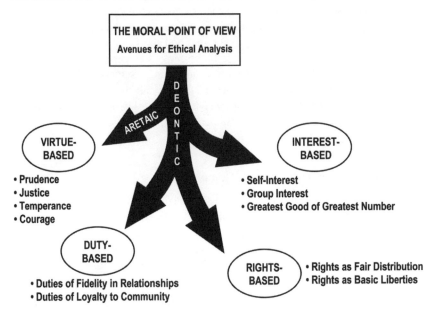

mitment to the social value of market forces, competitive decision making, and regulation in the public interest. Some of the problems and questions regarding interest-based avenues of ethical analysis become as follows. How does one measure utility or interest satisfaction? For whom does one measure it? What about the tyranny of the majority in the calculation? Can there be true ethical analysis when majority interests outweigh the interests of the minority groups? Do the interests of a few impact the decision making of a manager or a family leader? These questions often frame the dynamic difference between governments and private organizations, between the individual and the family. There is a belief that governments must be more concerned than private corporations about interest issues and people concerns. Minority interests must be considered within government, whereas private organizations consider the interest and monetary concerns of stakeholders—thus stakeholders' rights.

Rights-Based Avenues of Ethical Thinking

A second influential avenue is rights-based analysis. Its central idea is that moral common sense is to be governed not by interest satisfaction but by rights protection. The relevant rights are (1) rights to fair distribution of opportunities and wealth (contractarianism), and (2) rights to basic freedoms and liberties (libertarianism). Fair distribution is often explained as a condition achieved when all individuals are accorded equal respect and an equal voice in social arrangements. Basic liberties are frequently explained in terms of the individual's opportunities for self-development, property, work rewards, and freedom, including that of religion and speech. Liberties also extend to race, creed, sexual orientation, and disability. The rights-based actions of our society are mandated and implemented by governments, the courts, and the legal system.

In management practices, rights-based reasoning is evident in concerns about stakeholder rights (consumer, employees, suppliers, vendors) and stockholder (property) rights. The primary question for ethical analysis is as follows: *Is this avenue too focused on individuals and their entitlements, with insufficient attention to larger communities and the responsibilities of individuals to such larger wholes, or vice versa?*

Duty-Based Avenues of Ethical Thinking

The third avenue of ethical analysis is duty based. Although this avenue is perhaps the least unified and well defined, its governing ethical idea is equal duty or responsibility to the community and other individuals. This issue, coupled with rights-based avenues, creates a real opportunity for communal change within the society and within business. However, the ambiguity about duty drives continual misuse of ethical principles and analyses that one faces within corporate and business environs. Ultimately then, critical thinking turns on individuals conforming to the legitimate norms of a healthy community (which leads to interpretation and misrepresentation). According to the duty-based thinker, ethics is not about interests and rights. Instead, it is about playing one's role in a larger enterprise—a set of relationships or a community. John F. Kennedy expressed this notion eloquently when he said, *"Ask not what your country can do for you; ask what you can do for your country."*

In practice, duty-based thinking underlies appeals to principles of fiduciary obligation, public trust, governmental management and action, and corporate community involvement. The question that arises from this approach is, *Will individualism get swallowed up in a kind of collectivism, making it difficult for conflicting priorities to be achieved?*

Virtue-Based Thinking

Virtue-based thinking lies on the expressive side of the distinction made earlier between deontic and aretaic outlooks on human action. The focus of virtue-based thinking is on habits of the heart and character traits. Most recently, then President Clinton and Rudy Giuliani, the mayor of New York, presented the ethical challenge of virtue. Their actions and policies have been subjected to ethical scrutiny, not on the basis of consequences, but on the basis of their genesis—the degree to which they reinforce a virtue or character trait.

Virtue-based thinking emphasizes cultivating traits and habits that lead to actions and policies on the belief that too often the right thing to do cannot be identified in advance. Witness the fires in Los Alamos in 2000. The manager who decided to create the controlled fires was terminated because he violated virtue-based thinking—hindsight thinking. This in many ways describes the virtue-based thinking process. The most traditional short list of basic virtues includes prudence, temperance, courage, and justice.

In managerial context, the language of virtue is frequently encountered in executive hiring decisions as well as in management development training. Another management context that may prove to be more amenable to virtue-based thinking is environmental awareness. Often, debates over the impacts of business behavior on the environment have focused on the economic inclusion of special stakeholders (future generations). Questions associated with virtue-based thinking include the following: *How is one to understand the central virtues and their relative priority in a secular world that does not appear to agree on such matters? Are there timeless character traits? Can an emerging awareness change the virtuousness of an issue (such as sexual orientation or domestic violence or corporal punishment for children)?*

In summary, the impact of ethics on organizational congruence is the challenge to address thinking that guides personal and organizational choice. One is hard pressed to understand the issue of congruence without balancing thinking challenges that impact the creation of an internal state of harmony. The secular concerns of money, wealth, entitlement, fairness, belonging, and inclusion are all components of creating harmony. As Paulo Freire stated in his book *Pedagogy of the Oppressed* (1973) and as quoted in Williams, *Business Decisions, Human Choices* (1996),

Money is the measure of all things and profit the primary goal. For the oppressors, what is worthwhile is to have more, always more, at the cost of the oppressed having less or having nothing. As beneficiaries of a situation of oppression, the oppressors cannot perceive that if having is a condition of being, it is a necessary condition for all men. This is why their generosity is false. To the oppressor, humanity is a thing and they possess it as an exclusive right, as inherited property. . . . Over time, the oppressed gravitate to the behavior of the oppressor as an irresistible attraction, for being one of the haves is important. Self depreciation is another characteristic of the oppressed, which derives from their internalization of the opinion the oppressors hold of them. So often do they hear that they are good for nothing, that they cannot think, that they cannot write, that they know nothing, that they are unproductive, that they are lazy. They are peasants and feel inferior to the boss because the boss seems to be the only one who knows things and is able to run things. . . . The peasant is a dependent. He can't say what he wants. Before he discovers his dependence, he suffers. He let's off steam at work, at home, where he shouts at his friends, his co-workers, his spouse. He beats them, yells at them and is in despair. He complains, but doesn't let off steam at the boss because he thinks the boss is a superior being and he is afraid. (pp. 44, 49, 51)

Incongruent actions and thinking create a disharmony in the lives of people as evidenced by the Freire statement. Congruence and ethics are inevitably tied to one another and thus impact the success of personal and organizational choices.

THE IMPACT OF ANTHROPOLOGY ON THE ISSUE OF ORGANIZATIONAL CONGRUENCE

The history of anthropological research on organizations can be understood in terms of some important anthropological perspectives on the topic. An increasing number of anthropologists today question the validity of traditional, all-encompassing, functional-structural-configurational paradigms. To pursue systematic observation and analyses of cultural phenomena, social-cultural anthropology has diverged into various subfields. Some anthropologists have constructed theories of contradictions and contested identities (Rosenthal, 1985; Wolf, 1966), cultural materialism (Harris, 1979), structural analysis (Levi-Strauss, 1963, 1966, 1969, 1978), cultural ecology (Steward, 1955), ecosystems (Moran, 1983), and adaptive process (Rappaport, 1968, 1984). Other anthropologists have moved into cognitive anthropology (Clifford and Mercus, 1986; Geertz, 1973), economic anthropology (Dalton, 1961; Polanyi, 1947, 1957, 1959; Sahlins, 1958, 1961, 1972, 1976), anthropology of works (Applebaum, 1984), and other related fields.

Gregory (1983) critiqued past organizational studies done by industrial researchers, pointing out that many were still based on older anthropological paradigms and failed to explore multiple native views. She argued for a native view paradigm to explore a multicultural model of organization. Indeed, in many modern organizations, multiple identities and separation of formal and informal organizations (Homans, 1956) are often important and even necessary phenomena.

THE BEGINNING: FUNCTIONALISM AND INDUSTRIAL ANTHROPOLOGY

The concept of culture was first developed by the British anthropologist Edward Burnett Taylor (1871), who defined culture as "that complex whole which includes knowledge, beliefs, art, law, morals, custom and any other capabilities and habits acquired by humanity as a member of a society." In England and in the United States, the functionalists and holistic adherents regarded culture as an integrated system. Anthropologists posited that one aspect of culture was invariably related to others, and all aspects of a culture tended to function as an interrelated whole. The task of functionalists was to seek patterns of integration.

Anthropologists continue to be interested in the integrated totality. Issues of culture as a complex network of social relations, composed of partly autonomous coordinated institutions, or as interdependent parts of a social system or as the integrated totality of standardized behavior patterns, still frame the issues of cultural anthropology and social anthropology.

Beginning with the Hawthorne Studies on management conducted in the late 1920s and early 1930s, the issue of applied functionalism and participant observation theories have characterized society's understanding of social-cultural anthropology. However, the use of social-cultural anthropology to help explain the issues of culture within organizations has not been very clear. In the 1950s and especially after 1960, the human relations school of the study of organizations started to decline. But there was a resurgence recently as persons of color and of differing subcultures began to raise the issue of anthropological and sociological intrigue into the business environ. "The challenge of business is not about objects or products; it is about people—individual, groups, systems and cultures—and we don't know enough to make sound rational business decisions using only a business paradigm. . . . we are failing at business and in so doing, we are creating our own death!" (Adams and Whyte, 1991). The idea was that business would be unsuccessful and destroy a society if it did not use psychology, anthropology, and sociology as its real underpinning for the development of organizational strategy and process. The lesson of these two pioneers has continued to fall on deaf ears, as is evident in the actions of business today. The history of how these paradigmic fields have impacted organizational phenomena can best be seen in Table 3.2.

Each of the organizational paradigms listed in the table has anthropological, sociological, and psychological bases that frame the issues of people and culture in the organizational process. Hence, the critical question to be addressed seems always to be, *Can an underlying theoretical frame consistently and continually predict or describe what is likely to occur in the organization and among its members?* Theoretically, the answer should be yes. Unfortunately, when the theoretical frame is driven by an action rather than a consciousness, it is more likely that the descriptions of organizations and its leaders will be skewed to the actionable issue. Only when the theory describes actions, thoughts, and feelings can the system be called a paradigm of change and development (Williams, 1996). From the viewpoint of organizational culture, the question in cross-cultural management research seems always to become, *"Do universally applicable structural variables determine people's behavior in organizations, or do national, racial, or ethnic cultural conditioning influence organizational activities?"* Azumi (1974) suggested that if the perspective of social science as developed in western culture was inadequate, that must be demonstrated by creating a new and better social science rather than developing separate social sciences for different societies.

ORGANIZATIONAL ANTHROPOLOGY AND SOCIOLOGY IN THE CURRENT ERA

Within the disciplines of anthropology and sociology, research on North American work organizations flourished in the 1980s, and many scholarly societies experienced a renewed infusion of organizational energy. Key to this was the mandate (Hamada, 1989) to not separate organizational culture from the concept of culture. It opposed the notion of corporate culture as an additive or as a factor to be manipulated for organizational competitiveness. Instead, this

Table 3.2
Major Paradigms in Organizational Phenomena

Paradigms of Psychology, Anthropology, and Sociology	Founders	Advocates
Scientific Management	Taylor	Mooney, Reiley, Gulick, Urwick, Brown, and Koontz
Action	Weber	Silverman and Bowey
Systems Theory	Parsons and Bertalanffy	Merton, Etzioni, Gouldner, Blau, Selznick, Miller, Rice, Burns, Stalker, Crozier, Lawrence, Thompson, Lorsch, and Duncan
Expectation Theory	Lewin and Tolman	Vroom, Porter, Lawler, Evans, and House
Needs Theory	Maslow and Murray	McGregor, Argyris, Herzberg, McClellan, Cumin, Litwin, and Stringer
Influence Leadership	Lewin	Cartright, Sander, Bales, French, Raven, and Tannenbaum
Exchange Theory	Homans and Blau	Whyte and Jacobs
Resource Dependence	Blau, Emerson, and Merton	Pfeffer, Salancik, and Hickson
Conflict Theory	Marx and Simmel	Dalton, Walton, Mouton, Coser, and Dahrendorf
Decision-Making Theory	Simon and March	Cyert, March, Lawrence, Galbraith, and Duncan
Bureaucracy	Weber	Udy and Hall
Technology	Marx and Veblen	Woodward, Thompson, Perros, and Harvey
Contingency Theory	Fiedler	Thompson, Duncan, Kagano, Tannenbaum, Lawrence, and Lorsch
Congruence Theory (developed in 1993 by this author and Jack Gibb, his mentor; development is ongoing)	Williams and Gibb	Saxxon, Hampden-Turner, and Sommerville)

new movement began to advocate the organizational culture study as a way of understanding organization not as an economic or political entity, but as a sociocultural entity placed in a particular society within a particular historical context (Hamada, 1989). One continues to explore and understand the contextual issues of organizational psychology, social-cultural anthropology, and business ethics on the emerging landscape of organizational thinking. In doing so, I am struck by sociocultural entities continuing to emerge in one's thinking and behavior as ongoing relationships among subjective experiences of its members— symbolic communications and representations, manifested political alliances, behavior patterns, collectively expressed artifacts, and physical, social-political, and economic environments. The challenge is to understand the organization and create effective change that encompasses the present and the future.

In 1982, interest in corporate culture exploded with the publication of popular works such as Deal and Kennedy's *Corporate Cultures* and Peters and Waterman's *In Search of Excellence*. Their works explored the relationship between productivity and culture and created a desire for additional research into these relationships. One theory (Schein, 1985; Sathe, 1983; Frost et al., 1985; Kilmann et al., 1985; Garsombke, 1988; and Hebden, 1986) suggested that organized action is the product of consensus among participants who act in a coordinated fashion because they share a common set of meanings or interpretations of their joint experiences. Following this perspective, a number of researchers explored a multilevel topology of culture that proceeded from abstract, unconscious assumptions at one end of a continuum to concrete expressions of culture at the other. Schein (1985), for example provided a definition of organizational culture and described the processes of formation, emergence, and change. His structural model of culture operated at three levels: (1) the uppermost levels of artifacts and creation, (2) the next level of values that are the conscious, shared group beliefs, and (3) the third and deepest level of basic assumptions that are invisible, often unconscious, and taken for granted. The dynamics of his model are that culture emerges from small groups within organizations but that its leadership helps change, shape, embed, and transmit the culture.

Other scholars, taking the perspective that culture is a different concept, began to compare and contrast strong and weak corporate cultures according to the number of important shared assumptions. The more shared assumptions, the more pervasive the culture. According to this group of theorists, culture is a variable that can be manipulated by management, a value supposition that may be a product of the American management subculture itself. Davis (1990), for example, believed that culture is something an organization *has* that is manifested through its myths and rituals. Of greater concern is his underlying theme that corporate culture is merely a pattern of shared values and beliefs, and reducing workplace behavior to a homogeneous, monolithic entity created by senior management.

The movement for organizational culture has produced four different ideas about the usefulness of the culture concept. *It is an analytical tool, a managerial tool, a tool of change, and a cognitive sense-making tool.* Management scientists have not reached a consensus on the definition of organizational culture, and most research methodology is still directed toward assessment questionnaires and surveys (Rousseau, 1990). The general scarcity of the long-term, organization wide participant-observer studies may be due to the organizational scientists' cultural orientation, objective data gathering, and hypothesis testing techniques as well as monetary support.

THE ISSUES OF CONGRUENCE AND THE NEED FOR A NEW THEORY

The cultural perspective leaves an enormous void. Consider the following as you think about culture and organizations. From all perspectives, organizations are examples of sociocultural development. From many perspectives, the thoughts and behaviors of management may create the management culture within an organization but not necessarily the organizational culture. Organizational life is more than just a linear or single thought perspective. Decision making, planning, roles and accountabilities, inclusion and representation, a sense of belonging and participation can propel an organization to new heights and understanding based on the interrelationships of all these factors. Values are subconsciously perceived, yet this learner (the author) senses that the critical issues are the underlying beliefs of the organization *and* its members that truly frame culture and process. Meaning and wisdom are more important than events in understanding culture. Just because something happens does not mean that it has any real meaning for the organization or its members. Cultural integration is not the same as alliances that are created within organizations to retain one's power, control, or authority. The same events can have different meanings for individuals within an organization based on ethnic, racial, environmental, and other schema frames of learning, growing, and understanding. People will alter the perceptions of what they experience to create their own levels of comfort, or will become more congruent with their belief structures. The contradictions of organizations mirror the contradictions of its members, and only through an understanding of the contradictions can movement within the organization occur.

Apparently missing is a sense of holism and comprehensiveness. The struggle for congruence, therefore, seems to provide an avenue for framing organizational cultural understanding *and* comprehensiveness development and synergy of the members of the organization. *However, the furtherance of both the organization and its members is based on the relationship between the two entities (people and systems), not the separateness of either entity.* The desired outcome of a congruence theory is the unification of numerous aspects of organizational "life," including different languages and symbols; behavioral actions and outcomes; sociopolitical structures that embrace issues of power, authority, and control; inclusive issues of ethnicity, gender, race, and age, and sexual orientations; and other environmental factors within *both the system and among the people.*

The phenotypical intent of a congruence theory is to continually reveal dy-
namic interrelationships between culture and process, thinking and action, feel-
ings and emotions, processes and practices, outcomes and planning, objective
and subjective realities, symbolic interpretations and representations, connec-
tivities of personal empowerment and systemic commitments and specificities
that can occur between locations and regions. Through this effort to understand
or embrace connections, the opportunity and capacity to grow and change become more possible for the organization and the person, for the society and the
group, for the culture and the region.

Concepts of culture, groups, gender, and sexual orientation are all anthropological ideas that can influence one's understanding of personal and organizational congruence. If congruence is the creation of the state of harmony, balance,
and alignment, then businesses and people are less likely to achieve congruence
without an understanding of gender, culture, groups, and sexual orientation as
components of effective business decisions or transformations when these factors are critical to achieving an understanding of congruity.

INNOVATING AGAINST THE NORM

Rosabeth Moss Kanter, in her groundbreaking book, *The Change Masters*
(1983), stated: "the degree to which the opportunity to use power effectively is
granted to or withheld from individuals is one operative difference between
those companies which stagnate and those which innovate. The difference begins
with a company's approach to solving problems and extends through its culture
and structure" (p. 18). The more a company invests in its people, she claims,
the more success the company achieves. Companies with reputations for pro-
gressive human resource practices have significantly higher long-term profitability and financial growth than their counterparts. In fact, the more inclusion,
the greater the potential for effectiveness.

In spite of Kanter's glowing statements, almost twenty years later, little has
truly changed in the behaviors of organizations and even less has changed regarding an understanding of the impact of organizational culture on organization
and people processes. Instead, it appears that the trend in industry is not to
address the impact of culture on the organizational and people processes, but to
confront cultural issues via two roles; a management tool or a change tool to
achieve control, power, and authority (in that it limits the potential for understanding and establishes a process for exclusion) without the benefit of the other
two roles of culture—a cognitive sensing tool and an analytical tool (potentially
growing an understanding that can lend itself to holistic learning) (Williams,
2000). When ambiguity or confusion occurs, innovation is a critical juncture
process for movement beyond confusion. Innovation refers to the process of
generating and embracing any new problem-solving idea and placing it into
practice. Ideas for reorganizing, reducing fiscal burdens, creating and implementing new systems of budget management, enhancing and advancing com-

munication, understanding and improving team performance, or refining products and services are all forms of innovation. Innovation is the generation, acceptance, and implementation of new ideas, processes, products, or services (Kanter, 1983: 20).

The challenge for anyone choosing to embrace innovation and change within organizations and among people is to "tread where others fear the outcome." Risking, being, becoming, learning, changing, growing—all represent concepts of innovation in people and systems. *What is emerging is the belief that the innovation is sustainable only when the people and the system are growing and changing together—congruently, if you will.* So how do organizational psychology, social-cultural anthropology, and ethics create change in this dynamical interrelationship? How does one grow? How does one prosper?

CREATING CHANGE

Attempting to change a culture in order to increase its effectiveness is a hazardous undertaking. As consultants, one has the advantage of seeing organizational dynamics as vivid, unanticipated, and different, yet the process of seeing is often limited for organizational members, long caught in the culture of the organization. Members of that culture may take everything around them for granted and be so accustomed to limiting conditions that they're seen as necessary and normal. It is the outsider who often sees more. Psychological, sociological, and anthropological understanding is the process of engaging, understanding, reporting, and sharing the parameters and frameworks that guide the development of cultures. Anthropological understandings are those that focus on the developmental parameters that uniquely frame the culture with its myths, archetypes, rituals, and beliefs. Sociological understandings are those unique criteria that frame the actions and thinking of the groups within the culture. Psychological understandings are those that embrace the issues of individuation and how those individuation issues impact concepts of trust, fear, doubt, hope, love, peace, power, control, and authority within the person or the person's interaction with others. Table 3.3 depicts the issues involved in creating change and includes both anthropological and psychological factors of change. Interventions are psychological; cultural phenomena are anthropological.

The challenge in a change process is mapping the culture. The process is basically understanding "where man is willing to risk his future," or as Hampden-Turner (1990) termed it, "where angels fear to tread."

Both Hampden-Turner (1990) and Kanter (1983) speak of the concept of segments and segmentations (terms that can be called compartments or compartmentalization) as critical to the issues of change. In their writings, organizations and sometimes organizational leaders look for strategies that free them from risking innovation in the workplace. This (the author) learner senses that the real issues are based on compartments (which are more than the segments–external influences) that encompass the internal blocks to innovation and aware-

Table 3.3
The Mechanics of Cultural Change

Types of Intervention	Cultural Phenomena Elicited	Cultural Change Induced
Locate the Black Sheep or the Aberrant Thought of the System	Taboos and violations	You can now tread more safely
Interview and observe	Values, conflicts, and dilemmas	Substitute dilemmas for social conflicts
Review findings with the group	Theatrical and dramatic scenes	Suggestions of happy endings
Review past and present history	Surface myths, stories, and scenarios	Reinterpret myths, retell stories
Explore all higher logical types	Metaphors, images, symbols, ceremonies, and rituals	Revision, create new images and symbols; renew rituals
Discover logics by which the current system can learn new ways of being and acting	Old paradigms of manipulating employees and customers unilaterally	New paradigms and epistemologies created for better innovation and quicker and more sustainable learning

ness (Williams, 1994, 1996). The mapping process for innovation, change, understanding, or awakening is based on breaking through the compartments one creates to discover the connections to the compartments. In that discovery, risk becomes easier because isolation is not the primary factor driving the actions and thinking of the person or the system.

The critical issues that any individual, student, researcher, manager, leader, or system must consider are the following.

1. Breaking through the compartments reduces the issues of isolation by the person.
2. Breaking through the compartments reduces the protective stance of "I am the only one who can know," the belief that by not sharing one becomes indispensable.
3. Breaking through the compartments requires the sharing of information to obtain more knowledge that will inform one's strategies.
4. Breaking through the compartments allows others to explore and each decisions, freeing one to collaborate and see a larger whole that can influence issues.
5. Breaking through the compartments allows exploration of open spaces rather than continual placements of issues or people into comfort or existing boxes. One does not always have to have the answer; thus the exploration is real.

The Demonstration of the Discipline—Movements to New Ways of Knowing

The process of new learning and innovation in the field of social-cultural anthropology and its influences by psychology and ethics reveals a new way of understanding. Hampden Turner (1990) provided a manageable diagram to help understand what happens when people hear information from a stance of either fear or trust. He called people who are fearful his vicious circle and people who are trustful his virtuous circle.

Figures 3.3, 3.4, and 3.5 depict the struggles of understanding culture and creating movement in the process of systemic development. Figure 3.3 shows the issues of viciousness and virtue. The challenge is based on the ability of individuals to hear and respond versus listening and reacting to information that can alter one's history, climate, environment, or culture. In the chart, the vicious circle focuses on harsh realities or critical dilemmas created by the process of openness. The challenge in that circle is the lack of clarity, as well as the innuendoes that are created by vagueness, which generates retrenching behavior and fear in the development of solutions. The virtuous circle is predicated on the concept of clarity—the cognition process, if you will—that can free one to hear and not just listen to words. Whereas little connection is readily apparent in the vicious circle, connections are experienced in the virtuous circle. This is the process of innovation and movement.

Figures 3.4 and 3.5 speak to models of thinking in the development of resolutions to issues within a culture. McKinsey's diagram in Figure 3.5 shows that leaders who want to focus on distant, or nonhuman, interactions within a system look to structure, strategy, and systems as the decision points of learning and change. *This focus is critical because it represents a rejection of the human connections that are critical to the change process within an organization.* McKinsey calls these three issues—strategy, structure, and systems—the cold triangles of business: "strategy, structure and systems are the favorite elements of the hard crowd, who believe that the rest of the organization will fall into place if the cold triangle is constructed properly" (p. 84). Human resource types and the vast majority of the organizational behavior types represent the warm squares within the organization. They tend to believe that a vaguely human style and overabundance of skills development for people will automatically create a benign culture from which strategy and structure will spontaneously emerge, with systems generating all the right numbers. But both perspectives are wrong, perpetuating compartments and connections that will never be made.

Figure 3.4 represents the pull technologies that seem to drive top leaders in their thinking about the work and culture of their organization. When the cold triangles polarize with the warm squares, a clash occurs. The cold triangles subjugate the warm squares, and the necessary learning does not occur. There is a disconnect between thinking and action. There is a quantification without qualitative considerations, and in the process there is a loss for humanity.

Figure 3.3
Where Angels Fear

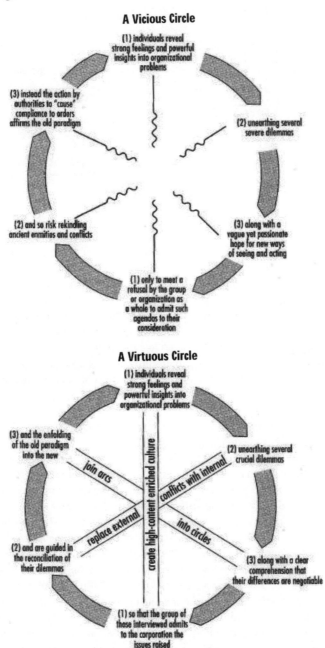

A Vicious Circle

(1) individuals reveal strong feelings and powerful insights into organizational problems

(3) instead the action by authorities to "cause" compliance to orders affirms the old paradigm

(2) unearthing several severe dilemmas

(2) and so risk rekindling ancient enmities and conflicts

(3) along with a vague yet passionate hope for new ways of seeing and acting

(1) only to meet a refusal by the group or organization as a whole to admit such agendas to their consideration

A Virtuous Circle

(1) individuals reveal strong feelings and powerful insights into organizational problems

(3) and the enfolding of the old paradigm into the new

join arcs

create high-content enriched culture

replace external

conflicts with internal

into circles

(2) unearthing several crucial dilemmas

(2) and are guided in the reconciliation of their dilemmas

(3) along with a clear comprehension that their differences are negotiable

(1) so that the group of those interviewed admits to the corporation the issues raised

Figure 3.4
The Dichotomies Between Cold Triangles and Warm Squares

Analysis	Interpretation
Quantification	Verbalization
Measurement	Evaluation
Control	Guidance
Science	Arts
Top-down imposed	Bottom-up participation
Big brain	Little people
Design	Implement
Bold	Deliberate
Win/lose	Win/win
Competition	Cooperation

American corporations and government continue to polarize their design and work, creating an individualistic macroculture. As a result, corporate leaders, both men and women, prefer the cold triangles when thinking about work. In addition, in any struggle or conflict between the cold triangles and the warm squares, cold triangles win. The real challenge becomes that of assessing whether or not the two sides can work together—whether a balance can be reached between hard and soft, loose and tight, strong and weak, power and influence.

MOVEMENT FROM DYSFUNCTION

Where do these perspectives of culture take us? How does one look more to cognition and analysis to create an effective balance to managerial tools and change models? Remember that culture is a difficult concept to grasp and that the problem lies in the fact that it is basic to human societies and organizational societies, thereby demanding an understanding of interconnections. Culture is made up of traditional ideas, related values, and intentional and unintentional actions. It is learned, shared, and transmitted from one generation to the next, and it organizes life and helps interpret existence. Cultures are driven by paradigms—a set of shared assumptions and beliefs about how the world works, its structures and the perception and understanding of what is and what should be. Psychology, on the other hand, sees paradigms as worldviews through which human beings relate to their world. Anthropology sees paradigms as worldviews

Figure 3.5
The McKinsey Seven S Diagram

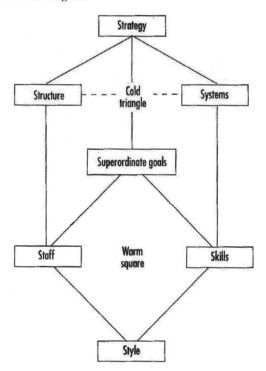

through which societies frame sustainable actions and structures for the present and future, incrementally focused. Sociology sees paradigms as the worldviews through which peoples and groups understand their interrelationships. Finally, ethics sees paradigms as the underpinning that frames relationships for thought and action. All are correct, and all are connected. Therefore, an exploration of culture, a new theory, or an exploration of underlying beliefs about an organization are connected and necessary to understand the "true reality" of the organization and its members. Whether looking at managers, leaders, or politicians, understanding their beliefs and assumptions often frames the issues of McKinsey's seven S Diagram (Figure 3.5). It is at that point that an exploration begins to describe the culture of an organization and the culture of the members and that one is able to create avenues for change. It is there that one begins to intrude into the culture to create options for understanding. Most importantly, only with that understanding can change and growth take place.

STRUGGLES WITH THE ISSUES OF CONGRUENCE

It is at this point that new challenge emerges: the challenge of transformation and congruity. A little known work by Jack Gibb, *Trust: A New View of Per-*

sonal and Organizational Development, began to create theoretical waves in academe in 1983. Gibb postulated that the lack of congruity prevented people and systems from being effective in the workplace as well as in day-to-day living. Gibb wrote that organizations and individuals operate from a stance of either trust or fear. His premise focused on the value of trust versus fear and on how those stances framed all work within organizations and all actions and thoughts of human beings. Books like *The Neurotic Organization* (Kets de Vries and Miller, 1984) and articles by Kets de Vries, Miller, Gibb, and Williams all attest to a "missing link" in the literature on transformation and congruence.

Since 1983, the void in the literature surrounding congruene and transformation has continued. Senge speaks to some levels of transformation in his book, *The Fifth Discipline*, and for beliefs about congruity, see Williams, *The Congruence of People and Organizations* (1993), *Organizational Violence: Creating a Prescription for Change* (1994), and *Business Decisions, Human Choices* (1996). Yet no other substantive work on congruence or transformation exists. *The challenge in congruence theory has to do with a movement away from the compartmentalization that occurred from the time of Hammarubi in 2100 B.C. to the creation of a collaborative-inclusive theory of people and systems today.* Because people spend more than 78% of their lives within organizations (Harman, 1990), there is a need for a theoretical base for the integration of people and systems. The present volume therefore focuses on the creation of a body of knowledge that balances and requires the nexus of multiple disciplines to create a theory of congruence and transformation.

THE CHALLENGE OF THEMATIC ANALYSIS

If congruence is about the interrelationship between people and systems, then at some point, what people say about themselves and their experiences becomes critical to the dynamic of understanding and searching for congruence in the actions of leaders and organization. In reviewing the existing literature, little, if anything, is said about the lived experiences of anyone within an organization.

The phenomenon that arises when dialogues on employee thoughts and feelings are breached focuses on discounting employee perspective for the sake of "credible numbers." Business leaders and managers traditionally tout the success of their numbers. The Baldrige Award for Quality consistently identifies the issues facing organizations, yet its process of interfacing with companies only involves the stage of identification. The "numbers" show that actions by organizations designed to implement systemic changes subside within two to three years. Sustainability is not there.

Hampden-Turner's virtuous circles require that people *listen and hear* more deeply than is the norm. The research paradigm behind that thinking is phenomenological research. In his treatise, *Critique of Pure Reason*, Kant maintained that "Human perception is more than seeing. Human perception derives from the mental apparatus that serves to organize the incoming sense impressions. It is based on understanding, an intellectual state that is more than just a consequence of experience" (p. 94). "Kant's model of human rationality was built on the process of knowing, and the emergence of knowledge was built on an epistemology that transcended empirical inquiry. Kant believed that the perception of the researcher or investigator must be considered because empirical inquiry alone cannot yield meaning. Max Weber used the German word, *"Verstehen"*— the grasping of intersubjective meanings and symbolizing activities that are constitutive of social life. Schultz later wrote that *Verstehen* referred to the "experiential form of common sense knowledge of human affairs" (Denzin, 1994: 120). Husserl's notion of *Lebenswelt* (life world) expanded the concept of *Verstehen* to suggest that understanding the lived experiences of human beings was critical to the development of meaning in the lives of human acts and thoughts: "it is these thought objects of theirs—their lived experiences which determine their behavior by motivating it" (p. 94).

Of great interest here is the distinction between phenomenological interpretation and the hermeneutical position. Frederick Taylor (1971) defined the activity of interpretation as hermeneutic because the process of interpretation was in itself biased. Phenomenological descriptions, on the other hand, are perspectives of others' lived experiences that shape our knowledge of the world. If the perspective of congruence is to be visible in the lives of organizations and leaders and if the paradigmic process of seeing the world in a certain manner is to reveal itself, then revelation is a process of description—not analysis.

We are therefore left with of phenomenological practice, which focuses on the ability of the human being to construct and give meaning to the appearances in life in their concrete actions. Each action by a human being is a biographical process, revealing what one understands and how one senses action and thinking. *Phenomenology is the study of appearances and experiences* (Husserl, 1970). Husserl stated that human consciousness actively constitutes the objects of experience. This perspective has become basic in the qualitative study of reality-constituting practices. Schultz took the philosophical perspective of Husserl and stressed the constitutive nature of consciousness and interaction (Schultz, 1967). Schultz argued that the social sciences should focus on ways that the life world—the experiential world everyone takes for granted—is produced and experienced by the members. Subjectivity of the members is paramount as the scientific observer deals with how social objects are made meaningful. The emphasis is on how those concerned with objects of experience comprehend and act on the objects as "things" set apart from observers. Schultz stated that as individuals approach life with a stock of knowledge composed of common-sense constructs and categories that are social in origin, their theories, images, ideas, values, and attitudes are applied to aspects of experience, making them meaningful. This is most important for families, individuals, leaders, and managers: People are the single most important factor and ingredient in personal and organizational success. When organizations rely on the business paradigm to decide on organizational process and change, businesses lose. When individuals and families discount and refuse to listen to the members of the family, then families lose.

The process of describing the meaningful lived experiences of members of an organization and families provides the opportunity to learn real value for the members. The experiences reveal information that supports or detracts from an organization's strategies. The identification and recognition of the existence of these meanings for organizational members may one day bridge the gap between empirical and social reality.

This discussion of congruence in organizations and among people has come full circle. From the writings of Weber to the writings of Husserl and Schultz, the discovery of congruence and the discovery of social reality are connected. The desire and need to discover meaningful data are best explored through the thematic process of phenomenology. It is that sense of closing the gap—of exploring the missing link in congruence theory—that becomes the challenge of this book.

THE MAKINGS OF C⁶: BUILDING PERSONAL AND ORGANIZATIONAL CONGRUENCE

You may have noticed the chapter's subtitle, "The Making of C^6." The concept of extended power is in effect the challenge and the perspective of the six levels of thinking. The old adage, "the whole is greater than the sum of its parts," here is represented by the perspective of clarity, collaboration, complements, choice, complexity, and congruence—when added together. That is, the six components of thinking are stronger and more engaging when added together. They unleash in all of us an awareness that allows for greater utilization of our feelings and our behaviors, creating greater opportunity for congruity in our lives and our work.

The challenge in most of my writing, and in this book in particular, is to move beyond our compartmentalized manner of functioning. As a society and as Cartesian thinkers, we have focused on the content of conversations and writings in compartmentalized ways. We often take information out of context, separating the ideas to gain advantage, yet in our desires to gain that advantage, our compartmentalized approach often changes both the meaning and the value of what has been said, written, or developed for action. C^6 is a chance to move from our historical approach to one that demands a connectivity and understanding of the components of creating congruence as a holistic and systemic endeavor that expounds and enhances rather than just explores the pieces.

We must now create a new paradigm of thinking and being from what exists in our society. Each thinking paradigm discussed in Chapter 2 represents a way that people in our society currently look and operate within the world. In responding to the issues of my corporate, nonprofit, government, and individual clients, it is important to craft a framework that will allow each client to create a different level of balance. Williams (1996) develops a system that examines how people and organizations must act. This book focuses on how people must shift their thinking.

The first thinking change is the creation of *clarity*. Achieving clarity in one's thinking is predicated on discovering the factors impacting thought and action. Some key principles are necessary to achieve clarity. First, always identify the original symptoms that create dissonance and incongruence. Second, map all the quick fixes to the symptoms that have been used by organizational leaders—personal and systemic—and then discard them. Third, identify the undesirable effects of the changes and congruence issues. Fourth, map the addictive side of the quick fixes so that you have a better understanding of the hooks that continually trap your ability to effectively diagnose what is happening personally and organizationally. With this understanding, the fifth step is to find the interconnections to the fundamental loops of the organization and the people. Last, identify all the high-leverage actions (communication, mapping, etc.). With these steps you now have clarity for yourself and the organization.

The second thinking change is *collaboration*. Collaboration is not easily accomplished because organizations and family systems are trapped by the rewards of individuation. The concept of individuation has outweighed the nuances and enlightenments of joint or collaborative efforts and ventures. To move to a stance of collaboration, first describe the constraints and dilemmas. Nothing gets someone's attention better than describing what they are up against. Sometimes we oversimplify a problem, and in so doing, we create more of a problem than we are trying to resolve. Underlying most problems are complex dilemmas that must be taken into account. Therefore, doing it alone often means that we miss critical information that would block a sustainable solution. Second, focus on the reasoning and actions required for success. Too often, the diagnosis we give is abstract and vague. Describe at a concrete level how the issue is without reason and action and identify what is effective reasoning and action *related to* the problem by reviewing aims, assumptions, and actions. Third, connect reasoning to actions. Each person's actions and reasons are based on his or her world view and may be realistic from his or her perspective, but may not necessarily be what the data supports. The issue involves recognizing and including other points of view in the assessment of what is possible. Fourth, and most important, connect actions to unintended consequences. An effective diagnosis has to address the consequences of the person's actions in terms of how they affect their own and other people's ability to learn, grow, and move to a new space based on the proposed congruence and change. Helping others see how their actions are inconsistent and incongruent with their aims and how their assumptions are incongruent with their objectives often allows them to see the unintentional problems they create.

The next thinking change is creating *complements*—the anchors that enhance the ability to create change while remaining congruent in our process of action. The first step is thinking in terms of loops. If one can get other persons to describe what they are thinking, what their dilemmas are, and what the consequences are, one can begin to connect the strands. By learning to think in casual loops and being able to draw these loops for client, boss, peers, family, or other significant relationships, one can help clarify complex situations in a useful manner identifying leverage points for change. The second step is to describe how all parties are contributing. This reduces the need for blame and shame in the thinking and acting. Therefore, describe the way that the impasse has occurred and map out what is going on, remembering that most people are visual, not auditory.

Now you are ready for the movement cycles. The next thinking change is *creativity*. The most critical aspect of creativity is posing alternatives. Remember, every diagnosis is an intervention and every intervention is a diagnosis; alternatives therefore provide options for how to think and respond to the issues at hand. When you try to figure out what is wrong—what is out of sync—you are creating the conditions for congruence and change. When you make suggestions, you are moving toward congruence and you are moving with the change. And when you select an alternative, you are creatively implementing change. Second, creativity is based on our learning process.

The three levels of learning in relationship to our creative thinking are (1) knowledge acquisition and insight, (2) habit and skill learning, and (3) emotional conditioning and learned anxiety. Knowledge acquisition and insight are based on reading, schooling, and memorization. It is the process of cognitive learning. Insight is the information or knowledge that one gains when a breakthrough occurs, expanding our container of knowing. Habit and skill learning is obtained through trial, error, and practice. Although it is a very reliable form of learning, it is limited because only your history is valued in the process of learning. The difficulty is avoiding the learning of bad habits and not having the opportunity to make errors. Emotional conditioning and learned anxiety are the most potent form of learning. Emotional conditioning occurs in response to rewards as well as in recognizing when we are unlearning. Issues of shared assumptions, cultural norms, and process development are critical to framing what one can learn and what must be discarded. Anxiety develops in three phases. The first is anxiety associated with feeling an inability or unwillingness to learn something new because it appears too difficult or disruptive. My father learning how to use a computer is an example of this anxiety. The second phase is anxiety based on the fear, shame, or guilt associated with not learning anything new. My father waiting five years to learn about computers increased this level of anxiety. The most insidious level is asking others to learn something new if we have not learned something new ourselves. The best example is leaders in an organization creating training opportunities for employees, yet choosing not to participate for their own growth and development.

Two other levels of thinking change are *complexity* and *choice*. Sometimes, my clinical clients say, "Doc—I need a break. The changes and the thinking are pushing me too fast, and I just want to slow down." The difficult tension in choice is recognizing when one is abdicating personal and professional movement, creating codependency and systemic moroseness. People and organizations commit this omission every day. From statements of "we can't push faster and harder—the organization cannot stand it (meaning I really cannot stand it)" to "Joe likes to get information this way and this approach will push him over the edge (meaning I have been pushed over the edge)," every day people and organizations make choices to limit their options and possibilities, creating more difficulty in the development process. Complexity is the movement beyond the sound bites that we experience every day. Simple answers to complex information are not often available. Therefore, looking for the simple is anathema to congruence. When you are asked to submit two pages to describe thirty years of work experience, you recognize that the human resource department doesn't want to know who you are, how complex you are, what choices you have made, and how the choices are complemented, creating anchors that allow you to respond rather than react to ambiguity.

In effect, we are challenged to look at our thinking and our actions and to determine where and when we began compartmentalizing, controlling, and boxing our thinking. When did we begin to focus more on protecting and limiting than on understanding and growing? This process of imbalance, misalignment, and incongruence occurred a long time ago, and as a result, we lost! We must begin to change that.

Chapter 4

Getting Systems Clarity in Our Lives

Achieving clarity in your personal and organizational system is essential to the effective creation of strategies that move one forward toward a goal or dream. Often in our lives, the discovery of critical information that turns the lights on is an arduous task—wrought with historical tapes, fear experiences, loss or lack of support, and no sight of rewards that often are the catalyst for continuing the search for understanding.

Organizations are masters of lack of clarity. From the bottom levels of the organization to the executive tier, information and data are codified and cajoled until the data that reaches the top for final decision making has little true meaning that can benefit either the organization or the employees. In their development, individuals and groups experienced the same lack of clarity in their approach to communication, interaction, and relationship with people. What someone believed often drove the framework in which information could be shared or understood. Yet, there was no assurance that the information shared focused on creating clarity to enhance personal behavior, personal performance, or clearer understanding. What was allowed focused on discussion, possible conflict resolution, or individual growth, as long as the outcome met the perspectives of the person or group giving permission. Yet in both organizations and individuals, achieving clarity—a full understanding of the issues and concerns—was rarely a finding.

What makes it so difficult for people and organizational systems to achieve clarity, that is, a full understanding? What is the cost in personal and system terms for less than all of the information or less than full disclosure? When does the filtering process stop governing the development of a quality decision, becoming instead the block to personal and organizational movement, the block to personal and organizational decision making?

Clarity is the development of comprehensive, accurate information to ensure that the information received allows a person or a group to create a context for reaching conclusions and developing actions. The context of that information generation is based on the thinking style that one uses to inform or create action strategies. Clarity focuses on recognizing who we are, how we operate, and how we utilize the drivers of our thinking to propel us to a level of decision making and action that honors the uniqueness of the person with the uniqueness of the information to make an informed choice. For example, if one operates from a communication cybernetic thinking frame, the underlying reason for the creation of more and more data is to ensure *caution and safety*. Therefore, this individual skewes the information to ensure that safety and caution are maintained in the analysis of the information. For someone who is a process thinker, information is framed in the analysis to ensure that *integration and transformation* are the drivers of the information. Regardless of what framework the information has, being conscious or having consciousness around the rationale used for accomplishing clarity becomes a critical concern.

You might ask why becoming conscious is an important factor in the development of clarity. Let's take two examples for enhancing clarity. The first is a young man struggling with developing some intimacy in his relationships. Throughout his history with his family, he experienced communication as a manipulative and guilt-ridden process. Throughout his life, his father consistently spoke in riddles or in guilt-laden language. The young man learned to feel shame and guilt in his interactions and went through life manipulating people, looking for an edge in every relationship he formed. All the women who have entered his life have left because they feel that the games he plays and the manipulation he employs make him untrustworthy in his conversations, intimate developments, and actions. They report that he circumvents any interaction and that they are tired of the game. When the young man comes for therapy, his thoughts, feelings, and actions are without clarity. In the therapeutic process, he learns that he is acting out the thinking and practice mode of his father. His unconscious thought of manipulation and his habit of inducing guilt block him from achieving his desired outcomes. While in therapy, he rewrites the psychological pathway by achieving clarity—making conscious what has been unconscious, being aware of his abuse of others rather than not knowing or understanding that his manipulation was abusive. By achieving clarity, he is now free to join with others rather than seek power over others.

The second example is the director of finance and administration in a corporation. Unsure of what is needed to reduce costs and increase software sales to major corporations, he contacts three divisions in his organization. One organization is responsible for sales training, the other for marketing products, and the third for enhancing the effectiveness of software upon its release for sale. To each organization, he states that he believes the company is losing market share because of the way products and services are managed internally and that a cost savings must occur. Each organizational entity believes that it is working on this issue alone and that only their area of the company is misaligned with operational targets. They work furiously for two months developing their response to the director. They arrive on the day of a planned meeting, realizing that other groups are present and have a part in the same issue. Members of all three departments feel set up, scared, angry, protective of their information, and sensing competition as a key underlying issue in this meeting. Because of the nature of the assignment, two strategies with regard to clarity can occur: (1) open sharing by all three departments to assess what is common and what is unique to the operational issue that can make a difference in market share, or (2) withholding of information. In either situation, the director's thinking style was not understood. He operated from a scientific dynamic thinking style driven by *political skill and aptitude.* The result that people see is cause and effect and blame and shame. Where opportunity might have occurred to advance clarity of information and thereby create an effective decision, opportunity was lost because the thinking motivating the assignment was not focused on clarity. The thinking was focused on blaming and shaming, with assigning fault and punishing the group found to be the cause and effect.

Clarity therefore becomes a critical first step in achieving personal and organizational congruence. Lack of clarity is not always deliberate, however. In fact, often people are unclear because they focus on only part and not all of the information needed. In 1999 and 2000, I conducted a phenomenological research project to assess the value of thematic analysis as a strategy for achieving clarity and impacting congruence in a governmental agency. The premise of the study was that qualititative information, the lived experiences of employees and managers, is often not used by organizational leaders or consultants who are historically and traditionally hired by organizations. Without that information, organizational leaders rarely, if ever, achieve clarity. The critical premise was that clarity requires the utilization of quantitative and qualitative information to make an informed choice. Without that data, organizations and the people within them suffer. In actuality, as the employees suffer at work, their families and children as well as the friends who try to console them, suffer as well. Let me tell you about the research.

This study sought to identify the presence (or lack) of congruence characteristics in the interactions of managers and executives in full-service county government. The study also included a comparison of the emergent congruence characteristics from the interactions of the study participants to the congruence development model created to assess the efficacy of the model in organizational incongruencies that impact performance. The study also sought to demonstrate the use of the thematic analysis method in an organizational setting. By comparing the emergent congruence characteristics of managers and executives with the congruence development model characteristics, the research sought to identify the existence or nonexistence of congruence characteristics of the model. Where findings indicated that the model characteristics were aligned with the managerial success determinants, it was believed that the model accurately described the key congruence characteristics necessary to shape organizational behavior. The study had the following objectives.

1. To determine the relationship (congruency) between managers' thoughts (as revealed by their definition of management success determinants) and their actions (as revealed by analysis of their correspondence over a nine-year period—1991 to 1999—using the modified Van Kaam technique of thematic analysis).
2. To determine the relationship of the congruence characteristics to the congruence development model in order to validate this model for assessing congruence between managers' thought and actions in organizational settings.
3. To demonstrate the use of the thematic method in an organizational setting. Although the Moustakas method has been used to address individual or group awareness, the method has not heretofore been used to address the issues of awareness or understanding in an organizational setting as a method of understanding an organization's performance issues.

The study examined the emergent congruence characteristics of managers and executives in their lived experiences as shown by secondary source data (memos, e-mail, other documents, etc.) selected from the participants over a nine-year period. The research was conducted as a representative case study and sought to describe the characteristics essential to the creation of alignment and balance among executives and managers in a government agency. This was accomplished by assessing five primary determinants of organizational behavior as compared with the twelve congruence characteristics developed in the congruence development model.

TYPE OF RESEARCH AND METHOD

This was a qualitative research study and focused on human judgments and perceptions within its natural settings. Qualitative studies generally attempt to make sense of or interpret phenomena in terms of the meanings people bring to them. Qualitative research involves the studied use and collection of a variety of empirical materials—case study, personal experience, introspection, life story, interview, observation, and historical, interactional, and visual texts—that describe routine and problematic moments and meanings in an individual's lives (Patton, 1990: 40–44).

The method used in this study was the case study. A case study is not necessarily a methodological choice; instead, it is a choice of object to be studied. A study is considered a case study because it tells a story of a group of persons who are alike in demographics and focus. It is also a case study because its purpose is to understand more fully the unique characteristics of a given entity— managers and executives in a government agency. The most unique characteristic of the case study is that it becomes both the process of our learning and the product of the learning. In effect, the case itself is of interest. The technique for use in the analysis and interpretation of the data was a phenomenological inquiry process. The specific technique was a thematic analysis as applied to a representative case using the modified Van Kaam method by Moustakas. It is identified as a process of phenomenological inquiry because the steps undertaken are just as important as the findings of the process. In addition, what the researcher experiences is equally important as a lived experience to the actual findings in each step of the process (Patton, 1990: 53, 55, 98–102).

This technique is used because it allows detailed descriptions of situations, events, people, interactions, and observed behaviors, in verbal or written form; direct quotations from people about their experiences, attitudes, beliefs, and thoughts; and excerpts of entire passages from documents, correspondence, records, and case histories. It should identify the value of lived experiences in the determination of organizational action. Lived experiences represent qualitative measurements and raw data from the empirical world (Patton, 1990). This method was selected because it permits the use and collection of accounts, that describe turning-point moments in individuals' lives. Paraphrasing Patton, we can say that the collection comes from interviews, written reports, focus group discussions, and other forms of communication that can inform the researcher about the lived experiences of participants in an established parameter. The method is used to explain phenomena that can be generalized to the larger population. It also allows for the utilization and delineation of emerging and diminishing themes within a population regarding organizational rules and practices to explain where success or failure occurs.

This method then focused on the revelations of congruence factors (developed by this researcher in the congruence model) found in the written stories, rules, and practices of the participants. Where there is alignment between critical emergent congruence themes among people within the organization with the characteristics of the congruence model (based on five managerial/executive determinant factors—decision making, structure, people behavior, environment, and satisfaction), the research will have answered the questions of the usefulness of the congruence development model.

Moustakas (1994: 44) states that "perception is regarded as the primary source of knowledge, the source that cannot be doubted." Intentions, united with sensations, make up the full concrete act of perceptions (p. 52). On this subject Merleau-Ponty (1962) says:

perception opens a window onto things. This means that it is directed towards a truth in itself in which the reason underlying all appearances is to be found. The tacit assumption of perception is that every instant experience can be coordinated with that of the previous instant, and that of the following, my perspective with that of other consciousness is one unbroken text, that what is now indeterminate for me, could become determinate for more complete knowledge.

Moustakas' approach has heretofore focused only on the perceptions of the person, not a group of persons. The utilization of this method for a category of persons—managers and executives—to describe a composite of their lived experiences to project impacts on organizations has not been done. Therefore, this approach represents a new use of the method.

The premise of this study was that the thematic analysis of the interactions of the managers and executives will reveal congruence characteristics through the stories and accounts of the managers who described managerial determinants in their organizational and personal lives. This was achieved by a thematic analysis of patterns established in the data that reveal organizational and personal themes. The thematic analysis identified underlying core statements or experiences that enhance the opportunity and perceived mindset of managers, drive their decision making, enhance their people behavior, frame or alter structure development, establish environmental settings, and acknowledge satisfaction parameters. These managerial success determinants represented the participants' stated success factors for interfacing with their employees. Each phase presented was a further deductive process of identifying patterns, identifying themes, and evaluating primary, secondary, and tertiary themes that inform the actions of people and systems. The same data were evaluated against the characteristics of the congruence model to identify alignment or lack of alignment. The intent was to determine which characteristics of the congruence model impact congruence in organizations and people.

DESIGN OF THE STUDY

Managers and executives developed these five primary managerial determinants in 1998 as part of a consultation and stated that the determinants would guide their organizational success. Managers and executives were given a list of thirty terms cited in management studies as determinants of manager/executive success. From this list, they identified five determinants that impacted their success: (1) an effective organizational structure, (2) clear and concise decision making, (3) effective management and understanding of human behavior in the organization, (4) safe and liberating organizational environments, and (5) clear satisfaction parameters as stated by employees and managers. The managers and executives stated that change would occur as successful implementation of these five determinants became more evident in the organization.

As a qualitative study using the case study method, the research was designed to analyze the organizational and personal communications of twenty managers and executives in a governmental setting. A governmental entity was used because historically government's stance has been to provide a connection between the needs of citizens, the ease of data collection and analysis, and the statement of the county administrator regarding the success of the managers of the department. This selection was further supported by the National Forum of Black Public Administrators' (NFBPA's) statements of accomplishing community need measured by managerial success (NFBA and the International City Managers Association, 1998). The conventional wisdom of private corporations and many leaders was that managers and executives in government were not concerned with the "bottom-line economic goal," but with the more global goal of human and organizational satisfaction.

Executives, as well as managers, were used because a theme could be identified only if more than one level of the organization generated the same patterns. The generation of patterns at two levels would constitute a theme.

The case focused on the critical areas of alignment, based on the congruence development model, and of congruence that could be revealed through a thematic analysis. The rationale of this approach was that adherence to the development of congruence in this research would be accomplished in the areas of decision making, people behavior, structure, environment, and satisfaction parameters. This was the area of description and analysis from the case. It was expected that the findings of this study would support the congruence development model as a method of developing and understanding congruence within organizations and among individuals.

Figure 4.1 depicts the design of the research project. The *first step* of the research project was to select the agency for the collection of data. Data were collected in three ways. The first data collection was the identification in 1998 of the five managerial determinants of success. It was accomplished by providing the managers and executives of the study with thirty categories of organizational and managerial success factors. The executives and managers identified the five managerial success determinants that they valued as most critical to their success in the organization. This approach represented a facilitated process of consensus. Managers and executives identified and agreed on five determinants of managerial success that would guide their organizational performance: Organizational structure, people behavior, decision making, people satisfaction, and environment. The second data collection was the identification of secondary source data from nine years of correspondence to the researcher and to the other participants, focused team dialogues that occurred among the participants with this author present, team process reports, and a focused group discussion of the managers and executives. This data source was used to assess the congruity of participant correspondence with the five managerial success determinants identified in 1998. The third data collection was the synthesis of what the author learned from this study as a participant and primary source of data.

The *second step* was to analyze that data. Initially, the data sets were sorted into the five managerial success determinant categories of decision making, people behavior, environment, structure, and satisfaction. The horizonal experiences of each participant was listed in a descriptive format. The *third step* was to review the data to determine the horizonal experiences of each participant by managerial determinant categories. This was done by focusing on statements or words that matched or aligned with the determinant categories. The *fourth step* was to reduce or eliminate extraneous material to develop the cluster frames from the horizonal experiences. The clusters were determined by the closeness of words and phrases in the writings that reveal key words from the congruence

Figure 4.1
Research Design

RESEARCH DESIGN

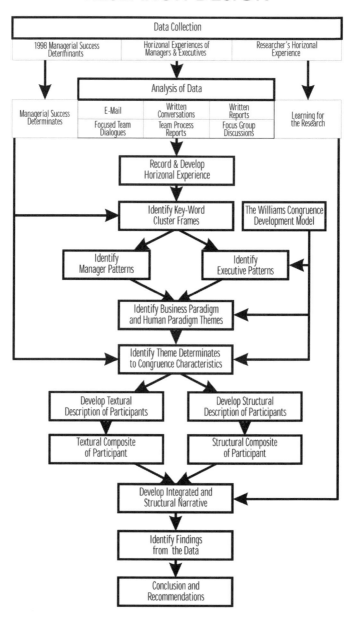

development model. Each of the key word congruence characteristics represents declaratory statements or descriptors of definitions of the key words or phrases of the horizonal statements. The researcher then looked for matches to the definitions or declaratory statements.

The *fifth step* was to determine patterns in the words by participants where a frequency score represented a pattern within the study. These patterns were determined for both executives and managers. To determine the pattern, the researcher counted the number of times study participants stated clustered words. Based on the total number of times, the frequency was identified. The researcher then described how many times each participant stated the clustered word or phrase to determine whether a pattern had been established. The *sixth step* was to determine themes from the patterns of executives and managers. Themes existed only if the patterns occurred at both the managerial and executive level. The *seventh step* was to match the themes to the congruence characteristics of the congruence development model and the themes to the managerial determinants of the study. The *eighth step* was to identify the textural descriptions and the structural descriptions of the participants by type—manager or executive. The textural descriptions help in understanding the context of the participants. These descriptions were based on existing data about each participant gathered at the interview process for developing the five managerial/executive determinants. The *ninth step* was to identify the textural and structural composites of the participants by type—manager or executive. This step was critical to the research design, for it established the "categorical description" of the managers and executives. If the method is used to describe organizational impacts, then composites of the participants will be essential.

This process set the stage for *step ten*. In this step, an integrated textural and structural narrative was generated, including the lessons the researcher learned for synthesis. This step represented the primary source data of the researcher synthesis (called lessons learned) and was presented in both table and narrative format. *Step eleven* began the process of identifying the findings from all the data. Findings were identified in response to the six questions that are stated in the data analysis section of this chapter. Findings were also identified based on each table developed in the creation of patterns and themes. *Step twelve* represents the last chapter of the dissertation where the researcher states the conclusions and recommendations from the study.

The congruence development model used in this study was a dual-process paradigm that assesses the lived experiences of people and organizations[1] through an analysis of their responses and their behaviors.[2] This assessment model was projected to enhance the sustainability of organizational decision making, structure development, people behavior, environmental design, and satisfaction issues—the five determinants for employees and managers.

This study was based on the following three facts:

1. Human beings must experience alignment with their own values in order to achieve turning points in their personal and professional life.[3] Numerous studies have investigated the impact of fear on the effective performance of organizational members. Other studies have suggested that a number of organizational leaders enjoy the restricted stance of employees when they fear punishment in organizational settings. Gibb (1983) postulated that trust must govern personal and organizational action in order for growth and change to occur. This assumption is predicated on that writing. If alignment is possible, then movement is possible; if trust is increased and fear is reduced, then success in performance is possible.

2. Organizations must experience alignment with their expressed policies and procedures (the structural strategy dictating organizational and personal behavior) in order to achieve turning points in their managers' and employees' lives. Organizations have historically used policies and procedures as control functions within the organization in order to ensure compliance with organizational rules and strategies. Yet, organizations have continually touted that flexibility in these policies, and procedures have allowed for respect of individuals and their unique needs.[4] Should correspondence be aligned with thought, then employees should experience increased alignment in their own actions in the workplace.

3. Congruence is achieved when decision making, people behavior, structure, environment, and satisfaction become verified facts and anchor points for individuals and organizations.

These facts suggested the following for this study.

1. Congruence characteristics from the congruence development model must be present in all five managerial success determinants in order to indicate success in the managers' organizational performance.

2. All five managerial success determinants contributed equally to organizational success and performance.

3. All characteristics of the congruence development model must be present in the correspondence of managers and executives.

Because there were two levels of employees, the analysis focused on identifying issues present from each group (managers and executives) and showing how that identification informed the development of congruence characteristics in the data.

NATURE AND SOURCES OF DATA

The first data set for this study was qualitative and consisted of interview responses from the participants in 1998 that comprised the five managerial success determinants (structure, people behavior, environment, decision making, and satisfaction) for organizing the data. These data involved the participants' consensus assessment of thirty determinants of managerial success to create the five determinants of managerial success for use by the managers in their organization. The managerial success determinants were developed by the managers of the study and used to establish the categories for sorting data from the secondary sources.

The second data set consisted of (1) written organizational conversations, (2) written organizational reports, (3) e-mail conversations, (4) focused team dialogues, (5) team process reports, and (6) focused group discussions, or combinations of these discussions as revealed in the data. This data set was critical to the full assessment of the organizational themes. The data were generated from a single department in which the communications were between the researcher and the participants or among the participants themselves.

There were 340 written organizational conversations over a nine-year period; 37 were written organizational reports over a nine-year period; 470 were e-mail conversations over a four-year period; 24 focused team dialogues over a three-year period; 12 team process reports over a three-year period; and 15 focused group discussions over a three-year period, for a total of 898 pieces of correspondence from 1991 to 1999. Although nine years of data were available, in some instances only a portion of those data were used, as required by the Van Kaam method for theme identification.

These data sources were secondary sources inasmuch as they were developed or conducted during consultations with me in the role of consultant over a nine-year period. They were originally used as data for organizational consultation and for varying reports that the researcher developed for the organization in the role of consultant. They are now being used as secondary sources for this research study. Denzin (1989: 319) states

that secondary sources are most legitimate when one has read or understood enough history to have some familiarity with a period . . . thereby allowing for a change from primary sources of data. He also states that the value in secondary sources is the frequency of the citation.

The third source of data was the synthesis of the author, accomplished by compiling the personal notes and observations, and participant conversations with the researcher to create a succinct and accurate listing of success determinant utilization. The synthesis represented the researcher's initial learning about the study. From 1991 through 1999, the researcher's personal notes focused on the performance and interpersonal skill changes of managers and executives. They were used to guide the writing of reports about organizational change, organizational development, personnel selection, and training development programs. They were used to develop the descriptions of the participants to better inform the correspondence analysis. All three data sets were qualitative and secondary in nature; none was originally developed for this study.

The data have been accumulated over a nine-year period from my practice as a consultant. This time period established familiarity with the subject sources, as well as consultation intervention, organizational development design, conflict

Table 4.1
The Van Kaam Method for Analyzing Data

---

1. List all relevant experiences (*horizonalization*) and attach the relative importance of the experience in given sets.
2. Eliminate any information that is abstract, extraneous, vague, or insufficient to understand or categorize (*reduction and elimination*).
3. Cluster the remaining information and identify themes (*thematizing*).
4. Develop a *textural* description.
5. Create a *structural* description.
6. Create a composite of the *textural* and *structural* descriptions to obtain and synthesize the essence of the experiences.

---

resolution sessions, and interviews with managers, the county administrator, and the Board of County Supervisors.

DATA ANALYSIS AND INTERPRETATION

Patton (1990) stated that qualitative descriptive data should be presented in such a way that anyone reading the data could both understand and draw their own conclusions from their lived experience with the data. The written text and analysis of that text would therefore lend themselves to an interpretation of the text in question (Miles and Huberman, 1984). When coded (in this case, mined data), manageable units and sorting of the units into thematic categories would therefore be possible (Moustakas, 1994; Strauss and Corbin, 1990).

Using only numbers to represent the participants in the study and to protect the anonymity of each participant, the researchers analyzed actual written and verbal communications using Moustakas's modified Van Kaam method. The Van Kaam method for analyzing data is outlined in Table 4.1 (Moustakas, 1994).

The data were analyzed in the following manner. First, the sorted information was presented in a spreadsheet table. The table identified the types of data versus the sources of the data. Examples can be "decisions made that impact organizational strategies; increased or decreased employee participation in legitimate decision roles; increased structure designs to match organizational work." Second, a numeric check from review of the data determined where existence of the patterns occurred or did not occur. Key words, key patterns, and potential themes were sought. There was no coding of the data in the traditional sense of coding. Rather, this study focused on "mining the data" to identify the patterns. Third, upon completion, the themes identified were compared to the twelve points of the congruence development model. It was suspected that themes would reveal themselves in both the business paradigm and the human paradigm, suggesting stronger alignment to the issues of congruence. Fourth, the data were presented according to the twelve points of the congruence development model. The model identified a business system paradigm and a human systems paradigm (described in synopsis form in the presentation of data chapter which follows). Fifth, upon presentation of the data, tables were created to determine the themes of managers and executives with a calculation of the numerical presence of the themes in each of the success determinants for managers and executives. Upon identification, themes that correlated to the congruence development model characteristics were determined as the first step in creating a baseline for either modifying the model or establishing a pattern for assessing organizational congruence to manager/executive congruence in the areas of identified success determinants.

As can be seen, the process of identifying the qualitative data is as comprehensive as any quantitative review. The leaders of the organization and the consultants who had traditionally provided advice expected that their findings of fact for the organization would remain as such—accurate findings. They believed that taking actions around structure, decision making, and satisfaction would correct the balance in the organization. They were very wrong.

What was amazing were the findings that began to drive the organizational decision making of the participants. The research had revealed data that quantitative information had missed. It showed mainly that people behavior was more critical to organizational success than were the determinants of structure, satisfaction, or decision making. This was an important finding because the organization had designed its programs and its strategies to focus on structure and decision making. The organization was utilizing fiscal resources to revamp the structure. The organization was making decisions without the advice of its employee population, and the organization was setting itself up to fail. When the research showed that people behavior was the most important criterion for success, the organization determined that money critical to employee development, organizational communication, skill matching of employees to the proposed work, and belief strategies that displayed how employees looked at the world were more important. They shifted their thinking and their behavior because qualitative data expanded their consciousness and they achieved clarity.

So what does this suggest for us as we think about clarity? First and foremost is the requirement to gather sufficient data to ensure that one did not participate in the "sound-bite economic process of analysis." Too much of our organizational and personal development has been based on little to no information—or sound bites is created in the media. From sound-bite resumes to bulleted items in reports, people and organizations make decisions without accurate information. Decisions continue to be made without clarity, and everyone suffers from the lack of clarity. Second, it is necessary to take the time to explore the obvious and the unknown *before* assuming that all the information critical for a decision is available. Third, when the clarity has been achieved, one should recognize that clarity is the beginning of the process of congruence—not the end. To move forward, issues of historical power and control must be addressed. In effect, moving through the process helps more than needing an answer.

NOTES

1. Lived experiences of people and organizations reflect the themes and patterns that emerge from the conscious aspects of the person and the actions of that person. Often, lived experiences explore the issues of spirituality, faith, hope, and awareness that inform people action and thought. In this study, these concerns will only be addressed as they become reflected in patterns reported by employees and managers. Should they become patterns, there is no assurance that they will present themselves as themes for evaluation as nexus points.

2. The dual-process paradigm system is a comprehensive congruency model for people and systems.

3. Jack Gibb (1983) focused entirely on the transformation issues of people and systems. His premise was that more things can occur in behavior, thought, and feelings when one operates from a stance of trust versus fear. He identified multiple stages for transformation and the impediments to that development.

4. There is a difficulty in the analysis of organizational valuing of employees. Numerous theorists from Gibb to Argyris, Cross, and Williams et al. have presented rationales for the differing experiences of people. These experiences have emanated from manipulation, control, abuse, usury, and other negative terms of expression to describe the issues of violence that often occur when organizations operate from misalignment. The challenge in this assumption is the requirement that where alignment occurs within organizations, there is a direct impact on people behavior, decision making, environment, structure, and satisfaction for employees and managers.

Chapter 5

Embracing the Art and Hope of Organizational and Professional Collaboration

The first concern that may impact the concept of collaboration is the organization's and individual's current use of power. The news television programs, and athletics have all taught us to seek out power as a strategy for winning and being on top of things. Power is perceived as the ultimate goal in business and in athletics showcasing personal strength. When we win market share in our organization, we have power. When we win in basketball, baseball, football, soccer, or other sporting events, we also have power. When we are in therapy and the therapist exalts the client's achievement over self-defacing behavior, the therapist often says to the client, "feel the power in you!" There is a sadness in these words, and more importantly, they reflect a dysfunction that has consumed us all.

Power is the process of winning or controlling others to achieve a given end, and as such it is not a good process for any of us. Power is a lose–lose process both personally and organizationally, for when one wins over another, the loser resents, regrets, and seeks strategies to win the next time. Power breeds resentment and creates competition as the end-all activity. For those of you who have graduated from universities with business degrees and are in busines, consider the terms of power that have driven your approach to business. Mergers, acquisitions, corporate takeovers, corporate raiding, industrial espionage, legal challenges to affirmative action, and diversity struggles are all examples of an inappropriate focus on power. The business mindset supports the attainment of profit and control through the destruction or competitive whipping of others in the marketplace. Even if the mergers and acquisitions fail, our infatuation with winning has created a society of organizational and individual misfits. We don't help one another; rather, we gloat over the failures of others. We don't assist in the sustainability of others; we seek ways to amass wealth when others are down. Take the stock market, for example. When unemployment is high, the stock market jumps. When companies merge and raid the pension plans of employees, the stock market jumps. When wars erupt, the stock market jumps. When pain and sadness abound, our society seems to revel in the misery of others.

Consider some of the delusions we have created. Our society has raised each individual to achieve the most he or she can personally, intellectually, athletically, and professionally achieve. When you go to work, your individual efforts are rewarded; yet somehow, your team performance is perceived as essential to the organizational effort. We are supposed to collaborate with others help each other, share with each other, participate with others. Yet, no where in our growth and development have we been taught to share. From our communication to our work, from our development in the family to our relationships with significant others—*collaboration* is the hardest activity to achieve. Even more difficult, historically thinking in Eurocentric society has been Cartesian—that is, individually focused. We continue to fail to join with another.

The counterside to the issue of power is acquiescence and hopelessness. Consider the children in the United States who are violent toward other children and society. In their sense of hopelessness, in their reactions to the bullying of the other children, in the teasing and taunts that block a sense of self, these children lash out inappropriately—harming to the point of death people whom they feel have participated or supported the abuse. Also consider the case of corporate abuse against Microsoft and its founder, Bill Gates. Court records document Microsoft's pattern of abuse, arrogance, control, and power over competitors and partners. The result has been the creation of a coalition of varying businesses in concert with the government to break (powerfully) the corporate entity that is perceived as piranha in corporate America. In both instances, society and the participants incur multiple costs in their attempts to "right the power perspective" for all to see.

There has been an increased incidence of personal violence by children in schools and family situations, by adults in reaction to organizational firings, and by corporations seeking to create a sense of equalness in the playing field. From mergers and acquisitions, from union lawsuits regarding equity in the workplace, from employment lawsuits challenging the layoff process by organizations. (Remember Computer Associates giving employees personal high marks for performance and pink slips for not meeting organizational targets—creating a belief that the organization just didn't want to pay severance packages?), the issues of empowerment, reciprocity, and equality in the organizational landscape have given rise to greater struggles against concepts of power or abuse.

Studies indicate that the average cost to hire a replacement for each employee released from an organization is $50,000. The cost for the actions of our organizational leaders is over $20 billion. For each child brought in court to account for "fighting back," the court costs are $500,000 to $2 million. The community cost is increased fear and the creation of more restrictive practices systemically. The political cost is a retrenchment to a more conservative stance that reduces the opportunity and capacity for creativity and change. The human costs are incalculable. We lose in every way when we continue to support power as the approach for living and being in our society.

DEVELOPING A PERSPECTIVE OF COLLABORATING WITH ONE ANOTHER

In our society we create coalitions and call them partnerships or mergers. Coalitions are single-focused issues that cause groups and individuals to join together to attack or address the single issue. Partnerships are equity relationships created to respond to multiple issues that impact the life of business, community, or sustainability. Mergers are agreements to join two entities together to create a new entity. *What we as a society have termed mergers and partnerships are in actuality coalitions. We have very few partnerships and mergers.* When Mercedes Benz acquired Chrysler in 2000. it was spoken of as a merger, yet the two became Mercedes, not something different. Corporations gobble up their competition or some other entity which they sense can help them with a singularly focused attitude—control the competition, control the industry, control the people—and life and business will exist as we want it. Schools, communities, and churches equally conduct the same activity. *Control the thinking, control the behavior, and create standards that fit a narrow norm— making every other approach or strategy suspect and punishable. Being different, thinking differently, and behaving differently are not valued.*

So how do we move toward collaboration? How do we achieve some form of connectedness? How do we move from coalitions to collaborations? *First, we should look for a sense of wholeness and not compartments.* Descartes began the process of assessing psychology from a Cartesian perspective, depicted in Table 5.1. As can be seen from the table, theorists throughout time have maintained a linear dualism in assessing the development of people within a cultural context. Over the life of a Cartesian approach to understanding human performance and development, humanity embraces a cultural intent around natural law, a world view that perpetuates and embodies compartmentalized development as pieces of the whole in the material world: an either/or perspective in the self and other dualism domain, a spatial dimension in the transformation domain, and a cause and effect process in the organizing ethos domain.

What is unique about the model is the integration of a global linear process that binds and blocks the fluid development of man. Dr. Grant Venerable, a provost at Morris Brown College in Atlanta, Georgia, developed a matrix model of humanity (the Ven Matrix, 1995) that "lays over" one another as parallel systems of development for people, systems, and chemical organizing principles. Dr. Venerable calls this process the tripartite dualism. The focus of the system created is the nonexistence of a beginning or an end to the development of humanity. His terminology is rich and expressive: he speaks of "living in har-

Table 5.1
Linear Dual Realities versus Tripartite Dual Realities

CARTESIAN—Linear Dualism	KEMETIC—Tripartite Dualism
Domain "A": Nature/Natural Law	
CULTURAL INTENT	
• Dominate/control nature.	• Live in harmony with nature (Ma'at).
• Tendency toward accumulation and exploitation of material and human resources consistent with domination and control.	• Tendency toward accumulation and exploitation of material and human resources consistent with Ma'at.
Domain "B": Material World	
WORLD VIEW	
• Universe is a vast mechanistic device composed of fixed operating parts, a whole equal to the sum of its parts.	• Universe is a unified, *tripartite* structure of the whole greater than the sum of its parts.
ONTOLOGY	
• Matter is "real" stuff knowable only through the physical senses. Material constants (image) valued over logical necessity.	• Matter is "spirit," purely an activity, a cosmic illusion—Logical necessity valued over material constants.
EXPERIMENTAL METHOD	
• "Objectivity"—observing subject split from observed object—no relationship between.	• "Relative Objectivity"—subject forms relationship with object's reference frame to obtain object's viewpoint.
• "Technique"—Speed valued often at expense of accuracy (time spent equated with lost money and efficiency).	• "Technique"—Slow, deliberate pace valued to not miss small, but possibly crucial details.
Domain "C": Self/Other Dualism	
SOCIOCULTURAL ORIENTATION	
• Linear (either/or), Male vs. female, egoic individuality, competitive, xenophobic, didactic.	• Complementary (both/and), male/female harmony, creative individuality, cooperative/group-oriented, xenophilic, dialectic.
• Zero-sum consciousness—Life is win-lose.	• (+) Sum consciousness—Life is win-win.
EPISTEMOLOGY (framework of knowing)	
• Logical-empirical, If A then B causality, fragmentive analysis and resynthesis of the whole.	• Holistic, metaphoric, relativistic—complementary rationality—field causality of sufficient reason—systemic synthesis; begin with universal and then assign component elements.
• Specialization, parsimonious deduction of data from general principle; limited induction of the general from specific data.	• Generalization, abstractive induction of universal principles from specific data.

Table 5.1 (continued)

CARTESIAN—Linear Dualism	KEMETIC—Tripartite Dualism
Domain "D": Transformation	
SYMBOLIC ORIENTATION	
• Logical-Digital/Literal-Realism.	• Analogic-Representational/Relative.
SPACIO-TEMPORAL CONCEPT	
• Newtonian; time is limited, linear in flow, separate from space. Form of change varies with circumstances.	• Einsteinian: time is relative and the complement of space; moment is infinite and cyclic. Change seen as cyclic, evolutionary, or instant.
Domain "E": Organizing Ethos	
• Universe is an efficient, utilitarian idea existing to serve the needs of (Judaeo-Christian) man.	• Universe is a God-centered, transcendent idea.
• God is a fixed, absolute "first cause"—The CEO of a male hierarchy of middle managers.	• God is a universal vibrating energy represented as different facets of nature.
• Salvation more dependent upon religious belief than personal conduct.	• Salvation more dependent upon personal conduct than religious belief.

mony with nature, universe as a unified structure of the whole that is greater than the sum of the parts, matter as spirit, people and systems as complementary, holistic, metaphoric, relativistic, universe as God centered" (1996 lecture). Taking the Cartesian approach to psychological and biological development, Dr. Venerable gives it a soul or spirit that has historically been missing from the developmental theories of human development.

The Cartesian thinking process, commonplace in American society, is a dominant/control thought and action process. Individually and systemically, it is human nature to dominate. Table 5.1 compares several theoretical and praxis strategies. What would happen, however, if we did not exist to dominate or to control? Actually, we do not exist to control or dominate. Although our society claims it is based on religious tenets, none of its actions follows the tenets of Christ, Buddha, Confucius, or any other religious leader. Our society also continually states that it wants to honor its employees, treat them as human beings, and live by a higher standard—but none of corporate America's actions mirrors that sentiment. In addition, our politicians from Reagan to the current president piously insist that the government is there to help our children. To the contrary, the children continue to suffer because our practices of power and control continue to teach abuse, misuse, and accumulation.

Organizational Violence (Williams, 1994) talks about the control parameters

Figure 5.1
Control Parameters

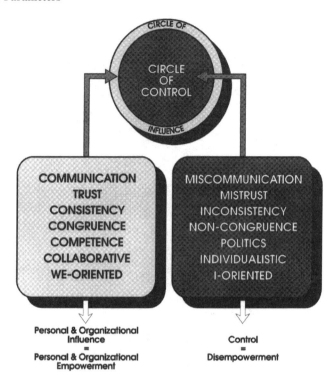

that block effectiveness. These parameters are still prevalent today (see Figure 5.1).

Figure 5.1 shows the control process as experienced by people. When any change occurs without attending to the unconscious issues of clarity, people experience an expansion of a circle of control. The control circle focuses on I-orientations, for the good of self—not the whole. The more control is expanded, the more employees within the organization experience mistrust, miscommunication, inconsistency, noncongruence, politics, incompetence and combative behavior. In effect, the expansion of control becomes a process of disempowerment. Change is successful because of careful attention to the tenets of violence.

Step two of the violence system occurs when anyone impacted by the change requests clarification regarding the outcomes desired within the change process. Each time clarification is requested; yet the answer given comes from the circle of control, [and] the violence paradigm is escalated. In step one, the tenets and vessels of violence are experienced by employees; in step two, the structure and process of violence become the strategies that escalate the system. The structure of violence is comprised of the varying standards that impact organizational functioning. In the case of the violence paradigm, standards are nonexistent.

The process of violence occurs through movement from the circle of influence toward the circle of control. The movement occurs because an aura of chaos has taken control of the organizational environment. The circle of control is actualized by the concept of inconsistency and noncongruence. Any action that appears I-oriented becomes a self-serving act. That act suggests that looking out for another is of very low value and protectionist behavior must be actualized. All actions are suspect; all behavior is mistrustful; all statements seem to have hidden meaning; and teamwork, collaboration, and we-oriented action have dissipated.

Our society has done little to shift from I-orientation or circles of control. The result is confusion, and both individual and organizational attempts to collaborate fail each and every time.

To collaborate requires the nonuse of power and control. Figure 5.1 shows a circle of influence as an effective strategy for empowerment. To collaborate implies clear communication, trust with one another, consistency in actions and performance, congruence where words, thoughts, and deeds match, competence in place of political action, and we-orientation that supports a win-win, not a lose-lose situation. When you hold a party to celebrate your birthday and to honor your development, people's participation at your party is a form of collaboration because through their presence they demonstrate their support. When you work with members of your family to heal the rifts that have occurred among you, you collaborate to achieve resolution. When you discover a problem at work and you develop strategies to resolve the problem with others—where the problem is the focus, not the individuals—you collaborate with one another. *Power and control focus on the individual, whereas collaboration focuses on the issues.* So to collaborate suggests that one supports the tenets of clarity; specifically, it suggests equality, reciprocity, representation, and empowerment. Power implies the antithesis of these emotional and practical frames. When one collaborates, the focus becomes humanness. When one uses power, the focus becomes objectification of the humanity into things. When, for example, President George Bush arrogantly avoided apologizing to the wife of a Chinese pilot for the loss of his life, his desire to appear powerful and in control was perceived as an objectification of the pilot as a Chinese thing, not a human being—and so the world reacted negatively to his power stance. A collaborative stance for resolving the issues between the two nations would have endeared others to Bush's "compassionate conservatism" rather than provoked frustration and anger at his discount of the human situation.

Remember the research study from the last chapter and the definitions of the congruence characteristics in Chapter 1? The findings from this research were as follows.

- *Managers were not as consistent or considerate of employees as they professed in verbal conversations.* The absence of reciprocity and equality from the business paradigm by managers in their actions within the organization strongly suggested that even-handed treatment of employees was not a reality. Just as the executives did not consider the skills and abilities of employees in their actions, so it appeared that the managers equally did not consider this characteristic. The characteristic reciprocity being absent was a total surprise. Conventional wisdom has often stated that give-and-take should exist in order to achieve employee loyalty, employee performance, and employee retention. Reciprocity was not critical in the actions of managers. There was an even greater surprise when one recognized that managers were less likely to value the concerns of employees or their comfort levels. Equality was also a surprise in its absence from the managers' success determinants. Equality was the business paradigm congruence characteristic that focused on the ability of the organization to ensure that people balanced effective work actions, strategies, policies and procedures. If the managers were unconcerned with equality, then the ability of the employee to meet the needs of the organization in accomplishing the work was not possible. Equality would require that every employee was well trained and understood how the work was to be accomplished. When little-to-no interest in the skills of employees emerged in the managers, success of the employees was very unlikely.

- *Discord and acknowledgment were absent from the patterns table.* The definition of discord stated that one was increasingly uncomfortable with emerging and changing factors in one's life. The absence suggested that managers were less concerned with what employees felt versus how employees functioned. This view supported the absence of acknowledgment which described the issue of comfort and its relationship to others. *Managers' actions therefore seemed to support having employees, individually and collectively, following the decisions whether comfortable or not.*

Regardless of the words they used, managers and executives made employees objects and through that action perpetuated power and control versus collaboration. It was when they understood the importance of people behavior to success that collaboration became an important practice.

Look again at some of the findings. Remember: The discussion here is supportive of a movement from power and inanimate thinking to collaboration and animate thinking.

- When the organization and the managers were experiencing effectiveness in people behavior and decision making, *empowerment was the congruence characteristic.*
- When the organization and the managers were experiencing effectiveness in people behavior and environment, *reciprocity, interpretation, commitment, and disclosure were the congruence characteristics.*
- When people behavior was the primary determinant present in a given event or act, *equality, representation, emergence, and acknowledgment were the congruence characteristics.*
- When people behavior and satisfaction were the governing determinants in organizational and personal effectiveness, *reemergence was the congruence characteristic.*
- When decision making was the primary determinant, *empowerment, representation, commitment, emergence, and reemergence were the congruence characteristics.*
- When structure was the determinant, *representation and self-indulgence were the congruence characteristics.*

The factors in the research that made a difference for employees and managers was recognizing the collaborative nature of the work environment. Feeling represented, empowered, committed, emerging, and reemerging in values and beliefs fostered personal and organizational success.

To collaborate represents an alteration in the balance of work and play. The current business paradigm is one of market share acquisition. This model focuses on competition and supply and demand as the final arbiter of business success. Unfortunately, this business model was created as an economic necessity early in the history of the United States when protection of the new nation's borders was a critical ingredient for societal sustainability. But times have changed. We now live in a global society and not just this continent. Organizations throughout the world create coalitions to achieve differing ends. Gemplus, a French smart card organization, has agreements with IBM and Microsoft to ensure the effective production, marketing, and distribution of smart card utilization worldwide. Cisco Systems has corporate alliances with major corporations to advance the sale and use of Internet technology.

In each case that you can identify, the paradigm of control when used causes the partnerships (actually, coalitions) to fail. When the converse occurs, thriving is the outcome. So what this suggests for the future of business is—*play fair, give and take equally, and find opportunity for shared thoughts, practices, and strategies that achieve an end for all; not just one.*

Collaboration requires looking at the issues of the world differently and choosing to alter the strategy. Every time one interfaces with an organization on a strategic or leadership issue, one is faced with helping the organization and the leader start from scratch. Einstein said that solving the problems of today with the strategies of yesterday that created today's problems is a psychotic adventure. While he was right, it is the hardest strategy to implement. Starting over means re-parenting one's approach to thinking and being. If competition, control, domination, withheld information, politics, and individualism are the frameworks that have created dysfunctional business and human performance, then it would behoove the organization and the person to try something new. Collaboration—the sharing of ideas, strategies, feelings, and action—then becomes a different way of functioning. In the Venerable model displayed earlier, the Kemetic mode of development was significantly different from the Cartesian model. As organizations continue to participate on a global scale, the Cartesian model will be regarded as an arrogant, self-absorbed, cognitive dissonant of interaction. As leaders focus on winning versus sharing, the arrogance of the company will become the arrogance of the individual. Similarly, on the personal level, as young people, and their families perpetuate the models of organizations that continually frustrate their personal sensibilities, their ability to work, grow, learn, and join with others will be thwarted by a dysfunctional paradigm that truly has never worked for sustainability.

Collaboration initiates a system rather than an individual approach. Collaboration occurs because attention is given to four capitals in thought and deed.

Figure 5.2
The Four Capitals

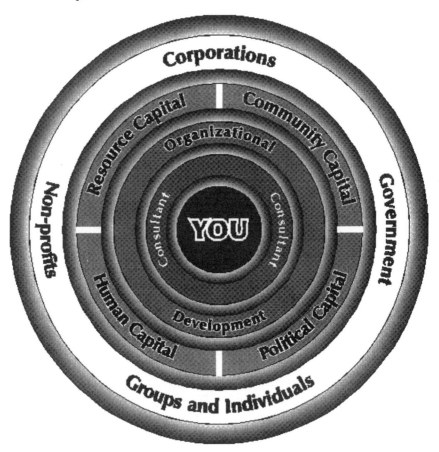

These capitals are human, political, community, and resource capital (see Figure 5.2).

THE FOUR CAPITALS

Human capital is the compilation of all the facets of humanity within an organization, community, or family that focuses on the personal and group effectiveness of people within organizations, communities, or families. How groups form, how people embrace the organizational/systemic process, how people sense inclusion and participation in the actions of the organization, how people find themselves being heard within the organization, how diversity is embraced, how consistency is implemented throughout the organization—all are critical criteria for the effective management and utilization of human capital within an organization. Who the person is and how the person is valued, embraced, and enhanced frame the human capital of the organization. The question that arises is to what degree for the extent do we embrace the human capital within our practice as consultants, leaders, managers, family leaders, siblings, groups, and educators to the people and groups we serve?

Resource capital is the composite of all the equipment, fiscal, and time resources that are utilized within organizations, groups, and families to achieve the timely, qualitative, and quantitative outcomes of the entity. Focus is more on efficiency than on effectiveness within the organization. The issue of resource capital is corporate sustainability. How the organization markets, sells, buys, trades, forecasts, and plans for the present and future with attention to the past of the organization is critical to the organization's overall success. The questions embedded in the resource capital are issues of balancing the values and integrity of the organization, community, family, or group with the fiscal actions of the entity. Resource capital focuses on the compartments of organizations rather than on the whole. Finance, accounting, marketing sales, administration, operations, inventory management, and other areas of the organization are the focus of attention.

Political capital is the consistent networking and development of influence relationships within the organization and other influence brokers to impact the resolution and management of critical conflict, resource, human, and competition issues that arise in the life of an organization. How one develops political allies affects the overall success of the company when legislative or other factors impede the success of the organization's strategies. The questions that arise focus on the extent to which political capital is effectively managed for all versus that which we use to manage and control the relationships by which we further our own individual ends. Can any of us effectively manage political capital with integrity without trashing and disempowering our colleagues in order to get ahead?

Community capital is the composite ethnographic, demographic, ever changing diversity of the community that supports the existence of the family, group, or organization. The image of the organization, participation in the surrounding community, valuing of the diversity and differences of the community, and understanding of the culture of the community and the organization to intentionally collaborate with one another are all key considerations in developing the overall infrastructure of the organization. To discount the community issues ultimately creates poor relations within the community for the organization. Community capital is about the learning potential of the organization and the community and the extent to which a shared meaning and relationship exists between the company and community to create new opportunities for reflection and transformation. The questions for we all must ask is whether we effectively balance all four capitals in our practice.

All four types of capital are necessary for organizations and their employees if they are to satisfy the needs of the organization. Devaluing any component for another is an ultimate breakdown in the system of the organization and the community. Challenge yourselves to look at your behavior and thinking in your daily lives. Where do you place your energies? How do you balance what is out of line? Have you considered any of the issues here before you?

THE IMPACTS OF COLLABORATION

So we are reminded that it is our humanity, not our objectification, that helps build congruence. The language we use, the actions we take, the approach for win–win all support or detract from the outcomes we achieve. As I tell students in class, "It is never your intent that people remember; it is your impact that frames your legacy." For all the good that President Clinton accomplished in eight years of office, it is the impact of the actions that people will remember. His intents around Monica Lewinsky will never replace the impact of his actions. Regardless of the intention of Charles Williams, the 14-year-old shooter in Santee, California, his impact will long outweigh his desire to get help and save his family from ruin.

Working with others is more sustainable than power over others. Regardless of Hitler's belief that purity was better than integration, the actions he took to achieve his ends will forever make him infamous. Family members, corporate leaders, managers, parents, individuals—you—are challenged to assess what your driver is for working with, around, or through others. What is clear is that if a shift in the process of success and congruence does not occur, we will again be trapped by our dominant/control paradigm. Descartes did us no favors, and we need to do some rethinking if his time has come and gone.

Mini-Epilogue: Putting a Face on the Process of Congruence Development

Creating clarity around one's history and one's pain in the workplace or in the family is often difficult. In the search for congruence, the task is an intense soul-searching process about the obstacles one creates in trying to be seen, heard, and understood. The challenge is to recognize that the search is within and that the exclamation is one's emerging sense of peace with a reality that is on a totally different path.

What might help with each person's understanding is the courageous writing of one of my students. Her exploration of her sense of congruence is taking her on a path beyond her wildest dreams. Hopefully, as you sense her emerging self, you will see where your pathways lie.

My experience in leadership and personal influence can easily be summed up in one word: frustration. My belief systems and thinking styles have not been congruent with the belief systems and thinking styles of the organizations I have been a part of whether they are the workplace or elsewhere. I have not been a leader since I cannot make things happen by "maintaining the beliefs and structures that the organization has established" (Williams, 1996: 123). Instead, I often ask the questions and raise the issues no one else wants to ask or address. Consequently, I end up frustrated because I do not "fit in" with the status quo.

I remember, even as a twelve-year-old, in girl scouts and later in high school when I served on committees, how badly I wanted to be a leader and influence my peers. Later as an adult in my different jobs and volunteer work I again wanted to be someone people listened to. Sometimes they did and sometimes they did not listen. Unfortunately, my frustration often grew in situations where I did not feel heard. As a conversation would progress my tendency was to become more intense or forceful in trying to prove my point. I would try to use the power that I watched everyone else use to win over a situation or a person. I did not understand how I created walls by continuing to use the same approach and over again to get my point across. I now realize I scared some people with my intensity and others got disgusted with me, consequently they stopped listening and never heard my point. It was a destructive cycle for me and it has been the manner in which I addressed my personal and professional life.

My family style of communication and influence was straightforward and blunt. As a result I valued conversation that went straight to the point. "Beating around the bush" just confused me. Over the years, it has been a learning experience for me to learn to be diplomatic and to understand that people do not necessarily say what they mean. I expected people to be clear and direct and when they were not, I did not hear what they were trying to tell me. Slowly, I have learned to read between the lines and become aware of the nuances in conversations and to check out the intended message, and discover whether the message was supposed to be a power play or honest leadership. I guess that I am learning how to achieve the clarity in the situation.

My father was a strong military man with definite opinions and critical perspective of others. He was verbally abusive as well. As a result of his dominance I became uncomfortable with and afraid of authority. I also became scared of being blamed and of never being good enough. I never rebelled while growing up, but now in the workplace I hate rules and sometimes resist authority, particularly when it does not make sense or is abusive or when I am blamed for things I have no control over. I guess I have been hooked by the rules of engagement in our society and it has impacted me personally and professionally. It just seems that the workplace and sometimes, families, are controlled by this blame/shame thought process and I never knew how to get out of it. Actually, I didn't even know before this class that it existed. . . . I just knew how to feel bad and be angry at authority.

I grew up with a strong sense of justice, fairness, equality. My parents, especially my mother, valued fairness. At Christmas time she kept a list of the gifts she bought and added up how much she spent on my brother, sister, and I to make sure we had an equal amount of presents. She also taught me that honesty was the best policy and that people are good. It was devastating to me when I discovered and accepted that life was never going to be fair. Here again I assumed everyone else wanted fairness, justice, and truth, except for a few "bad" people. Because my personal belief system was that people are honest and up front and are trustworthy, I kept getting burned. I always wanted to believe the best of people and believed they in turn believed that about me. Sadly, I have often found out, too late, that people are more interested in themselves and I end up hurt. Now I protect myself and I am more careful about whom I trust. I guess, I have become like them and I hate the way it impacts me.

My hero was an Australian physician of the nineteenth century, Semmelweiss, who discovered the connection between germs, and washing hands in between patients. He was ridiculed for his suppositions and became an outcast, later dying from the very infection he identified. As I studied about his discoveries, personal trials and triumphs, I developed immense respect for his courage to speak out amidst great opposition. His courage was something I wanted to aspire to. Heroes, to me, were the people who stand up for what they believed despite the odds against them.

So, I entered the workforce as a dental hygienist with the aim of saving my patients' teeth and then later as a human resources professional wanting to ensure the organization was complying with employment law and treating employees appropriately. What a wild ride I have had trying to survive in a business world that is more concerned about the bottom line—money, profit and power—than the people they serve and the people who help them make their dollars.

I mention the history of who I am because it has impacted my ability to lead and be influential. My beliefs and assumptions about people and the way we should or should not treat one another were so naive. I started out life as an open, trustworthy person, wanting the best for others and myself and believing they had the same assumptions. I wish I had remained that way. Over the years I found out the hard way, through many painful experiences, that others assume business is competition and everyone has hidden agendas. Sometimes the workplace seems like a war; a game of survival of the fittest and who comes out on top is the winner. So there are only winners or losers, and the losers are blamed. Actually, when anyone loses, everyone loses!

I hate competition and politics. Probably because I hate losing and when I do not win, I feel like a failure. Another reason I dislike competition and politics is I do not like being the winner and watching the loser lose. The straightforward approach I value might also contribute to my dislike for and inability at politics, since hidden agendas are not a part a straightforward paradigm. My lack of political finesse has also created some disadvantage for me in my attempt to survive in the win/lose dynamic of workplace war tactics. I guess what really gets to me is trying to operate in a way that others do which feels so sick and dysfunctional.

The politicizing of decision making infuriates me. I have kept my mouth tightly sealed shut until I could no longer morally or ethically let an issue go by. When I said nothing, I felt I had lost my integrity and could not look myself in the mirror. But then when I spoke up, I hated myself for becoming the "problem." It is almost funny to watch the people that I work with finally realize I just want to do what is right for the organization and the employees and that I have no hidden agendas. Their paradigm does not allow them to believe people like me exist; they cannot believe that I do not have some underlying reason for what I do and say. Once they believe me and realize I am not out to get them, and understand I want everyone to win, their face and body muscles relax, and they start to trust me. Then I begin to have influence in the organization. I guess I do create collaborations in the work that generate new complements. Wow! I am getting it! The more I work to achieve ends that focus on the issues, not the people, I build collaborations with people and trust and integrity do become real complements for my life.

This cycle of distrust and trust occurred in my last place of employment with my direct supervisor who was the fiscal officer for the public works department. She believed the county director of personnel's point of view that I was incompetent and not to be trusted As time went by, I convinced my supervisor that I was not who the director of personnel said I was. My supervisor recognized my competency and started listening to me. Just before I left the job, I was beginning to see where my influence had impacted the organization in positive ways. Despite my change in influence within the department, I decided to leave because the director of personnel controlled everyone she believed might have impact on her power base. I found out she made it her business to know when I applied for other jobs in the county; consequently, I knew there was never going to be an opportunity for career and personal development beyond where I was in that organization. My supervisor also recognized there was little opportunity for me in the county and understood why I was leaving.

Because business operations are often reactionary and situational and do not consider the underlying causes of problems and issues within organizations, only the symptoms are treated. I often have been caught up in the symptoms and become the scapegoat in the dysfunctional system. I have watched the reactionary behavior and I shook my head wondering if someone would ever wake up from the delusions and denials of the truth. But no, a few powerful people controlled things and worked to keep their power. Then I would walk right into the dynamic and I became the perfect distraction for the few powerful individuals' manipulations of the organization.

The powerful used me, the crusader, who was unwilling to play by the rules, as the perfect patsy to keep their precious power from being challenged. When I asked questions, presented a different point of view, or stood up for myself when they lied to make me look bad, they would then paint a picture of me as a disruptive and defensive person who was "the problem." Since it is normal (but not maybe the best strategy) when one feels attacked to protect oneself, I fell into their trap and they made me look the way they wanted. But when I did not try to protect myself, I became depressed for allowing myself to become what they wanted, which was to be the "company person." It was a losing situation and there was no way that I could be congruent, so I was not happy with my life.

I also became defensive because I kept being accused of wrongdoing. I was ignored and criticized for my persistence in trying to do the right thing. I was on a crusade: the more I was told to keep quiet, the more I wanted to be the crusader. I think I understand that Dr. Williams was challenging our inability to be creative. When we struggle to find our anchors—our complements, we fall prey to the labels (classical thinking) that are given us and the attending actions (scientific/dynamic thinking) that become our problem process. We become the cause and the effect, the blame and the shame.

By being a part of organizations that were incongruent with what I believe, I have disempowered myself and have been unable to be my authentic self. One of the ways I was disempowered was by draining myself of energy when I tried to be a "good girl." Each day I went to work, I literally strained myself to keep in line with the status quo. I felt myself working hard at fitting in with the organizational norms. Each time I called into question the status quo, I received negative feedback from supervisors attempting to force me in with the rest of the herd of "company people," since they perceived me as a threat to their way of life and their success in the organization. In effect, I was always in classical thought organizations, but I wasn't a classical thinking person.

Frustration and depression set in, as I tried to conform or challenge the norm. There has been no middle ground in most of the places I have worked. Either you move with the masses or you are not accepted. Any personal power I have has been consumed by my efforts to figure out a way to survive and be successful. Lloyd Williams, in his book, *Business Decisions, Human Choices* (1996), discusses how organizations trap themselves from changing by their current belief systems. As I read this passage I thought about myself and asked how have I trapped myself through my current belief systems, keeping me from transforming myself and my life into what I wanted. After taking Williams' thinking styles and belief systems profiles, I discovered I am 55% psychological, 25% legal, and 20% theological in my belief system. My thinking style is 50/50 evolutionary and process. When I am stressed I will often move into the evolutionary style of thinking and I will push change at all costs. When I feel out of control and stressed I go into the legal belief system. For instance, in my current position I am caught in between middle management and one of my staff persons who has decided I am out to get her, even though I have tried to assure her, her belief is inaccurate. The pressure I feel to perform as my managers expect (which is vague to me even though I have asked for clarification) and the pressure to lead an employee who is sabotaging me, makes me just want to lay the law down with her. This desire of mine to tell her to "straighten up and fly right" is my legal side (and my father speaking). So my pressure points of pushing change to an extreme and becoming controlling could be keeping me from changing to more productive ways of relating to others.

The extreme effort of pushing change at all costs has created polarization and barriers between the "company" coworkers and me. When I first realized I was polarizing myself from others, I thought there might be a way to be myself and work within the organization, so I would not contribute to polarization and threaten people. I thought by finding middle ground it might be possible to be accepted through understanding the organizational dynamics and by not playing into them. However, now I am realizing I will still use a lot of energy to learn survival tactics in a place with a belief system and thinking style so very different from mine. As I have continued to contemplate how I will find congruency in the workplace, I am coming to the realization that it will come from being somewhere else than where I have been. Finding a new environment more congruent with who I am will give me more of an opportunity to have personal influence and be a leader.

I gain strength and have more personal influence when I work with others in a team. Although I work well by myself, I find I do my best in teams. I learn more when I work with others and am more creative. Bouncing ideas off of other people in a nonthreatening environment generates energy within me. For me, discovery and creativity arises when I ask a lot of questions and look at new ways of doing things. In many organizations, when someone asks a question, it suggests that there may be another way of doing something, or it points out a problem. There is the expectation that the person has to have the all answers. This construct that one has to know the answers, which is a hallmark of an addictive system, has been difficult for me to believe in—yet hard for me not to participate in. This distinction sets people up for blame and shame. I know I am not perfect and no one else is, so how can anyone have such an unrealistic expectation? Since I am not someone who has all the answers to my questions, I started thinking that I needed to, otherwise I might be perceived as weak or incompetent. I was afraid I would be misjudged or I would not be successful if I asked too many questions. One example of this was when I worked in fear of forgetting to tell a manager something that one of the Board of Supervisors might ask a question about and then I would be blamed, because the manager did not have an immediate answer.

While reading *Business Decisions, Human Choices* (Williams, 1996), I was relieved and encouraged to see that "just a strategy for framing the questions and walking through the process of discovery" was okay (p. 151). Some of the ways I am developing my personal influence is to find strategies for framing my questions and by learning how and when to ask the questions.

I have experienced organizational psychosis such as psychotic affect, loss of sense of self; and loss of volition as described by Lloyd Williams (1996) from working in environments incongruent with who I am. In particular, at several points in my career, I have lost the ability to sense myself as a competent and capable individual. I have found it is difficult to make decisions on my own, because if I do and it is not what someone perceives as politically correct then I am criticized. Yet, if I do not make a decision on my own, then I am again criticized for not being "independent" enough. My volition has been lost, as well, and I have difficulty getting started on projects and get confused about what to do next because expectations are always changing.

So far in my experience as a manager and a leader I have not been given the authority or support to implement a context for business and personal process paradigm that is congruent. When circumstances allow me to include my staff in decisions that will directly impact them I ask for their input. Usually what happens is I do not have the information either and I am given the news at the same time as everyone else in the work group. Then we make the best of what we have before us, so in that sense inclusion is important to me and is something I strive for. Inclusion has helped me to be successful in managing and leading most of my staff.

In the aspect of personal domain in business the fear present in the organizations I have worked in has been too great to conduct effective dialogue. Occasionally, there might be one or two people I trust enough and who trust me so we can dialogue openly with each other. I have included and encouraged the people I supervised to engage in dialogue. However, there usually has been at least one person in the group, whom others do not trust so the conversation becomes more of a careful discussion.

I have facilitated discussions in which people initially stayed out of the conversation, but over time they were drawn in and participated. In those situations the trust developed within the meeting. The trust was built by encouraging the participants to consider what was working well within the organization and use the insight as a stepping stone to the next level of growth. This approach was successful because people did not need to be afraid they might be blamed and shamed for problems. Instead they were able to celebrate what they did well and their self-esteem, individually and as a group, were raised. By taking an appreciative approach, hope rather than discouragement was generated.

Although writing this paper has been somewhat of a depressing experience from examining the incongruency in my work life and reliving the pain I have suffered from not being me, it also has been cathartic and affirming. It has been cathartic and affirming, because I realized I am not the problem and the dynamics that Williams attributes the problems are those which I suspected all the time. Now I know, without blaming myself; that I have been in places where I cannot be who I am, so it is no wonder that I have struggled and been unhappy in my work.

Writing this paper is a gift because it opened my eyes to see why I need to find a new path and it has given me a clearer picture of the new path I need to take. It also showed me that my assessments of the various situations were accurate and that I need to trust my instincts and believe in myself. I also gained awareness that one of my strengths as a leader is the ability to see the interconnections in a system and how they impact one another in the organization. My courage to ask questions is a strength that I can develop to help both organizations and myself use in the process of discovery and growth Now I just need to find the soil that I can grow and flourish in and find contentment, because I am becoming congruent! I like the changes and I sense that if I stay on the path, what a difference it will make.

Personal and systemic transformation, personal and professional growth, and movement to congruency are often about managing the chaos present in our lives. There is a clinical process called sitting with it—living with the tension— that allows people to explore the ambiguity of life rather than having to have all the answers in the moment. The challenge of the first part of this book is to recognize that achieving clarity, building collaborative experiences, and developing realistic and ethical complements is the hardest part of developing congruence and creating change. The reality is that congruence and change are processes that we work toward. Meg Wheatley, in her book *Leadership and the New Science* (1999: 12), stated that "organizational change is a dance, not a forced march."

Although our world of business and people still operates from McGregor's Theory X and Theory Y theorem, rarely does our world embrace the difficulties of a "black/white perspective." Complexity theory states that living systems are self-organizing with a capacity for adapting to sustain health, wealth, and life. In effect, the more one recognizes the ever-changing dramas in our lives, the more we can continue to become, grow, and evolve. Wheatley, Harris, and Owen—critical theorists of complexity—believe that understanding the complexity of organizations will generate autonomy, diversity, and learning. They are wrong, however. The challenge of complexity in their theories would suggest that the one still has greater value over the many in the development of key characteristics of organizations. I sense that the real issue of complexity is the development of authenticity—self-cognition, mutual collaboration, and systemic complements—sustainable forces that build from what is to what can be developed or formed.

We now face our opportunity for authenticity. This first section of the book has demonstrated and explored the underpinnings of congruence thinking—clarity, collaboration, and complements. We now move to the impacts of the thinking. If one can be clear, develop collaborations, and create complementary anchors, one can begin to explore creativity, complexity, and congruence. We go there in our next chapter.

Chapter 6

Looking at the Business and Personal Complements That Can Anchor Us

Anchors, complements—these are key terms that often elude business leaders, employees, and family members as they consider the relationships involved in their lives and work. In Chapter 5, the discussion centered on the impacts of power, authority, and control—its individual, group, and organizational focus. *The difficulty with power, authority, and control lies more in its impact on our lives than in its intent.* Most of you have experienced times in your lives—both personally and professionally—when you discovered someone using power, authority, or control over you to get their way. These experiences brought pain, hurt, and even trauma. Think of your reaction (not response) to the actions of these persons. Did you embrace them the next time you saw them? Did you forgive their indiscretion but not forget it? Did you avoid them in the future? Did you determine that what you experienced from them you would never do to another? Did you become fearful, slow down the work, select someone else to confide in the future? What did you do about your experience with power, authority, and control?

In the 1993 movie *Rising Sun*, Sean Connery and Wesley Snipes portray police officers investigating the murder of a woman in a Japanese company, an incident covered up by two other employees. The CEO of the company asks Sean Connery to assist in the resolution of the issue while helping the company save face. Near the end of the movie, the Asian employee who "had become too Westernized" was discovered to be the culprit. Interestingly, all of the other Japanese leaders backed away from him as he was confronted by the CEO. This process of distancing was deemed as disconnecting; they were removing all ties to this employee. This process was that of releasing anchors by the other Asians in the room. The Asian employee lost his anchors; that is, he lost his complements in his professional life. The CEO's final decision was to send him back to Japan and place him in an office in a far away corner to "learn the error of his ways." Key to this decision was the film's statement that he had lost touch with his culture, his way of being and knowing, and must now regain a sense of who he was in relationship to what he and his society valued. This challenge to the Asian in the movie is in many ways the challenge of this chapter.

THE CREATION OF COMPLEMENTS

Complements are those thoughts, actions, events, experiences, and persons we invite into our lives that create effective anchors for risking the development of change and congruence. Each and every day of our lives we face situations and experiences that establish or interfere with the building blocks we need for our psychological/personal/professional framework and world view on key issues. Each day we build either *membranes* that allow us to experience trust, fear, hope, compassion, fairness, and so on—helping us recognize how to use them effectively in our decisions and thinking—or we build tight *walls* that impede our ability to embrace concerns that impact us when we come in contact with another, often forcing us to focus on the strategies of protection, control, authority, or abuse in order to win and defeat others.

In our personal world, the way we make friends, learn to share, build relationships, and embrace love and loss are all strategies we use to develop complements, providing anchors that will sustain us in all our interactions. In the business world, the way we embrace assignments, respond to management complaints and to change and innovation, create linkages and partnerships, and bring our talents to the work are strategies for developing complements. Key to these areas is the issue of creating a *context for learning and development.* A context is an overarching frame or picture that informs our thinking and behavior in response to life situations. A coach can create a context for learning that says either that winning must occur at all costs, or that we are in a game and must be prepared to do our best to win, as well as respond to our losses as learning opportunities for growth. *The context sets the stage*, as the following example indicate. In 1998 and 1999, coaches around the country in Little League baseball were being criticized for the negative values they were demonstrating to children. Then there were the actions of corporate leaders who terminated employees to achieve a profit goal, blaming poor performance on the employees. In addition, we had Clinton blaming Monica Lewinsky or the Republican party for the demise of his legacy, and a little later George W. Bush alienated the environmental community by wanting to drill for oil in Alaska or for accepting arsenic levels in our drinking water. Each of these events alienated and defeated the opportunity for anchor building. Where is personal and systemic accountability for the contexts that we create? Is our way of being driven by the content factors in our lives often taken out of context?

Complements or anchors create contexts that expand our accountable connections in the world as critical to our world view. Contexts are about operating through a set of values that honor one's perspectives on life and about ensuring that the *contents and processes (strategies, methods, approaches)* employed honor the expansion of the anchors that drive your sense of self, group, and organization. Contexts establish a safe framework for us to embrace the world and its issues as experiences to be lived rather than as problems to be solved. Complements are about accountability and about how comfort with ethical and equitable strategies gives rise to an expansion of anchor development. Complements are also about seeing the whole of situations, not just the compartments or contents that often ultimately harm us in our everyday lives.

What are the contents that drive us? Think of the times in your lives when you have tried to get people to hear the overall story, and what you got in response was a discussion about the specifics that occurred out of context. Consider the school shootings that occur all too frequently around the country. Society's immediate response is to place the child in jail rather than consider the extent to which the child was harmed by bullying and taunting in the school. Consider the faculty and administrators of the school who have been found blameless for the actions of the child and the lack of an assessment as to the school's responsibility in not keeping the alienated child safe. Consider a society that downgrades the values of mental health, allowing accountants and actuaries to determine the appropriate treatment for dysfunction. Consider a government that for twenty years has avoided mental health as a realistic condition. Consider the court cases and states that are still under indictment and court order to "right" the mental health system allowing opportunity. Consider the mental health juvenile system that places children in jail rather than in mental health facilities. Consider your own desires for treatment and look at your organizational benefits. Where is the mental health component? How many sessions can you get on insurance? Look at the providers of service. Insurance companies have replaced psychologists with social workers and licensed professional counselors. Where is the comprehensiveness in the services provided? Why is less training valued more than comprehensive skill development? Pills versus therapy is the answer of today's mental health, even though all the research studies conducted by the National Institute of Mental Health and the National Institutes of Health explicitly agree that it is through the *collaboration* of the pills and therapy that people get healthy. So we again must consider the context—not the content which often is the decision maker in today's society. *It is not that the students kill out of frustration; it is that we all share accountability for the actions of the child because we focus on the content of the specific action rather than on the context of the entire situation. It is not that mental health is a pariah in our society; it is that treating the whole person for wellness is not valued as a prevention strategy—reacting to sickness is the paradigm of health.*

Look at your organizations. Each time problems arise, it is the employee who was not given full information, only content pieces, who suffers. Consider the leader who withholds information, avoids talking with the employees, relies on false information, poor information, and poor decisions. Yet it is the employee who is let go, not the leader. *Content drives our society, our families, our individuals, our businesses.* The piecemeal information that we use for decision making enhances the opportunity for dysfunction, pain, and trauma in the society. Every time you provide a two-page resume, you create dysfunction. Every time you create a bulleted memo, you create dysfunction. Every time you respond to the trappings of being rather than being itself, you create dysfunction and the society continues to grow in a downward spiral. Every time you compartmentalize yourselves and acquiesce to time-driven or singularly focused content about yourselves, you help create dysfunction in your lives—potentially disrupting the anchors of your life. In business, in intimate relationships, as well as in personal and professional development, your participation in the content facts of your life rather than the context whole of life creates dysfunction and the loss of your anchors.

We can talk about this issue in a slightly different but more searing manner. As a society we avoid accountability. Because we operate systemically from a Cartesian thought process, we have learned to use political skill and aptitude to address the issues of the past, present, and future. When interfacing with people in our society, the strategy most often employed focuses on control, manipulation, abuse, or flirting to win over another. This behavior is driven by the Cartesian model of thinking that says there is a cause and effect for whatever happens in life. The other side of the cause and effect is that someone is blamed and shamed for their failing. The political process replaces competence, creating political incompetence that says to individuals, managers, leaders, and employees: *fix the issue, take the blame, shame the affected person.* The process of political incompetence becomes that of obtaining power, raping the employees and stockholders, and creating bondage in the work process. Rather than add more anchors that can lead to future accountable personal and professional developments and change, the anchors one develops become a loss of trust and a loss of self esteem. Our corporate leaders become sadomasochists, punishing themselves and others and enjoying it all, saying that it is part of living. Comments such as "What did I do wrong? What can I do to fix it? How do I take the blame?" are commonly heard in the relational process of business and the unsatisfactory but stable development of families and individuals. Is it correct to say that everyone does it?

Listen to comments from the president of the United States, George W. Bush, to your boss. *Be efficient and consistent! Efficiency just means you did the task quickly, not effectively. Consistency means you did it over and over—not that it was congruent, balanced, and aligned. We have focused on the wrong issues and strategies in businesses, and we are paying the cost for that short-sighted process.* Yet we are proud of his direction and leadership. I think not! Whatever happened to effectiveness and congruence?

THE ACCOUNTABILITY PROCESS OF COMPLEMENTS

If we are going to achieve effectiveness and congruence, then we must look to the whole, not the pieces. The process of developing complements can be called the *congruency-accountability complement*. Accountability means that one or a group of persons are responsible for a defined set of actions, thoughts, and circumstances that establish an end point or outcome. *Accountability* is the primary factor used to establish effective interaction and performance, and *management* is the judicious use of strategies and technologies to accomplish an end. *Accountability management* is the process of ensuring that one person or group of persons responsible for a given product, and team performance strategy create an environment for the judicious use of human, political, community, and resource capital. Accountability focuses on the strategies designed to achieve predetermined or agreed upon outcomes through the effective management of human relationships and the effective implementation of strategies and technologies. Accountability management is a both and process and an outcome for people and work. To create complements in work management, development of human relationships and performance strategies is essential.

The key outcomes in this accountability process are as follows: (1) more effective work is accomplished when employees create their own strategies for accomplishing specific outcomes; (2) more responsible thought and behavior occur when employees recognize that success is based on team and individual effort induced by their planning efforts; and (3) creating trust options generates more avenues for collaboration and complement development than fear and blame strategies. In effect, creating complements requires looking to personal and team ownership of their successes and their deficiencies.

Accountability and complement development imply integrity, ownership, honesty, sharing as key to success, planning, effective communication, creative decisions, and risk taking. To become accountable, that is, to have complements, requires that each individual, leader, or team:

1. Work toward *harmony* to ensure that building relationships is devoid of blaming others for shortcomings in outcomes.

2. Enhance people's strengths and specific abilities to generate a willingness to take *risks* and actively take on challenges, recognizing that risks drive growth and learning.

3. Accept *responsibility for knowing and understanding* 100% of the work—not an incremental doling out of the work. To be successful in work performance, full scopes of knowledge are required to build skills necessary to accomplish outcomes and trust by employees in honoring their abilities to see the larger context for creating options for success.

4. Avoid fixing activities that lead to co-dependent dysfunctions, ensuring that *ownership* will become a key component of creating anchors in one's life and work.

Essential to the development of complements is recognizing and then avoiding the following inhibitors to complement development.

1. History
2. Blame
3. Fear
4. Sabotage
5. Shame
6. Jealousy
7. Unresolved conflicts
8. Miscommunication or false communication
9. Poor decisions or no decisions
10. Poor planning, no planning, or incomplete planning
11. Competition

Unfortunately, inhibitors are the norm in current organizational operations, ensuring that the life cycle of organizational and individual functioning will be controlled by ineffective leaders and managers. Alteration or elimination of these inhibitors is critical to the creation of anchors—complements in one's life. When these eleven inhibitors dominate organizations, effective anchoring is impossible.

The American Psychological Association and the Society for Industrial/Organizational Psychologists have long touted an imbalance in personal, group and organizational life driven by inappropriate personal and organizational strategies of control. Paulo Freire (1973), a noted sociologist, has discussed this issue:

Dehumanization, which marks not only those whose humanity has been stolen, but also those who have stolen it, is a distortion of the vocation of becoming more fully human. This distortion occurs within history. The struggle for humanization, for the emancipation of labor, for the overcoming of alienation, for the affirmation of men and women as persons would be meaningless. This struggle is possible only because humanization, although a concrete historical fact, is not a given destiny but the result of an unjust order that engenders violence in the oppressors, which in turn dehumanizes the oppressed. This then is the great humanistic and historical task of the oppressed: to liberate themselves and their oppressors. (p. 44)

Freire also pointed to the inability to create effective complements:

Money is the measure of all things and profit the primary goal. For the oppressors, what is worthwhile is to have more, always more, at the cost of the oppressed having less or having nothing. As beneficiaries of a situation of oppression, the oppressors cannot perceive that if having is a condition of being, it is a necessary condition for all men. This is why their generosity is false. To the oppressor, humanity is a thing and they possess it as an exclusive right, as inherited property. . . . Over time, the oppressed gravitate to the behavior of the oppressor as an irresistible attraction, for being one of the haves is important. Self depreciation is another characteristic of the oppressed, which derives from their internalization of the opinion the oppressors hold of them. So often do they hear that they are good for nothing, that they cannot think, that they cannot write, that they know nothing, that they are unproductive, that they are lazy. They are peasants and feel inferior to the boss because the boss seems to be the only one who knows things and is able to run things. . . . The peasant is a dependent. He can't say what he wants. Before he discovers his dependence, he suffers. He let's off steam at work, at home, where he shouts at his friends, his co-workers, his spouse. He beats them, yells at them and is in despair. He complains, but doesn't let off steam at the boss because he thinks the boss is a superior being and he is afraid. (pp. 44, 49, 51)

Our Cartesian desire to dominate and control therefore blocks our ability to create complements and anchors. As a society we seem to concentrate on gaining power over others, both personally and organizationally. We are often unclear and unaware of the impacts of our actions in the world. It is not that we choose to abuse; rather, that abuse seems to have taken a legitimate place in our society as an appropriate strategy for business and play. What is necessary is a "righting of the paradigms of operation" to create different technologies that can inform the human and business condition.

THE TECHNOLOGIES

Righting the current paradigms that operate in our families and our corporations requires that we shift the paradigms that drive our thinking. If the Descartes paradigm of domination and control over others is the performance and thought process of today's world, and yet the impact is less clarity, collaboration, and complement development, then it becomes important to rethink the paradigms in force. The challenge is to implement a paradigm that elevates balance and alignment over control, power, and authority. To make the shift from classical, scientific dynamic, communication, and field thinking to evolutionary and process thinking requires valuing the human condition and its development rather than stunting the human condition to ensure victory over others. Congress has recently focused on winning over China through intimidation and control. President Bush mouths on compassionate conservatism and yet reduces environmental, food and drug, oil and gas drilling restrictions that have short-term, content-based strategies. There is a context here, however: to create fear and to return to a previous time of extreme power and control. Each of these examples requires a loser—meaning all lose. The paradigm must assess the creation of balance and alignment as essential to personal and organizational sustainability. To accomplish that feat, winning and losing must no longer set the tone of the contextual goal; creating balance where growth and development can occur for all must become the contextual outcome.

Four technologies or four strategic changes have been utilized in varying degrees as strategies to achieve congruence: (1) the team approach, (2) the competence approach, (3) the matrix approach, and (4) the integrity approach.

The *team approach* focuses on empowering groups to accomplish outcomes. It has been in existence in some form since 1940 when Taylor outlined his scientific management theory. During the past twenty years, surveys, studies, and organizational strategies have focused on team approaches to the work. Unfortunately, a significant amount of team activity in organizations has been wrought, with competition as the primary strategy for innovation and excellence. Employees within units compete with one another and other groups; groups withhold information from one another to ensure their survivability; and leaders create competitive processes in companies within companies—as though the competitive process will permit growth and development. John Chambers, the CEO of Cisco Systems, has described the degradation of the industry at a pace that no one could foresee. The partnerships that they believed were forged with their alliance partners did not and could not yield positive results because the competition blocks any opportunity for true collaboration and the lack of collaboration, in spite of all the perquisites to employees, was not tantamount to complements that sustain people and systems. In the same way parents create competition in the family, pitting boys against one another in athletics, girls against girls in beauty pageants, and parents against one another for the compensatory levels that they achieve. In effect, teaming is a nice thought, but rarely is it a reality in the workings of organizations.

The *competence approach* focuses on determining the specifics that are above and beyond the skills of the group and reward the super skilled for using their competence. It has been in existence since the 1920s and was reinvigorated in the organizational process during the 1960s. Think of the teams that you have been a part of in your career. In some cases, the team was to create the strategy, but the supervisor, manager, or director actually relied on one individual–to perform the work. Similarly, a team effort will be praised, yet the evaluation and merit system rewards the individual contributor, not the team. For all the conversation in organizations about teams, the expert seems to take precedent over teams in organizations. Individual contributors expect and demand a level of flexibility that the team cannot achieve, and the boss presents a duality in the rules process to the advantage of the expert—the competent one—rather than sharing the advantage equitably with all.

The *matrix approach* assesses where skills exist in other divisions and creates options for utilizing the skills across the department and not just within the division. This approach was the beginning of the collaboration process for organizations, teams, and groups. It has existed since the early 1970s and has been seen as a strategy for getting more work accomplished without expanding existing resources. The challenges in the matrix approach arise from the competitive internal organizational process. Leaders want to explore numerous strategies and use the matrix to share resources. It would suggest that the most talented should be assigned to the matrix. Rarely is that the case, however. Instead, the competitive, power-oriented, unbalanced approach pits functional managers against matrix managers. Struggles to understand the roles and accountabilities become the challenge of the century, and as a result, the organization and the participants in the matrix lose. In the movie *The Matrix*, Keanu Reeves created a win–win for all because the collaboration and trust among the members of the rebellion was the binding glue. The movie's emphasis on trust, collaboration, sharing, and equity does not occur in the corporate world. Phenotypically, the issues are the same within a family or a group of friends. Competition rears its ugly head, and the collaboration necessary for interactive play goes out the window. One sibling mistrusts the other, the sports leader seeks glory over shared success, and the struggles of the matrix continue.

The last option for strategic change, the *integrity approach*, demonstrates personal or professional ownership of thoughts and actions that impact others by supervisors, leaders, and employees of the success and deficiencies of the group. It requires becoming involved, participating in planning, joining in the work effort, and building the appearance of team and group rules. This approach has existed throughout time in limited situations. It is the only approach of the four that involves all persons within an organization or all members of a family in developing anchors that honor everyone impacted by family, organizational, or personal decisions. It does not mean that all four approaches will not expand the congruency–accountability complement; rather, it indicates that the integrity approach gives a bigger success outcome than the others. The challenges of these strategies often fail in the business and family process because the underlying thought paradigm is designed to elude development and change. Ultimately, classical, scientific dynamic, communication cybernetic, and field paradigms are about no change. Thus, using them as the baseline for the creation of clarity, collaboration, or complement development will never get one there. Two perspectives are created that defeat accountability. They are balance of power and unresolved competition.

Balance of power focuses on the need of one group to develop approaches that will defeat the other group or keep it in place. Historically, unions hold the balance of power in organizations. The other factor, *unresolved competition*, focuses on the need of one group to say that unfairness has occurred, thereby shortcircuiting the need to build congruence in the way one works with another. In effect, both approaches suggest that power, authority, and control become the struggles of work and the downfall of accountability.

What is missing in the approaches currently used to develop anchors? What gets lost in the transition and transmission of strategies to create accountability and congruence? The hooks of power, control, and authority block the development of clear thought and strategy development. People continually state that their experience with people and systems is about the discount—to shore up self-esteem and ego. To create the complements, bonding and balancing are the critical baselines for developing self, group, teams, and systems. Without equitable relationships, bonding does not occur. In the absence of balancing employee and organization needs, or your needs with those of your siblings or friends, an underlying perspective is that the real outcome is abuse of you.

Understanding this issue of integrity and complements can sometimes be difficult. We therefore return to the integrity approach. Integrity falls in three categories.

THE APPEARANCE STANDARD

The appearance standard is the gauge of the organization and the community that establishes a baseline of trust in your actions, thoughts, and future projections. The appearance standard is critical because what is seen is as important as anything that you do. If you state that something will occur and it doesn't, then your value or worth is diminished by others' perceptions of your actions. You can do the right thing and still be wrong. Conversely, you can do the wrong thing and be right.

THE RULES STANDARD

The rules standard is the gauge of the organization that builds credibility through congruency and equity in the written rules, administration regulations, departmental operating procedures, and the supervisors' direct statement of how things will occur. The rules standards become critical because employees and the organization in general build faith and act in successful ways because they trust that the organization looks after their best interest through the rules that govern treatment, performance, promotions, and overall succession strategies. When you violate or constantly change the rules and treat different groups inequitably, then belief in the rules goes out the window.

THE PRACTICE STANDARD

The practice standard is the gauge of day-to-day functioning that demonstrates adherence to the organization's appearance and rules standards. If the organization states that it values and empowers employees, and yet those employees only experience power, control, and manipulation, then the practice standard is counterproductive to the rules and appearance of the organization. The goal becomes that of building a level of congruence between what have become the standards of the organization to the implementation of those standards through all actions of the organizational environment.

The blocks to the integrity option are as follows:

- Operating out of fear, power, and control
- Operating without balancing management and technical performance
- Creating avenues and approaches to blaming, shaming, discounting, and manipulating the employees and system

- Forgetting to accept ownership for your responsibilities, both managerially and technically
- Avoiding collaborating strategies, especially when the success of the work requires collaboration
- Showing poor skills in communication, decision making, conflict resolution

Therefore, to be successful, a balance of skills, management, and integrity is critical to effective performance.

To help you embrace the issue of complements, and thereby creating anchors, you should participate in the next series of exercises with someone in your office or a significant person in your life who can help challenge your thinking and acting.

As a member of a team of supervisors, managers, or directors, how might you respond to the creation of more integrity within your work environment, or how might you create more integrity in your personal development?

_____
_____
_____
_____

As a supervisor, manager, or director, what might you specifically do to build on and enhance the appearance, rules, and practice standards of your particular work group, or how might you enhance your personal standards in your interactions with family, friends, and loved ones?

_____
_____
_____
_____

As a manager, how might you lead persons under you to adopt actions and behaviors that will create more effective appearances, rules, and practices, or how might you congruently think and behave personally in such a manner that you can lead others important in your life?

_____
_____
_____
_____

Group Simulation: The Integrity Option

This is a two-hour exercise in which you are to look specifically at the work that you are asked to accomplish.

In your planning, delegating, monitoring, and evaluating the work, how might you enhance one-person, group, and organizational success through a review of appearance, rules, and practices within the organization? _____

_____

_____

_____

_____

Which of the issues you identify are based on team ineffectiveness, individual ineffectiveness, or system ineffectiveness? _____

_____

_____

_____

_____

What creative strategies can you devise to alter the current heading of those issues, and what specific things will you do to change the direction? _____

_____

_____

_____

_____

The challenge for you is to focus on the thinking that drives actions, not action to drive thinking. When we act first, we often resort to our history and the inhibitors without recognizing their control over us. So when you focus on the thinking, you can see the blocks to your anchors.

Accountability Management

Based on all the issues discussed in this chapter, the following technical skills are required to maintain success in your roles as accountable leaders.

- Coaching and counseling skills
- Planning and scheduling skills
- Time management and matrix management skills
- Earned value and percent complete skills

Each of the skills you use requires a genuine understanding of communication, conflict resolution, resistance, and customer accountability. This exercise focuses on understanding those relationships so that you can more effectively manage your areas. Remember: the employees who report to you are your customers; the clients you serve are your customers; your peers are your customers; and you are your own customer.

Your success is based on your understanding and ready acceptance of your accountability. We start with communication skills.

Table 6.1
Roadblocks to Effective Communication

Evaluative Responses	You should/You should know better
Advice-Giving Responses	Why don't you try/It would be best for you
Topping Responses	That's nothing, you should have seen/You think you have it bad
Diagnosing Responses	What you need is/Your problem is
Prying Responses	Why, Who, Where, When, How! (puts people on the spot)
Warning, Admonishing Responses	You had better!/If you don't!/You will (produces resentment)
Logical/Lecturing Responses	Don't you realize?/Here is where you went wrong! (produces inferior feelings)
Devaluation Responses	It's not so bad/Don't worry, you'll get over it (creates a lack of trust)

The purpose of communication is to get information shared from one to another! However, to be effective in that communication, you must ensure that the other person heard the information that you wanted to share. This means: Did you share the information in the way that *they needed to hear it,* or did you share the information in the way that you like to give it and receive it? Most often, we share information in the manner that is most comfortable for us rather than for the person we want to hear the information. Therefore, often the information is not heard.

Can you think of times when this has been true for you? _____

_____

_____

_____

_____

We often take communication for granted; yet it is communication that is the central skill necessary for creating clarity. It is also communication that drives our ability to collaborate with one another because we recognize the potential of joining with others rather than controlling others. Often we don't hear, and we just play at listening. Therefore, it is important that you think about your communication with others. Where are you in your ability to hear?

Each of us at varying points in our careers indulges in one or more roadblocks to effective communication (Table 6.1), and sometimes, we use all of them in one conversation. We need to look at how those comments impact our ability to obtain the *results that we want in a conversation.*

Communication between you and another person does not always mean that

Figure 6.1
What Did You Really Mean?

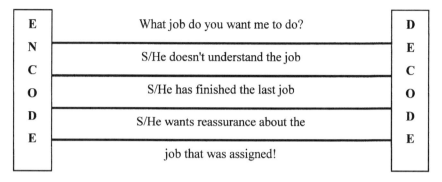

you heard accurately (see Figure 6.1). What did you hear? Mental listening is the key to responding accurately. Effective expression requires that you:

• Become aware of your thoughts and feelings.
• Feel comfortable in expressing your feelings.
• Be aware of the listener.
• Focus on the importance of the message.
• Use as few words as possible.

Points for the Listener

Be fully accessible to the sender.

• Develop a purpose and commitment to listening.
• Be aware of your feelings as a listener.
• Avoid distractions.
• Listen with a third ear.
• Wait before responding.
• Suspend judgment.
• Continually reflect mentally on what is being said.
• Develop paraphrasing in his or her own words and context.

You should also be ready to respond when the sender wants and needs comments from you. *This is often seen as simplified by many persons; yet the accessibility and the focus on the listening are often not accomplished. Because accountability includes creating trust options, listening is a critical component of doing so. In work and at home, we each have a tendency to become self-absorbed,*

Table 6.2
An Example of Effective Frustration Management

Specific Behavior	What It Does to Me	The Effect
Tony, when you are consistently absent from work	I get upset with your lack of responsibility	Because I have to find someone to cover your responsibilities and I can't trust you!

and what we consider listening and being present for another person just does not occur. This strategy process helps.

Frustration Management

The Importance of Giving "I" Messages

Often, what we want to communicate regarding our frustration or our anger is appropriate; however, *the way we share that frustration with another can create a major problem.* The goal in sharing our frustration is to *change thought and behavior* without destroying the relationship, friendship, or contact. We would not want to destroy their self-esteem. An example of effective frustration management is shown in Table 6.2.

"I" Messages

When you give an "I" message:

1. Determine for yourself what the conflict is about.
2. State clearly for the other person the behavior that is causing you the problem.
3. State the effect that the behavior is having on you.
4. Give a tangible effect; describe what it causes to happen to you.

Don't just say that you are bad, or wrong, or stupid. Don't bring in a long list of grievances, for it's overwhelming. Be honest about what happens.

If the message doesn't say exactly what you want, then restate it until you are sure that other persons understand your feelings and your concerns. If they don't understand, it is usually because you are not getting your point across well. Keep the following points in mind.

- Know what you are feeling.
- Be clear about what you want to communicate.
- Be aware of the listener.

Figure 6.2
A Problem-Solving Model

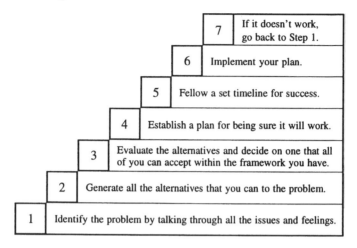

7	If it doesn't work, go back to Step 1.
6	Implement your plan.
5	Fellow a set timeline for success.
4	Establish a plan for being sure it will work.
3	Evaluate the alternatives and decide on one that all of you can accept within the framework you have.
2	Generate all the alternatives that you can to the problem.
1	Identify the problem by talking through all the issues and feelings.

- Don't assume—it will get you into trouble.
- Be open to what the other is saying.
- Don't make assumptions or second guess the sender.
- Avoid distractions.
- Wait before responding.
- Be committed to listening.

Roadblocks to Effective Listening

- Don't assume in advance that the topic/issue is unimportant.
- Don't mentally criticize the sender of the message.
- Don't get overstimulated when questioning or opposing an idea.
- Make sure you listen for the total thought.
- Be attentive.
- Don't over-react to certain words or phrases.
- Don't withdraw—Be present for the person communicating.

Once listening is enhanced, one needs a model for creating resolutions. Figure 6.2 demonstrates a model for creating resolutions.

Things to Remember about Successful Conflict Resolution

Conflicts arise on the job because of:

- *Poor communication.*
- *Making assumptions* about others and acting on those assumptions without checking it out.
- *Having expectations* of others and others having expectations of you that are not shared.
- People expect you to be *congruent in your thought and behavior.* When you are not, then their trust and risk factors decrease markedly and set up suspicions that you don't know exist.
- *Lack of Direction.* Everyone likes some guidelines and limits in which to work. It provides a goal and some objectives. Without them, frustration and potential depression set in.
- *Jealousy.* If you get more than I got . . . if you have more clout than I have . . . if you appear more in charge or responsible than I am, then jealousy is a definite outcome.
- *Lack of fairness.* When you operate with favoritism, then people become angry, hurt, and mistrustful.

The Importance of Humor

- Humor is the world's *"social lubricant."*
- We tend to be attracted to and like the people who make us laugh. Therefore, humor plays a valuable role in the support of group harmony and in the communication of information.
- Humor is an effective way of raising risky issues.
- Humor is an effective way of calling attention to areas in which people have become inflexible.
- Humor is an effective approach to establishing trust and frankness.
- Humor does not destroy one's self-image; rather, it provides a way to point out mistakes and problems gracefully.

Guidelines for the Effective Use of Humor

1. Start with yourself. "You grow up the day you have your first real laugh at yourself!"
2. Be able to take your work seriously but yourself lightly so that you can perceive and appreciate the humor in everyday encounters.
3. Be an observer. Be aware that you are surrounded by humor and notice that humor.
4. Think of humor as being of two kinds, public and private. Public humor is shared the moment it occurs, whereas private humor is experienced when something funny occurs, but it is inappropriate or harmful to laugh at the moment.
5. Use humor as a support for competence rather than as a means of masking a lack of competence. Humor at its best is one aspect of an individual's communication repertoire; its use should not be an alternative to giving direct feedback or to dealing with an issue!
6. Use humor with sensitivity and care so that it is likely to be appreciated. Otherwise, there are few useful generalizations about situations in which humor is clearly appropriate or inappropriate.

A Positive Approach to Resistance

In relating to customers/clients and peers, the issue that usually creates pain is the difficult experience. You do not seem to have problems relating to a pleasant person—customer, coworker, or boss. However, you find yourself struggling with the angry person, the distant person, the vengeful person, the loud person, the rude person, the royal person.

The real issue that confronts you is your ability to effectively respond to resistance!

There are low-yield and high-yield strategies for responding to resistance. Most of us use the low-yield strategies.

Low-Yield Strategies

1. *Break it down!* (Threats, coercing, selling, reasoning)

2. *Avoiding it!* (Deflect, don't hear, induce guilt)

3. *Discounting it!* (Dismissing, promoting tradition; appealing to the need to conform)

In dealing positively with resistance, two basic assumptions must be understood (1) resistance will always exist; and (2) resistance needs to be honored!

The positive approach has four separate steps:

Surface the resistance.

Honor the resistance.

Explore the resistance.

Recheck the resistance.

1. In *surfacing the resistance*

   A. Make the expression of resistance as safe as possible. State that you want to hear the resistance.

   B. Ask for it all. . . . Listen to all of it, working through it in pieces creates more trauma!

2. In *honoring the resistance*

   A. Don't try to sell or reason; just accept the resistance.

   B. Acknowledge the resistance! Acknowledging does not mean that you agree, but only that you heard what is being said!

   C. Reinforce that it is okay to resist!

3. In *exploring the resistance*

   A. Distinguish authentic resistance from pseudo resistance. Authentic resistance is directed toward the specific request, policy, or demand! Pseudo resistance usually originates in feelings. Ask, "What is your objection?"

B. Probe the resistance. Ask, "What would you prefer?" You are working *toward* the objection, not *against* it.

4. In *rechecking the resistance*

You wanting to assess whether the objection or resistance is the same. This is important because you are providing closure.

Remember that

- *"I" Statements* express thoughts, feelings, impacts, wants/needs, expectations, preferences, decisions, and consequences.
- *"You" Statements* express empathy or understanding of the other person's situation or experience. Grant the other person's position or truth, or describe the other person's behavior.
- *"We" Statements* express mutual options or alternatives, compromises, decisions, or actions. They affirm the relationship, or in question form, request mutual problem solving.

Make sure that you

1. Gather baseline data.
2. Discriminate among behaviors.
3. Demonstrate your assertiveness, not aggression.
4. Give feedback to others.
5. Establish an action plan.
6. Make sure you follow up.
7. Evaluate the outcomes.

The Art of Successful Intervention

Now that you understand the theory, the next step is practice to integrate the thinking and acting into your everyday life. The more you do this, the greater the opportunity to create anchors and complements in your life. People will trust you and you will trust yourself more. People will collaborate with you rather than resist you. You will complement you rather than defeat you.

We are going to experience multiple ways in which we can use these skills to best relate and be accountable. Some of the time you will be practicing with each other, and other times, you will be practicing with many persons in your exercise. Remember to acknowledge the resistance, use your humor, communicate and listen effectively, and problem solve—we are all in the business of relating to each other!

A Communication Role-Play

You will be divided into groups of threes. One person will serve as the observer and share with the other two a perspective on your ability to communicate in the role-play. Remember the roadblocks to effective communication.

John and David are coworkers in the Department of Public Works. John is a new employee, and David has been with the city for six years. John feels that no one likes him because he is very talkative. David is a quiet man and says very little. John has never had a problem with David and feels that he can trust him to tell him why people shy away from him. David has agreed to talk with John. You must share with each other how you feel and what you feel occurs in the job that makes people act the way they do. Remember: Hear what the other is saying, give direct feedback, listen to what is happening with you and the other person, and be open!

John is a loud man who acts as though he knows all. Coworkers find him to be a bore, and they resent his attitude that his way is the best.	David feels sorry for John because he used to be like John. The real issue for David is that he believes John is right, but is just going about it the wrong way.

You have thirty minutes to complete this short role-play.

A Conflict Resolution Role-Play

You will be divided into dyads—that is, teams of two. This exercise is an experience in resolving a conflict.

Your supervisor, Tony, has been consistently blaming you for work being turned in late. You have not wanted to tell Tony that the work has been late only because Tony has changed the rules or requirements of the work, without extending the time frame required to accomplish it.

You have decided that you will finally confront Tony on the issue. It is important to remember how to look at positive resistance, listening skills, communication methods, and in particular I-messages.

Tony has been upset that Mark's work has not been up to standards. Tony feels that Mark is doing so poorly that he is prepared to terminate him. This meeting may be the only saving grace.	Mark is angry and scared. He feels that Tony has changed the nature of the job and hasn't given him enough time to learn the ropes. He wants Tony to back off and give him some space.

You have thirty minutes to complete the role-play.

A Listening Simulation Exercise

As a group, you will be asked to listen to a conversation between all of you. I am an angry citizen, and I don't believe that you are treating me fairly. I believe that you have overcharged me in parking tickets and that you have not adequately notified me of the consequences of not paying my fees. I am friends with the mayor and have threatened to use my "influence" to make you set things right.

This is an exercise in listening. What are you hearing? What is going on inside of you? What are the rules? Can the rules be bent, or should they be bent? What do I really know about this situation?

You have thirty minutes to complete the simulation.

A Problem-Solving Exercise

Your boss tells you as a team that the city must reduce its expenses by 23%. All of you are supervisors in the Health Department, and your director has advised you that you must lay off twenty-three employees as your contribution to the city's reduction plan.

As a group of supervisors, you are free to look at any options that might resolve the issue. However, you must create a plan that you feel will accomplish the directives of your department executive.

Use the problem-solving model to create your options and resolve the problem.

You have one hour to complete the exercise.

Group Discussion

You have experienced four different practice role-plays or simulations. In each you were asked to use varying skills from the writings/discussions on accountability and anchor development. Now the questions are as follows:

How do I operate when I hear a threat, an angry response, a frustrated gritting of the teeth.

What do I do when my boss is discourteous, disrespectful, or ungrateful?

Where do I address the issue of frustration?

What was different about the role-plays and the skills I was asked to use?

How can these skills be helpful to me in the future in dealing with a citizen, coworker, subordinate, or boss?

Brainstorming the Problem

What is so difficult about dealing with our accountability?

What do you see as the problems of relating?

Where do we go wrong?

What are the issues?

Do we really care?

Is it a joint problem, or does the customer just have to conform to our rules and procedures?

In a brainstorming situation, someone usually tells you what the problems are without using the same skills to find out from you what can be the cause of difficulty. You are being asked to reach clarity on the problems and to collaborate with others on the solutions. You must remember that integrity, ownership, and sharing are key to your success. You are building anchors for your life, not silos that shut out your light to the world.

A Role-Play in Transition

You are all a special team of new supervisors within the organization, chosen because you are flexible, adaptive, interested in change, committed to service, and dedicated to improving the quality of work for all employees. The executive team and the managers and directors have praised you for your unique and wonderful skills.

Recently, the organization has had to address:

- A decline in the quality and productivity of the employees' work.
- An increase in the unions' reports of supervisors' abuses of employees.
- An increase in complaints from citizens regarding all levels of service delivery.
- The changing strategies being created by the hiring of a new city manager and executive team.

The organization is struggling with these new changes, and the executive team has requested that all of you create a program that focuses on customer service and service delivery. The executive team has also stated that you have $100,000 to implement a program over a one-year period beginning in September.

What are you going to do. How will you use the skills to help you co-create a program. What are the strengths of the organization? What are the strengths of the employees? Where are the deficiencies, and how would you create changes?

You have one hour to finalize a customer service process.

WHERE WE GO FROM HERE

The foregoing exercises focus on your ability to think about your professional and personal life. If creating complements—anchors—in your life is about integrity and ownership, how do you bring these qualities into your life? Is integrity the hallmark of your thinking and acting? When have you made allowances or taken a different path in defense of actions that you knew were not the best or ethical thing to do? If accountability is about sharing, effective communication, creative decisions, and risking, how do you experience that harmony, responsibility, and risk-taking in your work and play? An issue of authenticity drives the blending of these three "Cs" in your movement toward congruence: clarity, collaboration, and complements. These *are the seeds of personal and organizational discovery.* Without them, every individual, family, group, and even organization may regress to the age-old dynamic of narcissism. It would appear that each entity in our society has an ego that functions either as a supraordinate regulatory system or as a subordinate agency within the mind concerned only with gratification of self-absorbed drives (Gedo and Goldberg, 1973). Consequently, the more one thinks of self, the more likely the thoughts and actions will focus on gratification of the self to the detriment of others.

Unfortunately, our society's adherence to Cartesian thinking has perpetuated a self-absorption that makes everything and everyone else an object. As a result, little opportunity for the development of anchors exists. So as you consider the words of clear communication, clear decision making, clear planning, integrity, and ownership in the business and personal world—key words for the development of anchors—consider this thought: Domination, power, and control lead to psychosis and inevitable destruction. Every day we witness the destruction of individuals, groups, and organizations as they attempt to live out a psychotic vision of ego, which is a delusion that frames one's power—one being more important and powerful than reality dictates. We witness the consistency of that vision of ego each time the organization relives old strategies that advance only power, control, and authority. As the recessions of 1980, 1987, 1991, and 2001 make clear, nothing has changed in the strategies of organizations. The same historical tapes continue to run, and our ability to achieve clarity, collaboration, and complements becomes more and more elusive.

We have now presented the start of altering the paradigms—the first half of a different approach. What follows is a discussion that puts the process in perspective. We struggle for sustainability, not replicability; we search for authenticity, not consistency; and we will thrive because of congruency.

We seek the anchors that give us a sense of direction, using what we now understand to frame the direction through which we can advance.

Chapter 7

Experiencing Our Business and Personal Creativity: The Impacts of Emerging Strategies

THE CURRENT EXPERIENCE OF INNOVATION

Every day you hear business gurus and corporate leaders express their organizations' critical need to innovate. They tout a new strategy, product, and equipment as the next best approach to expanding and advancing their business. But often within eighteen months to two years, the new strategy, product, and equipment are already obsolete. And so the process of innovation begins anew for the organization and its leaders, but the result is the same for each new innovation. What is going on here? What is the problem with this concept of innovation that is so heavily endorsed by organization leaders and gurus?

Webster's Dictionary (7th ed.) defines innovation as "the process of renewal." *Webster's* further defines renewal as "the act of making young again that which is old." To cause to exist again and revive what has gone before is an additional definition of renewal. So this means that innovation is the process of taking what is old, outdated, and dead and reviving it as a form of improvement. These are all interesting definitions of what businesses and gurus advertise as the next best thing since sliced bread. The term *innovation* is not a good one, for it implies that one cannot think beyond what already exists. Innovation is a process of extension—bringing back in a dressed-up form that which has gone before and failed. This is a quite different way of looking at this critical business language and activity. It is a concept that businesses and leaders seem to have lost in their attempts to (1) quickly capture market share, (2) get ahead of the competition, and (3) ensure a profit outcome that is often unrealistic and is almost always based on the present rather than sustainability. *In actuality, corporations and their leaders renovate and innovate; rarely do they create.*

Fast Company in its April 2001 issue reported that there are four principles of life and business. First is equilibrium, which is a precursor to death. When a living system is in a state of equilibrium, it is less responsive to the changes that are occurring around it and it is most at risk when it feels most secure. Second, when threatened or galvanized by a compelling opportunity, living things move toward the edge of chaos. This condition evokes higher levels of mutation and experimentation and is more likely to result in fresh new solutions. Third, as living things move closer to the edge of chaos, they tend to self-organize, and new forms emerge from the turmoil. This property of life called self-organization and emergence is a major source of innovation and evolution. Lastly, living systems cannot be directed along a linear path. Unforeseen consequences are inevitable. The challenge is to learn how to disturb them in a manner that approximates the desired outcome and then to correct the course as the outcome unfolds. The article presents a very poor analysis of the process of living, being and becoming. *In fact, I the paradigm of living and being, of becoming, and of change that we adhere to as gospel are wrong.*

I am an organizational psychologist, a father, a consultant, a man, a black man, a brother, an uncle, and a significant other. How I live and sense life and living does not match the paradigms that govern business. Innovation is not a standard in my life. Nor is regurgitation of what has gone before or stirring the pot to see if some alteration occurs. My life is about creating and creativity.

Webster's is again helpful here. To create means "to cause to come into existence, to bring into being, to make." To create is to originate and cause something new. This is different from stirring the pot. To be creative is to have an intellectual inventiveness that stimulates the imagination and inventive powers. To have creativity is to have an intellectual inventiveness.

This chapter is about creativity, not innovation. It is about exploring your intellectual, emotional, and practical inventiveness, and it begins with a reminder of the chapter on thinking. The first four paradigms of thought—classical, scientific dynamic, communication cybernetic, and field thought—were and about change. Most individuals, families, groups, organizations, and governments operate from these four paradigms. Our society is one that does not value or understand change. Our society is one that looks to chaos as the catalyst for change and that utilizes dominance and control as the primary thought and action strategy for living and being. The more we try to understand our uniqueness, the more we become trapped by the rules and engagement strategies of the society.

When you come up with something truly new, you are often ostracized for your audacity to think. When you search for your balance, you are warned to follow the norm, to conform—never storm. The group theories of compromise, acquiescence, and silence are all designed to ensure that we only innovate and renovate. To create requires calm, peace, and equilibrium, and to change requires a serious assessment of one's authenticity. To create requires movement toward congruity—what the society and business often fear as "too far out there." So if you become congruent, you cannot be dominated or controlled.

Consider the example of Eastman Kodak. In the late 1970s and early 1980s, the corporation was approached by Cox Cable which had introduced a visionary approach to telecommunications and believed that its strategy was an extension of Kodak's vision. Although some of Kodak's leadership tried to get the organization to see the future, Kodak's senior leadership was mired in an incremental *innovation–renovation* thought and action process. Ultimately, therefore, Kodak rejected the challenge to *create* a different vision for the future. Diversification beyond the thought paradigms of *"no change"* did not occur. Over the past fifteen years, Cox Cable has become larger, more profitable, and more sustainable than Kodak.

Consider Gemplus, a multinational smart card corporation in France. Gemplus began thirteen years ago as a family business. Over the past few years, it has grown to almost 30,000 employees with operations in the United States, Canada, Asia, China (it separates China and Asia), and Europe. Although its growth has been phenomenal, it has become mired in innovation in its management and leadership and creation in its product life. The organization's technology is years ahead of the leadership. Without leadership that can think beyond the strategies and processes of yesteryear, failure for the future can be predicted

In government strategies employed over the past fifteen years in the areas of leadership and fiscal management have been based on the private sector model of effectiveness. Yet the paradigm of profit and its attendant strategies do not fit well with the paradigms of service—the charge of governments. Governments reinvent the wheel and accept the language of the private sector; yet innovation and renovation are the true results of their efforts. Governments need to *create* a paradigm that honors their roles and accountabilities, and not latch on to paradigms that have not worked well in corporate America.

SETTING THE STAGE FOR CREATION

Recently, my life and business partner talked to me about products and service. He said,

I want to have an organization where the leader of the organization selects the brightest and most diverse persons in the company to serve as a special "bust the gut team." As the leader, I want to charge them with one activity—take each product and each service that we provide and make it obsolete. Create newness for all that we do, so that we never stagnate and become comfortable with ourselves. I don't want to have you create change for change's sake; rather I want you to out-think what has already been done and create original products and services that make a difference. Your job is to create newness, not innovate or renovate what we have done before. Your job is to be nonincremental—give it all to me, not what you think I can tolerate. Your job is to collaborate, not compete. Your job is to build complements to what you create so that it has anchors in the business world and in the society. Dream and create—that is your charge.

Dreaming has always been exalted in our society. It is an essential component of emerging thoughts and fresh ideas. David Pottruck, chief executive officer of Charles Schwab, said that "the why, who and where questions need to be addressed on a continual basis and in such a manner that those around you take action on their own to develop the what and how to enhance the performance of the company" (Clicks and Mortars, 2000: 64). Harrison Owen, founder of Open Space Technology, says that the two critical ingredients of dreaming are passion, without which no one can make a difference or impact the society, and responsibility, without which no one can get anything accomplished. Owen believes that creation involves eliminating boundaries, and energizing and honoring relationships that are based on common interests and concerns. He says that leadership is dynamic when no one is in charge—effectually, that what is supposed to happen will happen, when it is supposed to happen, with the people who are supposed to do it. Nothing can be preordained, and freedom is the watchword. With this perspective, open space catalyzes innovation and creativity. When one is free to sweep the mind clean, creativity is born. If innovation becomes a part of the equation, creativity is lost.

The more common view of innovation and creativity comes from Senge (1999) and Owen (2000) both of whom believe that chaos theory, the explosion of one's actions, is essential to learning and growth. They are correct when they state that the concept of a closed system is an illusion. Not everything can be controlled; in fact, surprises always arise defeating the control, thus making it impossible for any system to be closed. Their perspectives are that organizational life flows from order to chaos.

Margaret Wheatley (1991) spoke of the creation of order in chaos by understanding that the change process is inevitable and constant. She believed that tinkering with the organization—only when everyone understands the values and beliefs of the organization—would result in a systemwide approach to congruence. She stated that any form of conformity would kill the system.

If these perspectives are true, then why have organizations and their members not moved beyond the spaces of history? The real issue here is that organizations have relied too heavily on order and chaos. Both require an understanding of rules, authority, power, and control. Whether one is fighting to break control or institute it, the results are the same—a duality between order and chaos. So I began to think about what makes a difference in one's understanding, and I thought of an African Kraal (or village) and a 1960s commune (communal living space). In both instances, some principles apply that move beyond self to community and communion that somehow get lost in the concepts of order and chaos. The first principle is that one purpose of the village is sustainability, with each individual and each home in the village accountable to everyone else in the village. The backs of all the houses support a section of the village wall. The building of the village huts is based on the concept that everyone must build what is strong and yet, fluid. These are built by the women of the tribes. The cooking in the village sustains all life and is performed by the young girls, while the crops and cattle are maintained by the boys under the age of 12. The boys older than 12 serve as the protectors of the tribe and hunt and defend the present and future of the tribe. The men and women over the age of 21 serve as the policy makers and strategists for the sustenance and sustainability of all.

In the 1960s, many of these same experiences from the African village were replicated in American communes. From Flower Power to Love Power to Peace Power and Black Power, the value of the many over the one, the sharing and collaboration of all, the anchoring of one's life with the complements one experienced was tantamount to Owens' system of open space. Yet, missing in all of these perspectives of change is the underlying frame. We have continually looked at creation as an external action for an external world. From the African village to the communes, from closed systems to open systems, from the classical organizational structures to the open wheel concepts of indigenous cultures, external frames are the drivers for action and thought. When the focus is external, we all lose and participate in lose–lose, competitive systems.

Creation therefore must come from within—personally, systemically, organizationally, societally. Creation is about the discovery of equilibrium, and balance and alignment. Congruence, not chaos, is a critical process of growth, change, and development.

So how does one begin to create, not innovate or renovate? How does one look at creation organizationally from within? How does one personally create without buying into the trappings of living and being that come from history, the television, or their friends?

Conventional wisdom has always held that one creates when there is a disruption to one's personal system. From a human dynamic point of view, conventional wisdom states that when a disruption takes place, people emerge to a different level. Over the past four years, I have moved away from that view. In business, when problem arises in the organization, the leaders demand that the staff create a different strategy to respond to the problem. However, history shows us that staff really innovates or renovates the product or service in response to the issue. It is an external action to fix an issue. In your own life, you consider the factors that cause your disruption, and you innovate or renovate your thinking or your behavior to deal with the issue at hand, and then you move on. In each of these situations, in your personal or business life, the impetus for innovating or renovating comes from the outside.

Take Wall Street, which goes up or down based on the actions of corporations' abilities to meet the expressed targets. When the market goes down, employees are let go, belts are tightened, consultants—different thinkers—are released from contracts, organizations merge or become acquired, and leaders either remain or roll over based on their reactions to the external influences before them. Quick desires for innovation become the norm, renovation of existing strategies takes the forefront, and the organization repeats with slight twists all that has gone before.

Creation requires first and foremost developing and making new thoughts and ideas in the calm, not the chaos! Creation can best occur when one is calm, when things are good, and when strategies are working. For all the talk of order and chaos and the balance between the two, either end of the spectrum as a space for building capacity is critically flawed because the impetus for both order and chaos is external pressure. External pressure, the process of generating innovation and renovation, is a process of prescription. External pressure is the relationship between the oppressed and the oppressor, and it is driven by a desire to avoid or control freedom and newness. External pressure is the prescription of one view over another to the detriment of the conformer. It is the prescription that transforms the consciousness of the person, business leader, manager, or employee into one that conforms with the perspective dose identified by the external evaluator. Each time one relies on the external evaluator to give direction or to set the standard, the prescription of the pressure takes over, causing all to believe that the prescriptor was right. We have all been taught to accept the precriptor's perspective as right. So, when your business competitor determines this is the path to take, all others within the business system go along and do the same thing. Witness the airline industry. If Delta raises its rates because of the jet fuel crisis, then all other airlines follow suit. For another example, look at the health care system. When someone stated that fee for service was too high, the reaction was to renovate and innovate the system, creating Health Maintenance Organizations. What happened to patient care, the purpose of fee for service? Did it go out the window and did patients get worse care? Yes. The reaction was the introduction of new legislation to reduce the number of lawsuits against the insurance industry. Every action taken in the industry in the past ten years has been an action of innovation and renovation. There has been no creativity in part because the external pressures have created chaos and order, not calm.

Creation occurs when there is authenticity and equilibrium within, not outside. The goal of any person or any work is ultimately to increase the opportunity for freedom. Whether it is freedom to make certain types of decisions, to think and be, to reduce the impact of work, to serve, or to conform, each individual, group, and business seeks to enhance the freedom options for people. Freedom does not occur without authenticity. We are oppressed by the external forces that dictate what is acceptable in our lives. From the way women and men are supposed to think and act—from the gay culture valuing youth over age, from television ads proclaiming that slimness and beauty are better than ugliness, from the corporate perspectives on dress, hair, and jewelry, from the family perspective about straight, gay, bisexual, transgendered living, from the concepts of faith-based strategies in government to atheist leanings, from speed and power over one's competitors—the issue of freedom is the ultimate driver of our being and our thinking. The need and desire for freedom is an internalized reality, not an external pressure. We desire to be free from the trappings of family, society, work, friends, and even loved ones—and we fear that which we desire such that our attempts to be free have historically involved our oppressing others. If we are to be free, then we must discover that freedom within ourselves. Only in that discovery of our freedom, becoming fully ourselves in the presence of people and system, can we truly create and produce original thought and action.

Does all this sound esoteric? It is not really. Freedom is about expunging conformity; it is about embracing authentic thought and action and about honoring your values and beliefs, not acquiescing to the whims of others who have different agendas other than honoring the person and the organization. Freedom is also about influencing your future in concert with strategies that help produce the outcomes you desire. Freedom is about risking moving beyond what is historically allowable to what is in concert with the dream that you have. When employees feel that what is allowable is already determined, they are operating according to the prescription given by the leader, manager, organization, or society.

When Cisco Systems laid off 8,500 employees in April 2001, it tried to honor the dignity of the employees with six-month severance packages, letters denoting a business decision, not on employee performance, and payment of COBRA. Systemically, Cisco daily informed the employees of its actions, strategy, and rationale and explained up front how it would honor the employees in the process. Cisco followed through on its statements. The result was a valuing of Cisco even by the employees leaving the organization; that is, the result was a congruency in its strategy and a congruence with the expressed values. No violence, no disruption, nonchaos—planned thought and action. Could this action have been seen as creative? I think so. Cisco did not follow the actions of its partners—Motorola who let go of employees without attending to their long-term needs. Cisco chose to work with employees in a way that valued the employees—open communication, clear information, linkage to the values and business strategy, above-board action, collaborative to allow for partnering in the future, anchors—complements that suggest that humanity is key. Though professing tight profit margins and a loss in the stock market from $110 to $18 a share, each employee being laid off was valued as all those remaining. This was a creative solution to a difficult problem. There was no need for control, for chaos, or for order; rather, there was a need for freedom for all.

Creation is about commitment to transformation. When one chooses to create, one commits to not participating in the oppressive prescription. This means that one must first focus on the nature of the oppression or the prescription. What is its intent? What is its impact? Is there a winner or loser? Or does everyone win? Is there capacity and opportunity for change and growth? Is there potential to experience the fullness of others? If the answer to any one of these questions is no, then freedom and transformation are not possible. Second, the origination of new thought and action must take into consideration what has occurred and identify the world view in operation. The third action is to expunge the violence (violence is initiated by those who oppress, exploit, and fail to recognize others as persons having the potential to be authentic beings) from the system or group that oppresses new and original thought.

One of my students is a member of the executive team of a major automobile insurance giant. His practicum assignment involved changing the planning and budgeting process of his organization to be consistent with learning theory and diversity inclusion. What he discovered was a struggle within his organization to let go of the historical strategies to participate in transformational ones. He writes:

As the leader of this change, I learned that to bring about organizational transformation, I had responsibilities that could not be delegated. It is the leader who has to make the case for change, has to enlist the support of others, and then has to follow this up with constant commitment and energy towards the cause. I learned that ultimately what matters most is the passion for the cause. Initially this passion may just be with the leader, but if the change is going to be sustained this passion must catch on with others and create a critical mass.

There were many times that I had to dig down deep within side myself and ask myself if this was worth it. When there were no easy answers to the issues that arose in this project, I felt vulnerable (walking naked), not knowing how to get the group to the promised land. Maybe that is why George Leonard (1992) in his book on Mastery states that "in order to grow you have got to be willing to look foolish on occasion" (p. 63). I had to learn to let go (which I still struggle with), and trust the change process to take its course, living through the pain of chaos and uncertainty. Letting go entailed changing my view on what leadership is from "I need to have the answers because I am responsible" to "We need to learn because we are all responsible." Letting go meant that the pain and chaos was not real. What was real was my need to trust me and others—not control me or others.

I mentioned in the previous section the difficulty of being in liminality, a space of unknowingness. Change is a process. I have a much better appreciation now of what creation looks and feels like. It is never going to be pleasant, but I do think that by recognizing what it is and its value in bringing about learning, I can grow more comfortable with being in this zone.

One of my key goals was to learn about leadership from the inside. I have read many views on this subject. From my experience, I better understand why leadership is so in demand and why there are so few who fit the bill. Given the "whitewater" that we are all trying to navigate, there is a lot of apprehension and fear. We are in uncharted territory, with none of us having the answers. We look to our leaders to give us a vision that gives us a sense of destination and of purpose. Good leaders support and guide so that the members of the organization have energy, passion and inspiration to build and do something meaningful.

Leadership is not easy. I underestimated how emotionally taxing change can be. Leadership starts with self-reflection. The energy and spirit for the change must come from deep inside. There are many forces that resist deep change. When we ask people to change the lens through which they see the world, they are going to resist and deny. It is part of the process. To gain this type of deep change is a delicate process. As Meg Wheatley (1998) says, "Organizational change is a dance, not a forced march."

Michael Eisner (2000), CEO of Disney, expressed the role of leadership in a way that struck a chord with me. Eisner looked at leadership as performing four main roles. First, the leader needs to "be in the weeds." The followers are reassured when the leader is with them, understanding their challenges, hopes and dreams. Secondly, the leader needs to set an example. The followers look to the leader for cues on how to act. In this role, the leader has great influence on the values and group norms. Thirdly, the leader needs to be a nudge. I laughed when I read this because I often have described myself as the corporate nudge—a person who pesters and pushes to move things forward. This role aligns with the strategic termite metaphor that guided my actions. Lastly, the leader sets a tone with idea generation. It is not that the leader has to have the ideas, it is rather that the leader has to set a tone that all ideas are welcome and even ones that seem to be outlandish may have merit.

Leadership relies on forming trusting relationships. I learned that this starts with being authentic at all times. So how do you build relationships? My learning is that there is no greater power than that of conversation. Simply by learning to ask for input and to check in on where people were at—and listening closely to the reply—did more to establish trust and credibility than all the knowledge and wisdom I might have shared.

I was not in charge but needed to get things done. It was through relationships that I was able to gain and use influence to help the group achieve its goals. I approached every interaction with my colleagues as an opportunity to gain new information. The feedback allowed for midcourse corrections.

I learned that my effectiveness as an agent of change depends on my holding on to curiosity. An aspect of Appreciative Inquiry that gave me pause to reflect was regarding how one views an organization. If I would have looked at the effort as a series of problems to be solved, I'm not sure I would have made it. At every step, there were new problems—some very messy—that presented themselves. Some were related to the group process, others to outside factors, others to cultural issues. Sue Hammond (1997) says "What you focus on becomes your reality." By approaching organizations as an endless mystery, I was much better able to keep my spirit and energy up (not to say I didn't have my moments!). By taking this tact, instead of solving problems, I focused on asking questions as a means of exploration.

I believe that all organizations, but especially larger ones like Anytime Automobile Association, are so complex and dynamic that it is virtually impossible to fully comprehend them. Spending time writing out a Causal Loop Diagram or a Force Field Analysis helped my understanding; I kept in mind that what I was representing was much simpler than the true dynamic. Nevertheless, the diagrams were helpful in asking the questions: what are the relationships going on here? What is my influence in this system?

One of my learning objectives was to apply Eastern philosophy to the effort. The wisdom of Tao reminded me to listen to my fears, and learn from them so that I could make wiser choices. I attempted to get centered, living from the "Hara," when under stress. I have a way to go, but I understand the value in emotional detachment achieved by staying centered. Zanshin means flow, the rhythm of life. Moving with Zanshin taught me not to fixate on mistakes or doubts, but use the energy to learn and grow. Like Bamboo (a metaphor used in Taoism), I learned about resilience, bending but keeping strength.

My experience on the practicum project reinforced my belief that Margaret Mead was right. There truly is no more powerful force in the world than a small group of committed people. The potential to make organizations great lies in the aspiration and passion of its members. I believe that people desire to contribute to something bigger than themselves.

The challenge of this executive team member was to reduce the conservative and functional silos that existed in both organizational thinking and organizational action to set a stage for transformation and for freedom within the organization. His learning came from his internal exploration, and that learning freed him to meet the challenges critical to the development of his people. Without that movement, transformation of the business was not possible. Thinking about creating something new was not possible without the movement internally. Becoming someone transformed, with new visions, was not possible without the internal exploration.

Creation is about curiosity. The greatest strength of creation is the exploration of the unknown. We run from the unknown, or we find that we must lasso the unknown and own it. Sitting with the unknown and exploring what questions arise are critical responsibilities of creation. I often wondered how the curiosity within me grew, and I began to recognize that when I could see the humanity, not the omnipotence, of people and systems, then I could ask those questions that everyone wanted hidden.

We perpetuate the unknown by being afraid of it. Creation is about asking the questions no one else wants to ask. Think of your work. How often have you wondered why it is conducted in the manner it is? How often have you asked yourself where a particular strategy originated? I often give my students the following play on Genesis to help them with their thinking and querying skills.

> In the beginning there was the Plan.
> And then came the assumptions, and the assumptions were without form,
> And the plan was completely without substance.
> And therefore darkness was upon the face of the workers. And they spoke amongst themselves, saying,
> It is a crock of shit and it stinketh!
> And the workers went unto their supervisors and sayeth: It is a pail of dung and none can abide the odor thereof.
> And the Supervisors went unto the Managers and sayeth:
> It is a container of excrement and it is very strong such that none may abide by it.
> And the Managers went unto the Directors and sayeth: It is a vessel of fertilizer, and none may abide its strength.
> And the Directors spoke among themselves, saying: It contains that which aids plant growth, and it is very strong.
> And the Directors went unto the Vice-Presidents and sayeth, It promotes growth and is very powerful.
> And the Vice-Presidents went unto the President and sayeth: This new plan will

    actively promote the growth and efficiency of this Company, and in these
    areas in particular.
And the President looked upon the plan and saw that it was good, and the Plan
    became Policy.

Anonymous

    Sound familiar? It is the method often employed in our society as we rely on
innovation and renovation. Exploring the unknown is essential to creating effective movements. Paulo Freire wrote, "Freedom to create and to construct, to
wonder and to venture is the pathway to authenticity. Such freedom requires
that the individual be active and responsible—not a slave or a well-fed cog in
the machine. It is not enough that men are not slaves; if social conditions further
the existence of automatons, the result will not be love of life, but love of death
(1973: 34).

    Creation is about emotion, passion, and reflection. If there is no love of or
enthusiasm about what we do, then we will only tweak what exists rather than
create what was dreamed. One must be able to reflect on the creation as the
end-all of the activity. One must think beyond the present and the past to generate options, opportunities, capacities, and transformations that matter. In this
way, one creates with others, not for others. A small trucking corporation in
North Carolina is an example of this action. The company is named Crook
Motor Company and was founded by an entrepreneur. He was bought out by
his son, C. B. Crook, who expanded the company to heights his father before
him never imagined. He had passion and emotion and needed help in reflecting
on what had gone before to jump the broom to what could be. The transformation that took place was from a trucking company to a transportation empire.
The creation was partnering with the community and the employees to dream
about advancing the social and economic conditions of an entire county. C. B.
worked diligently and dreamed ambitious plans, challenging his managers to
dream and explore the unknown. Each awareness created a new experience and
a new level of organizational and human performance, success, and balance.
His passion spread to his employees and the community. That's creation—for
he believed that he worked with and honored the community. He dreamed that
all could succeed and that transformation was the method of exploration. When
I left the company, he dreamed of helping welfare mothers become independent
truckers—selling them their first truck, getting the bank to finance the dream,
creating small businesses for disenfranchised women, empowering them to be
all they could be. He represented the women at the bank, creating equity with
them for their future and being committed to their success. His reflection was
seeing them grow as he had grown and wishing them well in a life of personal
and organizational empowerment. That's creation.

    Each of us must meet the challenges of creation if we are to achieve congru-
ence. It is not about the strategy alone: it is about the dream.

Chapter 8

Understanding Professional Choice and Creating Business Options

Now that we have an understanding of the thought requirements to achieve clarity, develop collaborations, implement complements and anchors, and generate creations, what do we do with this new knowledge? Where will it lead us? Hopefully, it will help us make better choices. This chapter is about choice. It details how stepping out on the cliff of challenge and choosing to jump over the age to create something new is critical to congruence development for people and systems. This chapter is about how to approach business and personal choice as a living embodiment of what is within us, not external to us, and in that recognition, how to risk becoming fully integrated with our dreams rather than giving up our choices to remain hidden in the woodwork of living.

Choices are the decisions and actions people take to advance an idea, block movement, and alter direction. Every day we all make choices that either empower us or inhibit our movement. *Choice in the context of this book is the acceptance or abdication of our responsibility to direct our role in life.* Each of us can choose codependent actions that disempower and yield to others the responsibility we have for choosing the actions that direct our lives; or we can choose to put our lives on a path that honors the knowledge, skills, abilities, beliefs, and perspectives that have determined who we are.

Choice is that critical place between thinking and acting. Throughout this book, we have focused on our motivators toward congruence in our personal lives and our business actions. Our efforts to achieve clarity, allowing us to focus on the contexts in our lives, not just the content areas, and creativity, enabling us to generate original and new ideas for products, service, and action—all of these thought perspectives lead to making choices. Think of the times in your life when you felt that it was safer or more appropriate to allow someone else to make the choices for you. Think of the times when in allowing others to choose, you felt helpless to reach a better decision. Each time you abdicate your responsibility to choose, you reduce your potential to be accountable. Each time you choose to allow others to act for you, you lose some of your integrity. Each time you allow the choices others make to frame your existence, you reduce your potential for making a difference in the workplace and your personal life.

Making choices is not easy. Choosing your spouse, getting a divorce, selecting a university, picking a career—all are choices that will establish the context for how you will live your life. Making codependent decisions or choosing to do nothing will minimize the creative influence that one has and stimulate the interests of those who want no change, growth, or development in the world. In effect, no choices or codependent choices focus on the reduction of transformation.

Consider the case again of Crook Motor Company. The owner was at a crossroads. He had to decide whether to grow the business through acquisition or merger; sell the business and pocket the earnings and move on with his future; or transfer the business to the managers who had worked with him for years, thereby ensuring that the organization would continue. What critical factors helped him in his decision process? The long-term sustainability of the employees was one primary concern. He had grown the building from infancy and had loyal employees who had been with him from the start. He had built relationships in the community by offering internships to the young people in the area. His company had been a principal contributor in development of the community's parks and recreational facilities. If the organization got too large, how would that impact the value base of the organization? If the organization was merged with another, which values and beliefs would drive the organization? If growth was key, could it be sustained in such a manner that the values and beliefs, corporate strategies, and leadership concerns that had made the company the largest used trucking corporation sold in a pamphlet marketing (every sale is through a monthly brochure) environment be sustained? These questions were key to the owner.

The owner was also concerned about the type of business that had been developed over the years. Innovation had driven the processes for years, yet it was not going to move the organization to the next level. This was a family-owned business, however, and so the needs and desires of the family were just as important as the business choices being made for the future. What role could or would the son play in advancing the business? Did the wife of the owner have a part in the decision process? What role, if any, did other siblings have in the decision and choice process? Over a period of eighteen months, the owner committed himself to experiencing a congruence process to answer both the business and human issues facing him, his family, and his company. Following is a synopsis of the initial cursory assessment that helped the organization decide to choose congruence development over traditional organizational development.

FINDINGS AND INTERRELATIONSHIPS FOR THE CROOK MOTOR COMPANY

There are significant issues with these organizational profiles. The largest issue is the possibility that the managers of the company are non-risk takers, thereby making them poor leaders of people and the future of a company but good managers of the specific tasks of the organization. There is an assumption that because they know the process of how things work, they will be strong leaders to work and move the process. This would not be true based on their profiles. Sticking to what exists is their mode of operation, not movement of the process.

Fiscally, this would suggest that over time, when stress is high, the managers will do little to improve the fiscal bottom line. Attention to nonrisk-taking activity will cause a potential loss of market share, and little value is added to the company.

For the owner/leader of the company, C. B. Crook, this will ultimately result in him being forced to resume roles that he has had previously within the company of making all the choices, creating the structures, developing the strategies, and ultimately trapping him in the history of the company, not the future.

Flexibility is needed at this point, so there may need to be a larger role played within the organization by the profile of Betty Crook [owner's wife]. Her legal belief structure allows for flexibility, with the added goal of assuring that no harm occurs in the decisions that are made. Secondly, there is a strong need to look at congruity in the organizational decisions being made. As this consultant focuses on a congruity decision model, it may be helpful to look at how that model can be used to:

1. Build congruence in the decisions of the organization, while creating more trust by the managers in the organizational decisions. This will allow the managers to develop needed skills in leadership and in taking needed organizational and personal risk.

2. Identify other potential leaders within the organization that can ensure the long-term sustainability of the organization to achieve its future goals and directions. This might suggest that the real leaders are persons underneath the current manager/owners who can truly make a difference.

3. Develop a realistic and comprehensive strategic plan that allows the leader and the managers to see a path that achieves the goals and futures of the organization AND the goals and futures of each person.

Summary

Although this report is written in this cursory format, a full-blown assessment and analysis of the organization is still needed. As the consultant to the process, approximately 30 days would be needed to develop and help set the framework for implementation of a strategic process [including training, coaching, mentoring, and developing of the managers to be effective].

This initial evaluation, based on the belief systems and thinking style profiles helped the executive achieve clarity in the choosing process. His desired outcome was to make the most effective and sustainable choice for the future of the organization. If sustainability, visioning, growing the business, and moving forward with a commitment to the community were important, then there were problems ahead with the existing team. So how did the executive choose? What were the drivers for his decisions?

As we continue with comments from the consultation, it is possible to see the interrelationships between people and business issues and how organizations move toward effective choosing that honors who they are.

Overall, I believe that repurchasing the stock is a sound idea, for without that action, little movement can be made to position the company for any action, be that action developing strategies to eventually sell the corporation OR developing strategies to build the corporation. I sense that there are options available that can move the company to new growth and development, yet management within the company would need to change. The movement, however, will require more of the family corporation than the members of the family will be willing to assume. Therefore, let me throw out some of my thoughts for consideration by people in the preparation for the weekend.

Thoughts for Consideration

First Thought

The first thought that comes to mind for me is repositioning what type of company we have in Albemarle. First and foremost in my thinking is looking at the company NOT AS A TRUCKING COMPANY, BUT AS A TRANSPORTATION COMPANY. To that end, the growth in the company can be movement to becoming a transportation holding company that focuses on the creation of new businesses, wholly or partially owned by Crook Motors, as a diversification strategy. Paint Shops, Repair Services, Training Services, Banking Services are all businesses that can be created to "grow the company" and truly position it for sale.

An *example* that might work that would allow CB and Betty to achieve some of their community dreams is an Education and Training Business. The business might look like the following as an umbrella service that has a non-profit component: Identify all the women and men on welfare within the county. Meet with them as a large group to discuss the creation of training services to teach them to become Truck Drivers. As independent truck drivers, negotiate with them that their first two trucks will be purchased from Crook Motors for which the company will help them with financing from the bank. Provide them with their first contract for delivering of trucks to customers. This effectually can create new customers, new partnerships, and a different business in education and training. Money from the school system, the county, the state and the federal government can be garnered to support the non-profit areas of the company. It would additionally show a community-based process for responding to welfare, and over three to five years would prove most profitable. All salaries could be paid out of the non-profit side of the business, reducing tax issues for the company, and expenditures would be audited at differing levels leaving more money within the company.

If there are 10,000 persons on the roles and you get 500 persons to go through training for a 3 month period . . . the federal government will pay you for their training at a cost of approximately $5000 per participant. The government may hold the note for the original truck purchase at an average cost of $30,000 per truck, and the government may insure or hold the note so that there is no loss to Crook Motor Company. Five thousand dollars times 500 participants is $2,500,000. Trucks therefore on the lot that are inventoried at a loss therefore become trucks for training purposes that can now be written off differently with the IRS. A new ready-made pool of customers is created.

The same type of ventures could be created with students from the high school in Paint Stores and Repair Shops, whether they are all in Albemarle or not. The difference is movement from a trucking company to transportation which opens up the avenues of thought and work. When you talk of using someone, the government becomes a perfect vehicle to increase the revenue of the company, build an image and publicity. This opens up avenues for speaking engagements for CB and Betty [usually at lecture fees of $2500 for a one and one half-hour lecture]. My guess would be that expansions in these arenas could generate $5,000,000 within three years.

Any number of thoughts can be created during the weekend as a potential strategy for organization development of Crook Motor Company. . . . the dreams you each have are critical to that discussion and set the stage for long term action. It also potentially sets the stage to reduce overall burnout of CB and Betty in the process of deciding the long term future of the company.

Recognizing that sale of the company may be the eventual outcome . . . diversification in the form spoken of previously could significantly enhance the attractiveness of the company to a variety of persons.

Second Thought

The second thought is about "As Soon As Possible Sale of the Company." I think that I am where Al [marketing consultant for Crook Motors] is in that thought process. We need the actual net worth of the company to look at a sale that would garner at least 1.5 times the value of the company. It could include membership on the board of the buyer company for stock and cash options as well as overall payout to the family. If the family is tired of the business, then this may be the best option. To achieve this option realistically, ALL THE STOCK NEEDS TO BE REPURCHASED from the managers to meet the best needs of the family. I am concerned here, however, with the issues of cash flow and flexibility that it reduces for the company. Although I have not seen the fiscal figures, cash flow is always the toughest component of business strategy development, so we would need to clearly look at the short and long term impacts.

The company, in my mind, is in a good position. . . . three years of solid growth, two years of sustained growth without "real losses" positions the company as a solid performer in the eyes of buyers.

Authors note: [There is a caveat here. Companies purchase the product, ethos, archetypes and values of an organization at the time of purchase. It is the organizational system that is of value to a new owner; therefore, what has made Crook Motors what it is becomes the "real juice" that is for sale. How we package that becomes even more critical than any other action is courting and cultivating a relationship with a buyer.]

I will need to talk with Al more about the marketing prospect here. This becomes a dicey process, but definitely doable.

Third Thought

The third thought is to do nothing except buy back the stock . . . ALL OF IT. I would not leave the managers with a kernel. The managers in my mind have hampered the true development of this company and as they are not members of the family, with the family's entrepreneurial strength and spirit, their participation in the decision making process has been an anathema to the successful movement of the company. The caveat here is the necessity for DATA, DATA, DATA!!!!!!!!

I sense that CB has the intuitive gut of the GODS! Somehow, CB has always known what was the right thing to do; however, when I met with David [one of the managers] over a year ago, it was apparent then that he had no idea what he was looking at in the data before him; therefore, his decision making was "history driven, not fact-present-future driven." This presents a problem. The company needs to utilize information in the choices that it makes, AND IT NEEDS TO CONSIDER THE VALUES OF CB AND BETTY more in the decision making process. The appendix attached to this memorandum suggests a strategy to ensure that the decisions and values are consistent and congruent.

I would not give the managers a raise. . . .they don't deserve it, and it continues to support their delusions about who they are and what they contribute to the situation. $200,000 is more than they ever deserve based on PERFORMANCE and the current GROWTH of the company. Their compensation continually skews what is being done, and I would strongly ask you not to do that.

Doing nothing then sets the stage to buckle down, tighten the hatches, AND BE BETTER AT WHAT WE ARE DOING. Managing costs [including compensation], changing relationships so that sales persons can make more based on what they sell and so forth.

The future of the company in readying it for sale becomes critical therefore, and part of what a buyer will look at is the overhead, compensation, growth and development and the systemic view of what it suggests. If you compensate these men more, it begins to appear as though you are afraid of some of the hard choices, and that spells *corporate culture problems for a potential buyer!*

Fourth Thought

The final thought initially is based on Al's comments with Chuck about the Maslow Hierarchy of Needs Theory. . . .I believe that you are right on there, Al. These men are at the base needs [survival] in their minds, and their actions support that thought. Psychologically, a team of survival-driven men become a dangerous group of men. We are fortunate in their choice to sell back the stock, however, the psychologist side of me says that I would want to know why so that I know how NOT TO CREATE STRATEGIES THAT WILL CAUSE THEM TO SABOTAGE THE PROCESS OUT OF THEIR FEARS.

Therefore, I will prepare questions for CB to use; however, I am not certain that they will be as candid with CB as is envisioned. I would almost suggest not doing that if Al and I are not the ones gathering the information. This is a tenuous time as a part of this crisis. It has amazing potential, AND it has amazing drawbacks. So walking carefully is the key here.

The Memorial Day Weekend

Current plans for the weekend involve Chuck, Al, Mary, Lloyd and Tony [Lloyd and Tony are both Psychological/Legals in the Belief Systems Audits] to meet on Sunday. We will be looking at finalizing the design for the Memorial Day process and looking at what are the unique issues that need to be addressed. I have included three instruments—Carol, Robert and Mary—so that we can utilize all the gifts of everyone there at the meeting.

Suffice it to say, the focus of the day should approach the issue of Stock Repurchase or not, decisions for sale within one year, three years and the development of strategies to bolster the sales of trucks, and possibly the assessment of other diversifications that can bolster the coffers of the company and the OWNERS of the company to ensure futures that make sense and meet personal and community needs.

To address the aforementioned, I would propose that *THREE SCENARIOS* be created to address these issues. One scenario is a worst case process, the second is a present day process, and the third is a best case scenario. The focus is to develop a process that allows each person in the weekend to assume differing roles to understand and focus on issues of change and development within the company to MAKE DECISIONS FOR THE FUTURE. Therefore, decisions should not be made until Tuesday morning from 9 until noon. This allows time to process Monday's activities; review the events of the day and then make decisions for the future and present.

The *tough issues for us to face at the weekend* are the following:

1. What choices should be made about the repurchase of stock? Is the repurchase going to impact the cash flow needs and the flexibility needs of the company?

2. What role will the family need to take for the future of the company irrespective of sale or growth of the company? What role will the managers need to take recognizing their limitations, their needs and the balance of those needs with the expressed desires of the family owners?

3. How do the skills, abilities and gifts of Chuck, Carol and Robert get used within the company to ensure that the outcomes defined are accomplished?

4. What role should consultants play in the future of the company's process of change and development OR sale? How important will additional data in marketing, sales, organizational process, training and development help the company for the future?

5. What long term strategy can be developed, and how does that strategy build realistic and ongoing contingencies so that crisis does not become the norm for organizational decision making?

6. If we embark on a given strategy, how do we monitor the strategy AND the organizational outcomes to ensure that we meet personal AND organizational targets?

7. What are the real goals of Betty and CB? Can those goals be achieved with any strategy or are only certain strategies helpful in the process?

8. What is the real marketing strategy? Here I am in agreement with Al. Latin America, Africa and the Middle East are untapped markets. The issues of inclusion around diversity will ultimately become issues in the development of an organizational culture for Crook Motors that can meet the test of time and the future. Hispanics, Africans, African Americans, Asians are all important issues here. Bahrain, Arabia, and other markets for Direct/Mail Marketing are possibilities, especially with the advent of the Internet. Therefore looking at what is realistic for the future of the company EVEN if you want to sell the company can be the development of emerging and attractive markets.

9. What are the real financing issues facing the company VERSUS the invest-
ment/retirement issues and values of CB and Betty? Can the company sustain
both strategies as a part of the development of the long term plan?

10. Is the company moving from a family business to a corporate business environment, and does that change the nature of leadership and management
within the company for the future? If it does, what needs to be identified to
secure that future direction, and how does that future direction change the
current organizational structure, compensation strategies, sales strategies, repair strategies and other issues within the company? Does the strategy alter
the relationships that we have with federal agencies and the like?

All of these are questions that need to be surfaced and thought about as part of the long
term strategy. I think it will be an exciting time together and we are looking forward to
it.

SUMMARY

So where is the process of choice at this point? The first thing to consider is
that *choice is about balance.* In the situation before you, the choice was balancing the needs of the family with the needs of the business. Each of us faces
that same dynamic every day. What is important to us personally, and what is
important to us systemically? The conflict lies in the choice between being
wholly oneself or being divided; between ejecting the oppressor within or not
ejecting it; between human solidarity or alienation; between following prescriptions or having choices; between being spectators or actors; between acting or
having the illusion of acting through the actions of doing nothing; between
speaking out or being silent. The choice is about being stuck or transforming
the world, the family, you.

Second, it seems that *choice, personally and systemically, is about liberation.*
To choose liberation—newness—requires that each person or leader make a
concerted effort to expunge the shackles of history, fear, shame, blame, control,
power, and authority. The struggle is tantamount to choosing between being and
being like someone or something. If the choice is *to be,* then it is about authenticity—internal factors and influences that frame being in the world. If the
choice is *to be like,* then it focuses on eternal factors and influences that frame
being controlled by the world. Look at yourself in the workplace. Which are
you—being you or being like others?

Third, *choice is about creating alignment between what is believed and valued
and what is operational.* In the case before us, it was insufficient to talk only
about what must occur. The owners and managers had to discover how their
beliefs and values were actualized in their performance. Each and every day,
you hear persons espouse a set of values and beliefs that seem inconsistent and
incongruent with behavior. Often what occurs in the workplace or the family is
a rationalization of guilt through being paternalistic. This was the case here for
the owner, and it is often the case in business. Leaders do a very poor job

of human resource management, development, and organizational change. Therefore, codependent guilt often rears its head, driving the actual decisions and performance issues of organizations. Even as this process is going on, the organizational leaders continue to perpetuate and demand positions of dependence from the employees. To change the systemic moroseness, leaders must join with employees in changing the situation by wrestling the issues together with the employees—instead of contributing to death, participate in creating life. This therefore becomes a process of creating reality to jump start originality.

So we are now back to our case. What was the conclusion? What was the impact? What was the choice? Although this writing cannot provide you with the specifics in the developmental process, suffice it to say that the following were the results of the case consultation.

1. The owner collaborated with the family to create real partnerships that were sustainable for the family. As a result, the family took a more active role in balancing their values with their work.

2. The family created roles in the family that balanced their personal choices with their new understanding of how they saw the world in work and play.

3. The owners committed themselves to a development process for the managers and the organization.

4. The owners and managers agreed that sale of the company to the managers would sustain the work of the founders and that sustainability was a key factor in all decisions for the future.

5. The family is closer than it has ever been, seeing real partnering as essential to their family congruence.

6. The owner has quit smoking after forty years of two packs of cigarettes a day, has gotten physically fit, and spends a lot of time with his wife and family.

7. Community work in the county has increased exponentially, as a result of which the owner is pleased, the family is pleased, the grandkids are pleased, the community leaders are pleased, and the managers are pleased.

8. A new foundation for community service has been created, and the company remains a driver for community.

This process of choosing yields fairly good results. Clear perspectives about choice have now been provided. One final thought strategy is essential in our work here. The last area is complexity, and it is where we begin with the next chapter.

Chapter 9

Enjoying Our Complexity and Creating a New Business Andragogy for Living

There is a concept in education that I aptly applies to the field of business and family development. The concept is called *banking education*, and goes as follows:

You are in my class, family or business. I determine what is appropriate, accurate, important, describable, discussable, and retainable. Do what I say, and you will be sustained. Challenge what I say, and you will find yourself singled out, ostracized, blocked, and unable to advance. Transformation from what has gone before is not an option. Reality is as I define it, not what you think it should be. This is not about liberating you; rather, it is about directing you and your actions. I think for you, I tell you what is right, and I establish the directions for the future. Live with my strategy and you will do well.

Banking education is in many ways the experience of our current business and family cycle. Doing what is expected and predetermined is more important than learning to think and develop one's own perspectives on issues. In effect, business and family development has created a "culture of silence" in our society.

What does this culture of silence suggest for us in our attempts to be whole, complete, and congruent? First, it suggests that we remain hidden by being un-unique. Be like everyone else and we will get along. Second, it perpetuates the system, thereby ensuring that no growth, development, or change will occur. Third, you should use only what is given to you—data and information—accepting the perspectives and analyses that are given rather than challenging the perspectives as skewed, filled with agenda, and designed to control. The culture of silence is designed for each of us to remain illiterate and pawns in a prescriptive system, not of our own making. The prescription says, don't make criticisms, for if you do, your status as a creator of the criticism will be challenged in such a fashion that you will be blamed for your perspective. Follow the rules and you will find yourself a member of the haves. You will find yourself a leader in the banking process, and you will continue what has been started. Bide your time, think as you are told, do what you are told, and the rewards will fall your way. Each time you acquiesce to actions in the organization that you believe are wrong and inappropriate, you are perpetuating the culture of silence. Each time you rationalize your actions as the responsibility of others, you are perpetuating the culture of silence. Each time you participate in stifling the thinking and actions of those trying to make a difference, you are perpetuating the culture of silence. When you allow your thinking to become compartmentalized, controlled, or boxed, when that thinking is designed to protect and limit, rather than understand and grow, the process of imbalance, misalignment, and incongruence occurs and people and organizations are the ultimate losers. So what is the necessary intervention in one's thinking to alter the current path of banking and silence? I think we are talking about *complexity*.

Complexity is the ability to think in connected membranes to enrich and challenge the known and conscious with the unknown and unconscious to bridge the past, present, and future in our personal, professional, and business lives. Organizations and families, groups, and individuals have lost their direction and connectivity to the issues of creation and entrepreneurship that pushed them. Organizations and families, groups and individuals have lost their responsibility to each other—their partners in life and work. Organizations and families, groups and individuals have abdicated their accountability to understand the relationships of self and others, rejecting their requirement to advance meaning into wisdom.

First and foremost, *complexity is systemic*. Everything in the lives and actions of people is connected. When organizations terminate employees, the statistical analysis states that at least four other persons are impacted times four other persons for each of the original four affected. When organizations change market strategies, the same analysis states that at least six other businesses are impacted times six additional businesses for each business impacted. Whatever one does impacts someone else. Simplicity is not the answer! When we agree to take an action, we must consider the true impact of our actions, sorting through the connections of what we know versus what we don't know or haven't explored.

Unfortunately, businesses and families, individuals and groups, business organizations and the legal system only purport to respond to facts—that which is known and often skewed—rather than a comprehensive exploration of all the facts and the innuendos that often influence action and thought. Consider the situation of a nonprofit organization dedicated to the eradication of prostate cancer. In the development of the strategies as a business, the organization developed processes and procedures that would only address patients who had a PSA count of 8 and above. The unwritten rule was that physicians needed to demonstrate PSA counts of African Americans over 12 before they were eligible for service from the organization. Physicians were unfamiliar with this unwritten rule, the unconscious, unknown rule. Somehow, the founders and the leaders believed that prostate cancer is different in men of color, and thus that service delivery is different. Upon being challenged about an apparently discriminatory policy, the leaders spoke of findings that were unproven in the medical arena. The organization was closed, the leaders were jailed for deception and medical mismanagement, and the cancer society had to rethink the assumptions that it operated under in relation to persons of color.

Next, consider a family in which every member of the family is heterosexual. The youngest son, 18 years of age, discovers emerging feelings of homosexuality. From the family to the church, neither acceptance, tolerance, nor appreciation of a gay lifestyle is forthcoming. He soon finds himself emotionally and systemically ostracized from his family, finally separating himself from the family to avoid abuse. In either business or family development, group or individual development, avoidance of reality is the norm; automaton performance—the negation of being human—becomes the norm of existence. When one uses the banking approach, one often fails to understand that self-denial and movement into the woodwork create the illusion that the simple approach or the simple answer is the correct one. Systemic development is essential to complexity.

Complexity is also about revelation or awareness. Seeking the known and unknown, the conscious and unconscious, is a process of building balance and alignment beyond facts to the totality of a given situation or thought. Consider organizations that every few years hire and then lay off employees. In each layoff, the corporation states how unfortunate it was that it had to resort to this approach. *But it didn't have to, it chose to! The organization did not learn, explore, traverse, alter, think beyond its history. It innovated; it didn't create.* Revelations in complexity suggest that people and systems are *with* the world, not just *in* the world. If revelation is the outcome, then there is a consciousness to ensure that understanding occurs. There is an attempt to ensure that one participates fully, and does not acquiesce to what has always gone before. When families seek to hold fast to their history rather than their evolution, they seek to be in the world—not live with the world. Revelation is recognition and participation with the rules that govern the world, the business, the family—not just resting in the world. Complexity demands operation with the world.

Complexity is multileveled. Communication that is one way, moving upward until what is released makes no sense, is often the strategy for business and family development. The general attitude is that those at the top know best. That is nonsense, however, for everyone can contribute. Every level has its own truth, every person has a perspective every outcome can be accomplished in multiple ways. The best answers seem to occur when all levels of the system collaborate to achieve a certain goal. Only through communication can human life have meaning. One's thinking is authenticated only by the thinking of all those whose lives one touches. Such is the case with both business and family development. Only when all levels are involved are the decisions of any level authentic and valid. Authentic thinking, thinking that is concerned about reality, does not take place in a vacuum or an ivory tower; rather, it takes place where the actions occur—in life.

Complexity gives credence to the necessity for clarity, collaboration, complements, creativity, and choice. Complexity is the basis for movement, for it is in the search for reality that we sense the congruence in ourselves and our work. We understand complex issues and situations when we can achieve clarity, collaborate and partner with others, identify the complements–anchors, become creative in searching for newness, and explore the possibilities in our choices. It is our complexity that gives us hope.

Finally, *complexity is about the andragogical [co-adult learners] process of learning together.* Andragogy is the process of learning from one another in an equity type of experience. We are all teachers and learners simultaneously. We learn from the theoretical and the experiential simultaneously. We participate together, recognizing that it is in the participation with one another that learning occurs. This learning process of joining and becoming is anathema to organizational life.

In 1999, I developed a cultural due diligence instrument for a consulting firm, Emerge-Collaborative Consulting, in Arizona. In validating the instrument and testing its results with executives around the country, I was struck by the extent to which a level of cultural congruence was lost at each level of the organization, in the executives' attempts to understand where the organization was going. There was a 19% drop in congruence from the governing board and senior executive team to the director level of the organization. The drop from directors to managers was 23%, from managers to supervisors 34%, and from supervisor to employee 43%. The firm used the instrument to help organizations understand the complexity of creating both congruence and change strategies.

What one senses is that the attempts of our society *to control learning, wisdom, and reality* actually works. Reality requires more work, learning, knowledge, exploration of self and others, and dialogue about truth and vision. Reality requires working with complexity, and the world in which we live abhors that concept. When thinking is compartmentalized, people and organizations are the ultimate losers. As in the case of Eastman Kodak, when it only wanted to innovate and did not approach the complexity of Cox Cable's offer, the employees and the Kodak organization were the ultimate losers. Similarly, in your family situation when you choose to be hard-nosed, rigid, and simple about a critical evolution in the family, the family loses.

When we are asked daily to narrow our approach, provide our professional history in one or two pages, provide all information to our leaders in bulleted lists because they will not read, think only as a team will think, dress only as the organization perceives dress to be appropriate, look as European Americans look in order not to offend or threaten, we are participating in strategies that dishonor the uniqueness and congruence of every individual. When we acquiesce to dysfunction and simplicity, we are asked to accept and perpetuate more imbalance and misalignment in our lives. The cost is the loss of the critical congruence essential to the fluidness and the flexibility essential to organizational and personal growth and development.

Being authentic and becoming congruent is a difficult task, yet it is the most important one we can ever assume—personally, organizationally, and systemically. The more we struggle to balance the conscious and unconscious, the known and unknown, the complex with the reality of our existence, we advance, grow, and change. Whether we function as janitor or chief executive officer, the challenges are the same: to achieve fullness in our experiences.

Chapter 10

Putting It Together: The Congruence Development System and Strategies for Building Congruence

UNDERSTANDING THE CONTEXT

The process of congruence building (see Figure 10.1) involves balancing thinking and acting. *Business Decisions, Human Choices* (Williams, 1996) describes the behavioral actions that need to take place for congruence to become actualized in organizations and people. That book did not fully describe the thinking that needed to take place in order for the process to work. The present volume tries to close that gap so that one can experience fully the concept of congruence.

Each of you has a thinking style fhat frames your perspective on thinking. Each of you also has a belief system that defines how you look at the world and take in information. In effect, both your belief system (world view) and your thinking styles (how you process information) set the stage for what you hear, when you hear it, how you hear it, and what you do with information. This becomes more important than most people would ever consider. Conventional wisdom says that we are a product of our environment, but this is truly not the case. *We are a product of our beliefs and our thoughts, and it is those two areas that frame our ability to hear, know, and become.*

Congruence contextually focuses on the next steps beyond what one believes and how one thinks. Systemically, it is not enough that you understand how you think or what you believe; rather, the conclusiveness is based on what you do with your understanding. For example, from a belief systems perspective, I am a psychological/legal person in my beliefs and a process thinker in my thinking. Thus, I initially look at the world through the lens of group and individual freedom. I do not place value on power, control, order rules, or authority. I look at the uniqueness of the individual and the importance of the

Figure 10.1
The Congruence Development Thought Process

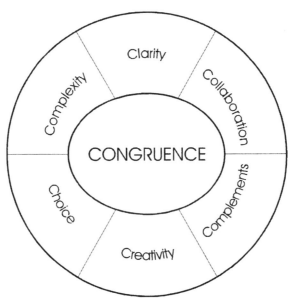

group from a proactive rather than a reactive stance. Empowerment and personal influence to make choices and participate freely are my highest values. Therefore, two value sets govern me: we-orientation and individuation. Who one is and how one feels are the highest priority for interaction and movement. Empowerment is the highest need, and understanding the system in operation is the second highest need, for knowledge of the surrounding leads to empowerment. Being creative and innovative is the third need, for it supports movement outside one's comfort zone to be effective. Getting the actual job done is the last component for me because there is no need to act and perform without an understanding of the other issues. All action should be based on the extent to which groups and people are made whole. It is not about getting to the end of a project; rather, it is about understanding the project and its desired outcomes.

As a process thinker, I look for balance and alignment between communication, evolutionary, and classical thinking styles. I recognize that change needs to occur, but it cannot be changed for change's sake. As this type of thinker, the goal for me is integration and transformation, moving consistently and congruently to new ways of viewing life, issues, strategies, and aspirations. I am always looking at information, data, and knowledge from the standpoint of integration of organizational and personal needs. However, data, information, and knowledge are not key for me. Meaning, wisdom, and a philosophical direction or system are essential. Thinking in this style focuses on creating harmony with one's values and beliefs *and* with one's sense of peace within the organization, family, group, or culture. Because harmony and meaning are important, this thinking style also supports the diversity of thinking of others. I don't have a need for others to think like me, nor do I need their perspective of forcing me to think like them. In my thinking there is no blame and shame, no cause and effect—just recognition that all things are possible. Because possibilities always exist, the strategy in my thinking is to understand the *why* more than the *what*, *how, who,* and *when* are equally important in my thinking style. Ultimately, in this thinking style, focusing on congruence in my life is an internally driven search for balance in my values, beliefs, and experiences. My thinking comes from an understanding of self and my internal influences.

So now we have a psychological/legal process thinking person. The first recognition for me was understanding that working in tiered, hierarchical, strict rules-based organizations was not a good match. Second, if organizations wanted me to just follow the rules and not think, that also would not be a good match. Remember that my thinking style focuses on the *why*. I want to focus on the congruity and comfort of employees and groups getting it in the workplace. It doesn't mean that I will slow down the work (I haven't missed a deadline yet in my work history); rather, it means that performing the work without understanding is not going to work for me. So if I had a supervisor or boss who wanted to control, I might be perceived as his or her worst nightmare. If I had a boss who liked to use power versus authority, my sense of the lack of importance of power would drive the manager nuts. If I had a boss whose thinking style was classical—follow the rules, don't make waves—or a boss whose thought process was scientific dynamic—cause and effect, blame and shame— working with me would give them fits because for me fear is not a personal inhibitor.

What does it suggest? First it suggests that integrity, accountability, honesty, intelligence, empowerment, representation, and equality are my motivators—not power, control, authority, blame, or shame. So if the latter tactics guide the organization, the managers and the organization will become frustrated. Tell me the truth and give me space to accomplish outcomes and the world will work great for me. What is not here is how would I walk a path to experience the congruence necessary? That is the purpose of this chapter—to finish the loop process that makes it all work together.

REVISITING THE BEHAVIORAL PROCESS

In 1996, I described a behavioral process for decision and action transformation. However, in using the system over the past few years, the dialogues have focused on the inability of people to think. The present book has therefore sought to close that gap in a manner that honors what has gone before—yet with creation of a different strategy for congruence development. Behaviorally, transforming decisions and actions are based on the ability of people and business to recognize the limits of a closed organizational process that tightly frames

Table 10.1
Paradigm for Business and People Development

The Process of Changing Thinking and Action to Process Development and Integration	
People Development	**Business Development**
Discord	Equality
Emergence	Interpretation
Acknowledgment	Reciprocity
Disclosure	Empowerment
Self-Indulgence	Representation
Reemergence	Commitment
Congruence	Wholeness

rules, regulations, norms, and behavior to achieve an outcome. In a tight and closed system, the ability to reflect and respond to changing issues and dynamics becomes a difficult and arduous process. Fluid and open systems are poised to alter components of the system to embrace and include change rather than fight, resist, and confront it.

Issues of emergence, acknowledgment, disclosure, reemergence, and self-indulgence become important for people in the transformational process. Issues of equality, interpretation, empowerment, reciprocity, commitment, and representation become important for systems and businesses. Congruence and wholeness become mirror images for the person and business and set the stage for framing long-term development. In this process, I have created a business paradigm that opens the organization to a new way of thinking about systems.

THE CHANGING BUSINESS PARADIGM

Business development can become more effective by altering existing business strategies from a closed to a more open and fluid systems process. This process requires that business rethink the approach currently used to understand and analyze the decisions that guide the business. In Table 10.1, business and people development focuses on the components of a changed paradigm for thinking and acting in business.

The process of development is a dual system of personal and organizational change. Being congruent and whole requires an integration of people and system development.

In this paradigm, business focuses on seven critical developmental processes as essential ingredients in effective business planning and implementation of products, services, management of resources, competition, and expansion.

Rather than looking at fragmented or compartmentalized elements, each element of the paradigm allows the business to frame decisions based on the potential of the decision to impact one of the seven underlying areas of development. Without the decision impacting an element, business must rethink the decision to ensure a level of wholeness with the decision in progress. The paradigm focuses on processes that are integrative and expansive, changing and continuous, rather than any set or static process. The paradigm has no beginning or end, just levels that must be adhered to in order to provide a level of understanding around the choices that we make in the business environment. Dissonances, incidents, and tangents of choice as described in Chapter 1 are not possible if you ensure that the levels of the business paradigm are understood, followed, and implemented.

This is a total *process business system paradigm* with membranes that expand ad infinitum. Closed systems restrict; open systems allow infinite experiences; fluid systems permit levels of integrations that cross the boundaries of all systems and, ultimately, all paradigms. That becomes the purpose and thrust of the new paradigm.

Business System Overview

The business system paradigm comprises seven levels: equality, interpretation, reciprocity, empowerment, representation, commitment, and wholeness. These are the levels of the business development process. Each is a separate entity framing business, and each is a part of the whole. When businesses make a choice regarding employees, products, services, strategies, competition, marketing, or any other decision, the decision should impact or be framed by one of these levels. Businesses never complete a level; rather, the levels are in tandem with one another in a nonstatic and continuous motion. Because there is no beginning or end to a level, there is no possibility for closure of any of the levels. Thus, a continual evaluation and reliability point in the developmental system is created.

Equality

Equality is the integrous [central integrity core] level of the system. It is the constant check and balance point of reviewing the congruity between what a business determines is valuable and the actions of the business to that existing value. If a business states that it values equity between genders, yet compensates one gender more than the other in the same classifications, then there is an inequity in the actions of the business and there is discontinuity in the values of the system. Equality is out of sync with the behaviors of the business system.

Equality becomes the "little voice in the background" for all decisions. Business leaders and employees are continually challenged to listen to the voice in the background and to determine the integrity of the decision. An example can be consultants who espouse a belief in the integrity of all business decisions, yet tell union leaders, "we can get rid of this general manager" on the one hand and state to the general manager, "if you just play along, we can get the unions to argue with each other enough about your demise and get them to lose their political influence within the organization." There is no equality in the statements by the consultant; rather, there is the antithesis of equality, which is manipulation.

Interpretation

Interpretation is the ongoing recognition that change is occurring. Environmental scans, visioning processes, strategic business modeling, functional outcome assessment, reengineering designs, strategic planning efforts, downsizing of staffing, eliminations of layers of an organization, and forecasting of future trends are all data sets that must receive interpretations in light of the nature of the business and the existing values of the business. Interpretations are the moving frameworks of business choice. Every action, planned or unplanned, can be evaluated through the interpretation level, with a constant check through the equality level of the system. As long as recognition of the integrity embodied in the choice is mirrored to the changing environment, then businesses maintain a pulse on the emerging dynamics of the choices that are made for the business.

Interpretations are essential to business choice because they represent an acknowledgment of the fluid nature of business remaining competitive in the work world. Who we are as a business is often framed by the changing and emerging world.

Interpretations are also critical because they allow business to remain inclusive in their strategies. Twenty years ago, the inclusiveness of domestic partner benefits would have been inconceivable in business. Today, 447 corporations around the country provide benefits to domestic partners. Thirty years ago, gender-based issues were not as prevalent as they are today, and interpretations allow business to reframe and rethink old analyses to replace their former decisions with a newer perspective for being and equity.

Reciprocity

Reciprocity is the mutual exchange of business action that moves forward and backward in time and action to ensure the ability of the organization to respond and frame effective business decisions. Reciprocity is the inclusion component of the business system, ensuring that all parties impacted by a given decision are included in the development of strategies surrounding the decision. It would be easy for people to suggest that reciprocity requires consensus; instead, reciprocity involves exchanges of privileges to achieve equivalency and inclusion.

Businesses must begin to assess the impacts of their decisions rather than just the intents of their decisions. The reciprocity level of the business paradigm is a check and balance to the impact of the decision choice before the decision is finalized. An example could be the implementation of the Omnibus Transportation Employee Testing Act of 1991 for the 7.5 million licensed commercial drivers throughout the United States. Implementation of the Act requires that employees in classifications within organizations requiring the commercial driver's licenses for safety-sensitive positions must participate in six drug and alcohol testing programs in order to maintain their positions within the organizations. Employers have good intentions in the development of programs in compliance with the Act. Employers must, however, assess the impact of the programs on the employees. Mutual exchange of information, values, beliefs, and strategies for implementation is essential to the reciprocity level of development. Through the reciprocity process, underlying paradigms of violence get superimposed on the organizational structure for the future, thereby avoiding impacting other aspects of business and business decision making (Williams, 1994).

Reciprocity therefore is the emotional balancer of the organization because it requires inclusion to ensure sanity within the organization.

Empowerment

Empowerment is the training and development component of any business decision. Businesses must ensure that decisions crafted include an assessment of the potential of the decision to increase the skill and influence parameters for employees accountable for development and implementation of the decision. Webster defines empowerment as the giving of official and legal power to others. For every executive, board member, stockholder, employee, or consultant impacted by any business decision, characteristics of systems become a critical and necessary dynamic. Every system involves *elements* (any object, boundary, or relation that can be articulated), *boundaries* (any idea that separates the elements), *relations* (any idea that associates the elements of the system—same thought, same shape, same boundary), *cause* (whatever brings the system into focus such as a condition, presence, absence, or issue), and *qualities* (characteristics of the whole that are evident only at the level of the whole). The process of empowering others becomes the nexus point in the process that activates an assessment of the entire system. When businesses empower, they share power and authority. This calls into question the elements, boundaries, relations, and qualities of the system. The constant revision of the system keeps the system open and reduces the overall fear factors that creep into systems development. As noted in the last chapter, codependence is the creeping disorder for business and restricts and compartmentalizes effective business decision making. Therefore, empowering others reduces the overall potential for codependent action and thought.

Most organizations in business operate from a classical paradigm. The systems thinking in this paradigm focuses on labeling, describing, and classifying things. Discovery of essential and true form was critical in this paradigm because clarity had to be established and framed—closed, if you will. This model of systems thinking was devoid of a model for understanding and embracing change. Therefore, empowerment of others in any organization would go against the grain of classical systems thinking.

As businesses continued to develop over time, businesses embraced the dynamic paradigm or scientific paradigm of system thinking. This is the conventional wisdom paradigm for current business decision making and decision action. In current business, there must be a *cause and effect*. Without cause and effect, no decision can be made. *Why* is no longer an issue of form in business; it has become the antecedent condition for analysis and decision making. This paradigm thinking perpetuates the compartmentalization and fragmentation of current business. In the dynamic paradigm, thoughts, perspectives, and assumptions about the structure of systems rested on the view, and sometimes the belief, that the elements of the system were clear and distinct. Fragmenting the process and only thinking of products, finance, marketing, human resources, cost assessments, and other issues were viewed from a singular system perspective. Only one aspect of business needed to be addressed. Change therefore would occur within the minuscule system rather than any assessment of the whole. Empowerment frustrates the classic and dynamic systems thinking model because it demands a review of the total system.

Representation

Representation is the process of ensuring that separate components of the business decision are connected to ensure a purpose. When the system operates, feedback adjusts and controls the performance of the system to be inclusive and comprehensive in the communication of thoughts, ideas, and future practices.

The communication paradigm of the 1930s focused on the concept of efficiency as embodied in the purpose and intent of organizations. As long as purpose and feedback were possible, organizations and employees would understand the directions and nexus of all actions.

The concept of representation goes beyond the traditional perspective and focuses on the expansion of boundaries of the decision-making system. Efficiency, formal, and expansion processes are the strategies for linking one part of a system to the other. Representation embodies the traditional communication, field, and evolutionary models of systems thinking and goes beyond them. The field model suggests that the boundaries of a system are not real; yet it avoids or discounts the values of the individual. The evolutionary model suggests that elements of a system are clearly defined; however, they may change or transform over time. What remains is a clear hierarchy of authority and control in order to reduce the concept of chaos. In effect, the history of systems thinking never changes.

This system of thinking in the new business paradigm suggests that the outcomes identified in all other theories automatically limited and trapped the thinkers and implementers of the system in actions and thoughts *because they had an end*. True systems work more effectively because the process of the system, not the end of the system, is what becomes important. Therefore, the representation level of the business paradigm focuses on ensuring the purpose as well as the communication of the purpose of the system, not the end of the system. The end never occurs. Only more intriguing and successful strategies for analyzing the issues to effectively develop a decision consistent with the system in light of the overall business direction.

Commitment

Commitment is the ongoing agreement to resolve issues and work toward completion of any given business and/or personal requirement that affects the overall business decision or business outcome. Most systems thinking models discount or avoid the importance of the human dynamic in the business decision process. This new system mandates commitment that focuses on blending system and human inclusiveness to achieve an overall organizational outcome.

Commitment is the embodiment of the entrepreneurial spirit and of the spiritual or living being within business. Business is a living process when seen in the context of an open system. Because business is not static, the potential to "give up" is larger inasmuch as no labels or ultimate descriptions exist to frame and define the business. Therefore, the process of committing to follow through, be involved, give one's all, and "be present, in the clinical sense" is essential to the overall success of business decision making.

The development of a new product, the analysis of a problem, the working to remain inclusive, and the need to integrate and acculturate the varying diversities of people and ideas require the process of commitment. The commitment also focuses energies on ensuring the equality, reciprocity, empowerment, representation, and interpretation of the business process and the business decision.

The civil rights, women's, gay/lesbian, international human rights, and environmental movements are all examples of commitment. What is essential about each movement is the awareness that it is an ongoing commitment. Governor Pete Wilson's response societally to eliminate academic and state utilization of the affirmative action policies and practices of organizations is an example of the classic and dynamic systems thinking that is devoid of fluidness and human recognition. Wilson perpetuates the old thinking strategies that continue to fragment and compartmentalize society and thwart the inclusiveness of people and systems. *Every time any politician, activist, or social scientist states that a system is complete or that an end has been achieved, there is an adherence to an old model of thinking that discounts the need for unity between people and systems.* Fear tactics continue to divide a nation around issues of race or economics, fear tactics strive for reorganization or reengineering of a corporation, fear tactics press for competition as the end-all of business action, fear tactics disempower, restrict interpretation, and avoid reciprocity, and each is an example of noncommitment to a living model with the expressed desire of closing the systems in operation.

Figure 10.2
The Process Business Paradigm in Motion

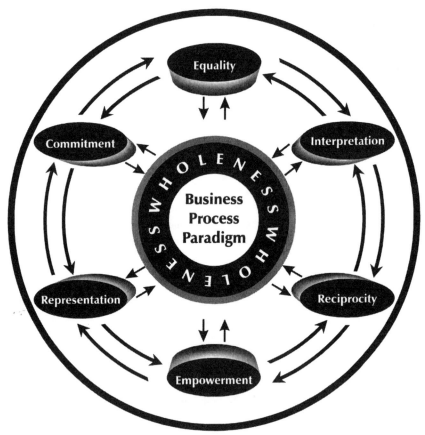

Wholeness

Wholeness, the last cyclical level of the new business paradigm, is a concerted and dedicated effort to package and review the actions and thoughts of business through a system of regurgitation. To be effective in the systems thinking paradigm of "process business thinking," a cyclical approach that is nonstatic is the ultimate level with no end.

Figure 10.2 depicts the total business paradigm in which all components are equal and necessary for a "whole" process of thinking and being.

The issue in this system is that business must begin to assess the value of humanity as a critical component of the decision-making process. Focusing on properties or qualities of business or avoiding seeing people as different from the organization represents critical changes from the traditional field theories that governed twentieth-century thinking models. Both cause and effect are important but not primary in the process of thinking. Again, Governor Pete Wilson of California believed that affirmative action was the cause of the angry white backlash. He did not look at the process of change and development to see that there was no beginning or end to the sense of equality, reciprocity, or interpretation. Rather, there had only been a shift in the thinking parameters that suggested that the old paradigm of cause and effect was no longer working.

The evolutionary paradigm has been the closest thing to a true transformational paradigm. Will McWhinney, the foremost theorist in this process, describes systems change as the movement to a higher plane of complexity. According to McWhinney (1991) and others, transformation is based on the system's ability to respond to more and more complex ideas and issues that confront the system. The second idea of evolutionary thinkers is that change is irreversible. Although those premises appear sound, in the development of this paradigm for business, the process of decision making became more important than the process of reaching a conclusion in the systems process. The strength of the process business paradigm is in its continual circle, not the results of any one component of the system.

INTEGRATION OF THE BUSINESS PROCESS PARADIGM WITH HUMANITY

The second critical strength of the business process paradigm is that it must work in tandem with the human process paradigm displayed in Figure 10.1. The process of development is parallel between people and business systems. You will note that people development and business development have similar issues from the titles of the levels of development. Suffice it to say for now that each needs the other, as will be shown later, and each requires similar levels of holism to achieve parity.

THE PEOPLE DEVELOPMENT–HUMAN PROCESS PARADIGM

Figure 10.3 depicts the process human paradigm that exists in the same time and space with the process business paradigm. This system is operational during the entire life span of a human's existence and provides the framework for human development that is nonstatic as the business paradigm is nonstatic.

The Human Process Paradigm in Motion

The human process paradigm shown in Figure 10.3 depicts a fluid system that has no beginning and no end. The system shows that people are thrust into a developmental process that demands that issues of discord, emergence, acknowledgment, disclosure, self-indulgence, reemergence, and congruence are fluid processes that guide human development. Early life, middle life, and old

Figure 10.3
The Human Process Paradigm in Motion

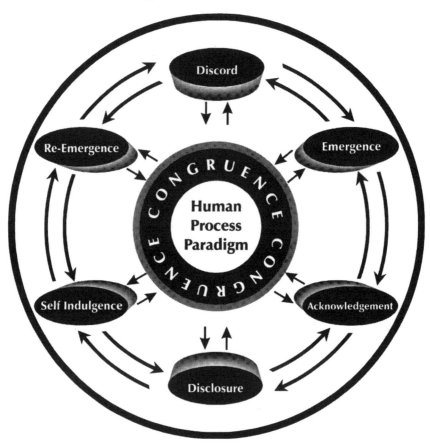

age are not the foci of the development process; rather, what one understands or does during their development matters most in the creation of a "whole or congruent" person. Married to the business paradigm, the congruence of the person is equal to the wholeness of the business system.

Discord

Discord is the internal development of persons from birth through adolescence. In this time frame of spatial development, lack of clarity surrounding role identity, gender understanding, sexual identity, career identity, relationship development, and other traditional developmental models is the predominant structure. People go through life without clarity in form or structure. Who we are, how we behave, what we understand as morality, what we understand as law, and how we frame that understanding in crafting internal rules is the focus of this process.

Discord represents the continual internal struggle and challenge to understand one's place in society, both personally and professionally. The struggle to find one's niche drives the continual discord within the person to institute limits and structures that will reduce the internal chaos that everyone experiences. Discord is neither positive or negative; rather, it exists merely as the framework of the development of people. Development of strength, internal focus, and coping strategies are all components of the process paradigm in the cycle of living.

What is wonderful about this paradigm process is the realization that businesses and people are always changing. The challenge is to develop blend processes for people to focus on their living as businesses must begin to focus on their living. No set pattern is right or wrong; rather, they all exist to mutate or continually change as tantamount to having purpose societally and personally.

In this connection, one can look at the changes the United Way instituted in the aftermath of the debacle that developed concerning the misuse of fiscal resources by the former chief executive officer. The United Way reaffirmed its commitment to the development of people and its commitment to be clearer in its approach to business. Discord existed among the employees because they recognized the taking for granted of givers to the institution and their responsibility for "right livelihood" in order to empower and impact society. The business recognized its role as regards "wholeness" and significantly altered its business practice to consider issues of equality, reciprocity, interpretation, and commitment. The processes experienced by the United Way were creations of a living spirit within the corporation for the business and the employees. The process of living and developing as parallel concerns became the synergies for continual living for both the corporation and the employees. Keith Green, an employee of the United Way at the Long Beach, California branch, said, "You know, I wasn't really afraid after the fall of the United Way. I actually felt that it gave us a chance to achieve our mission, and it gave me a personal challenge to balance who I am with what I do. I am actually excited." Process paradigms in motion allowed the employee and the system to build respectfully upon one another. Process paradigms in motion move the discord to the emerging process.

Emergence

Emergence is the flooding of the mind and body with new images, thoughts, and feelings that suggest that change within the human being is imminent. The emergence stage for adolescent girls begins as they experience their first period, and for adolescent boys as they enter puberty. For youth in college, the emergence stage could be the first sexual experience that empowers and connects the genders to one another; for gays and lesbians it becomes the emerging feelings of communion with another of the same sex; and for couples the birth of a child. Emergence is a critical and constant process throughout life.

Emergence is the beginning of comfort with discord because it creates clarity regarding the issues and perspectives that influence and control the discord phase of development. In the emergence cycle, light bulbs go off in the mind regarding issues that created depression and frustration in the discord phase of development. Feelings of connection, joining, comfort, awareness, and self-assuredness because of clarity are the essential dynamics of the emergence phase.

Employees sense the emergence when they give up fear in the organization, when they recognize that they can claim personal power over their own lives and careers, when they stop blaming themselves for the actions of the organization, or when they realize that doing their best does not involve castigation of the self. Whenever one recognizes that continuation of the discord phase is not essential to growth and development, then emergence is free to nurture and enhance the development of the person.

Emergence also frees and empowers the person to search for others with similar experiences and views, creating the joining and group process of development. Communication, listening, sharing, participating, and framing perspectives occur during the emergence stage. An excellent example is the emerging development of gays and lesbians in their "coming out stage of development." For the gay or lesbian, emergence is a process of accepting who one is without criticism or guilt. Being whole recognizes the existence of feelings and difference without fear of reprisal. For African Americans and Hispanics, the same dynamics are evident as they learn who they are, knowing that their history of thought does not have to embody a Eurocentric thought process. Emergence is the critical phase that drives essential growth.

Acknowledgment

Acknowledgment is the overtly conscious acceptance of one's emerging self, with a commitment to develop comfort with emerging views, attitudes, and behaviors. The acknowledgment phase is the most overtly parallel paradigm process within the person because acknowledgment is not a discount of how one has acted or felt historically. Rather, it is a parallel path being explored with full understanding and acceptance of one's current reality.

Acknowledgment is the personal acceptance and exclamation of who one is in spite of the views and attitudes of others. It is the African American who selects his own labels (in the classic paradigm) rather than letting others label him. In the 1960s it was the Negro selecting Black; it was the Latin male exclaiming himself a Chicano; it was the homosexual exclaiming himself a gay; it was the Eurocentric male asserting he was a "feeling man" in spite of societal pressures to hide his emotions; it was women announcing themselves as "equal beings entitled to all the benefits achieved by men." Each acknowledgment was and continues to be an intensely personal process.

Acknowledgment can be the professional determination that personal and professional decisions will be accomplished through adherence to personal values regardless of the political processes that exist within organizations—even to the realization that it could cost one a job. Acknowledgment is the development of internal influence and power in the self to the exclusion of others' perspectives.

Acknowledgment is the state that Malcom X, Martin Luther King, Robert Kennedy, Medgar Evers, and other civil rights leaders experienced when they recognized that they could be assassinated for their views. Yet they chose to forge ahead onto the path that made sense for them.

Disclosure

Disclosure is the public exclamation of the acknowledgment phase of the human development process. When one discloses, one must accept the consequences. Often people will go through the acknowledgment phase but stop at the disclosure phase because of the too great projected costs associated with disclosure.

Disclosure is no longer a private affair that builds on internal strength. Rather, it is the active seeking of others with similar views and perspectives in order to build personal partnerships that ensure survivability with a new perspective or a new view. Joining the Boy Scouts, the military, a basketball or a football team, a gang or a fraternity, or a sorority are all milestones that people reach, with which they build to their own perspectives with like-minded persons.

Disclosure becomes the recognition that clinical dysfunction may not be a reality surrounding one's personal view; however, there can be problems with the disclosure. Unions that develop and seek members often force their members to acquiesce to union views to the detriment of the individual. This becomes unhealthy disclosure, or being a member of management where participation in political decisions hurts others. There are so many examples of unhealthy and healthy disclosure, suggesting the critical nature of the disclosure process.

Each of us is accountable for our own actions and thoughts in the disclosure process. When we choose to include or find others, we must take responsibility for the impact of the intents we choose to implement. Too often, people want to change or grow within their lives, and yet they abdicate responsibility for actions that are the result of change. Therefore, the disclosure phase is constantly impacted by the acknowledgment and emergence phases. There is a constant reminder of the rationales that have driven personal choices. The more one abdicates, the more the issues of discord begin to creep into the decision-making and choice process for the individual.

Self-Indulgence

This is a critical and perhaps the most common phase of the personal developmental process paradigm. The self-indulgence phase of the paradigm is the pivotal nexus point of the system, for it is the resting place for personal development. Consider a young gay male discovering himself. He has worked hard to emerge, disclose, and acknowledge himself. He has joined gay and lesbian organizations, works for legal changes through gay and lesbian groups, and senses that he is a whole and congruent person. He also spends his energies being sexually promiscuous with multiple partners without looking at the potential of ultimate union with another. Over time, he hurts others in this phase because he manipulates the feelings and desires of others to achieve his sexual interests. He is self-indulgent and harmful of others. Or consider a married man who has worked diligently to develop a wonderful relationship with his wife. Yet he is unwilling to help his wife with responsibilities around the home, exclaiming that it is women's work. He castigates his wife for wanting help or assistance since he is the breadwinner of the home. He has adopted a self-indulgent life posture and is stuck in the developmental process because of views that are inconsistent with the rest of his developmental path.

Professional people are said to be in the self-indulgent phase when their actions are designed for self to the detriment of others. Consider the example of Joseph, a chief executive officer of the Family Foundation. Joseph brings to his foundation an outstanding professional instructor for his program to enhance the academic potential of disadvantaged children. Joseph continually promises Dale, the professional instructor, a contract for services rendered, yet avoids the consummation of the contractual process for self-purposes. The continual denial and discount of Dale is an example of self-indulgent behavior that detrimentally impacts Dale's trust in the relationship. Consequently, Dale finds himself becoming self-conscious in his relationships with others because of the uncertainty exhibited by Joseph. Dale asks himself, "Are all CEOs like Joseph? Can I trust the word of people or must I always test their commitment and honesty?" These examples of self-indulgence block the potential for movement.

Self-indulgence has a brother relationship with self-experimentation. The self-experimentation phase in the self-indulgent process is a testing ground for confident and effective choice or a testing ground for expansion of the self-indulgent. The more the experimentation focuses on healthy choice and movement, the more the person moves to the next phase of reemergence. The more the experimentation phase leads to expanded me-orientation, the less ready the individual is for movement to a higher phase. Rather, the person revisits discord, emergence, and acknowledgment. The less disclosure occurs because there is internal deceit in the developmental process. The more deceit, the more discord.

Reemergence

Reemergence is the revisiting of existing behavior and value alignment with historical behavior and value development. People often give up old behaviors and values as they discover and move through new thoughts and actions. It is like a child discovering beer or sex for the first time. Rather than listen to thoughts shared throughout time from the parents, the child explores on his own, often discarding existing family values.

Reemergence is the rekindling of history in order to build a balanced framework that maintains what is valuable and good about history with what is fluid and good about the present and the future. It is a psychological bonding of my historical life with my new life: filled with wonderment about what needs to be kept and what needs to be discarded because these trappings don't match or fit with my continually emerging self.

Joyce is the director of the Office of Management and Budget in a computer conglomerate in northern California. Over the past year, she has gotten a divorce from her husband and has been promoted twice in the firm. She had adopted behaviors to reach the top that she was not proud of. She both undercut managers and sold employees down the drain, and she had experienced a self-indulgent process that had a positive payoff professionally and financially. Along the way she lost the sensitivity that had originally made her the "darling manager" of the corporation. Joyce wanted her old self back. She liked the influence and power of her new role, and she believed she had a lot to offer the company, but she just wasn't sure who she was any longer.

In the reemergence, Joyce revisited the discord, emergence, acknowledgments, and disclosures of her emerging self. With a therapist she explored the self-indulgent behaviors she had adopted. Drinking, power manipulations, and compartmentalizing of communications and information had become the norm for her. She didn't like what she had become and she wanted to change. The reemergence stage allows people to rethink their development and to alter that development to a pattern that retains and expands on underlying values that guide overall action. When we emerge and change, we may not always bring with us the values that are essential to our total being. We may embrace values that move us through acknowledgment and disclosure, but we may be somewhat out of sync with what is really important to us. As we review and revisit, we often find pieces of our history that expand us as open systems, that nurture us as beings in the society, and that frame for us the whole that is critical to lasting comfort.

Reemergence then becomes the conscious in our development. It defines the sense of living spirit that allows us to meet the world head-on and to frame a true niche that works for who we are more so than what we do. In effect, reemergence helps us frame the balance that is necessary for continued development.

Congruence

Congruence is the development of the systems path within the human being. Issues of premises, assumptions, cultural transitions, professional and personal roles, behavior and communication, protocol, and etiquette help blend what one experiences in the other phases to this phase. It is not a static phase, but it is a more structured frame for balancing action with thought, personal with professional strivings, values with assumptions, and current reality with personal history.

In the congruence process, values and how one accommodates, negotiates, bridges one space to another, and creates new norms become most important. One's history, be it ethnic (race), economic (rich or poor), biological (male or female), ontological (young or old), familial (large or small family), relational (single or in a union), or psychological/cultural (gay or straight, domestic or foreign), impacts one's ability to be congruent. All parts of history are blended with emerging values and attitudes that may have changed one's perspective in any or all of the aforementioned categories. Dinah Shore, the television actress, once said that the recognition that she was African American versus Caucasian significantly altered her reality of the world and how the world responded to her. She felt that she had coasted through life without thought to who she was or what was important. The realization of an ethnic change altered her realities in every dimension. Discord became her norm, and only by "processing" her life and her needs was she able to rebuild a congruent life that meant something to her. Only then was she able to impact differently the realities that others wanted to create.

Each of us goes through a developmental process through which ups and downs frame our thinking. We analyze, we accept, we avoid, we cajole, we move forward; however, somewhere in the process, we look for congruity and we strive to make sense of what is. The making sense is the challenge of congruence. We challenge ourselves ultimately when we risk growing and developing from a process perspective rather than from a compartmentalized and fragmented approach to our development. Generalizations, abstractions, techniques, and xenophobic perspectives leave, and so we are left with the nakedness of who we are.

Congruence is the vigilant and constant movement in the process paradigm. People process in an intentional manner to ensure that all the parts make a larger whole.

THE IMPACTS OF A PROCESS PARADIGM APPROACH

Business is currently trapped in an analytical thinking approach to development of long-term strategies for the implementation and management of business. The analytical thinking approach feeds the process of compartmentalization, fragmentation, and detachment that haunts successful business venturing. In this approach, focus on control, structure, individual performance, semi-teams, power, directed approach, and other fractured terms become the norm for assessing and implementing new strategies. The failure of the fragmented functions is the inability to craft solutions to issues that cause businesses to succeed or fail.

Businesses succeed because they embrace new issues and craft different solutions from the past. Among systems-oriented terms are collaboration, cooperation, teamwork, partnerships, alliances, self-directed teams, self-regulated teams, process-oriented teams, process-oriented strategies, and open system strategies. Support systems and operating systems bridge history to craft parallel strategies for resolving of business issues to achieve realistic business outcomes.

In any business organization, the support functions of human resources, finance, legal, and public relations are critical to the overall success of the business venture. The operating areas of research, production, sales, and marketing are driven by support departments. Windows 95 and 2000 are excellent examples of the challenges of the two parts of a whole. Marketing and research identified a critical delivery date to the public. Research, production, and project teams drove the delivery process; however, the effectiveness of the structure was based on the ability of human resources to hire and retain competent personnel; the legal department to identify and resolve critical issues of patents to the technology being employed; finance to agree to the expenditure of resources for the product development and marketing; and public relations to maintain the high trust of the public. The product was released on time, but the effectiveness of the software was moderate in comparison to other releases from Microsoft. All the right things had been in place—strategic plans, business plans, individual plans, and goals—yet it was not totally successful. What happened to all the issues required in a business process paradigm? Did release of the product ensure that the equality of the product development process would mirror the history of the company? Were there misinterpretations of the roles and policies that guide overall quality testing and quality delivery? Although commitment seemed to be clearly in focus, did commitment overshadow reciprocity in the development, marketing, and sales process? Did finance drive the actions of the firm, or did product drive the actions? Where was representation and empowerment in the process? Did the organization allow equality in ensuring that the separate components of the business decision were connected to ensure the purpose of the product? Empowerment seemed to have been in place in the training and development of the employees to provide assistance to the customers. However, were the elements, boundaries, cause, and qualities essential to an effective system in place? Did the process drive the development of Windows 95 and 2000, or did the release of a new product drive the system? The fact that numerous issues are arising suggests the latter.

So what can the process paradigm generate that closed-end analytical paradigms seem to overlook? First is the empowering of individuals to move toward self-mastery. Human beings have an innate need to improve personal competency and effectiveness. The self-mastery process sets the stage for the individual to improve interpersonal and working relationships and the effectiveness of all persons on the team. The concept of excellence has meaning when people experience representation and empowerment. Second, intergroup relations are enhanced in such a fashion that business processes between teams and departments horizontally are enhanced, thereby increasing the quality of customer service.

Third, the total organization begins to experience a better "fit" than has been a part of its history. Systems, structures, and processes flow together because there is a greater commitment to the process than to the product. The commitment to process guides product development and delivery. Last, the environment surrounding the organization is enhanced because business leaders and business members—the employees—understand the direction and process of the organization.

The business process paradigm and the human process paradigm set the stage for organizational leaders and the organizational system to embrace the strategic process. Discussions of the future state drive the feedback loop process that assesses the current state. With some understanding of these issues, the organization can begin to focus on the critical issue of the transition state. The balance of all the issues creates a greater whole than has previously been experienced by the organization.

Vision, mission, customer focus, quality, service, environmental cost, profitability, stakeholder focus, and society become part of the future state. Critical values regarding how the future state is to be achieved become essential issues for the future state discussion. Teamwork, self-directed teams, process teams, employee empowerment, total quality management, quality improvement process, and communication strategies are all part of the future state discussion because it helps frame the process of equality, interpretation, reciprocity, empowerment, and commitment of the business process paradigm. Remember, it is the process that guides, *not the product*.

NEXT STEPS: UNDERSTANDING THE PROCESS OF THINKING AND ACTING IN CONCERT WITH CHANGE

Certain combinations of strategies must coexist to ensure effective outcomes in congruity development and management. Management (this is the first time that I have used that word in concert with congruence) requires development of different interrelationships from the norm of business functioning. Suffice it to say that this is a comprehensive-level system of personal and organizational change and development. The system helps you identify *what* is not working, *how* the organization created the rift, *why* the organization's strategies have been unsuccessful *who* is best able to alter the course of events, and *when* changes should be made that match the short and longer term organizational need. The system is based on the identification, recognition, and intervention of seemingly separate thoughts, actions, strategies, and capacities of an organization. These disparate parts are developed into a system of thoughts, strategies, and operational outcomes that allow the effective capturing of market share and satisfaction parameters in the organization.

Systemically, the congruence development system focuses on the creation of balance and alignment within organizations and among its members. Organizations historically focus on the compartmentalized strategies for change and

Figure 10.4
The Williams Congruence Development System

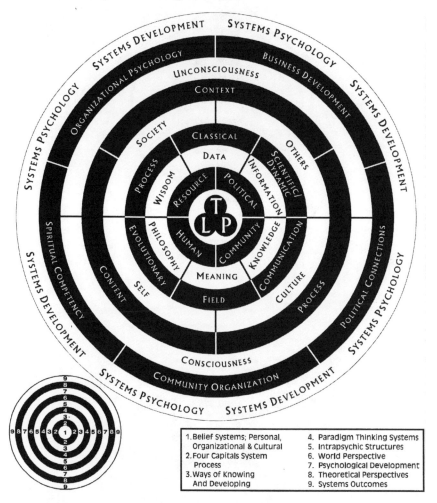

1. Belief Systems; Personal, Organizational & Cultural
2. Four Capitals System Process
3. Ways of Knowing And Developing
4. Paradigm Thinking Systems
5. Intrapsychic Structures
6. World Perspective
7. Psychological Development
8. Theoretical Perspectives
9. Systems Outcomes

development, believing that the strategies designed for the organization will achieve a better balance with the desired outcomes of the organization. Unfortunately, the planned designs for change, growth, productivity, and increased market share are less than successful because of the lack of congruence necessary for critical success. Issues such as the equity valuation of employees and the participation of employees are undercurrent themes that get left off the strategy chart. Organizations still get trapped in responding to *either* the organizational issues or the people issue, not both. Each retreat or deficit act creates less trust, less movement, and less success.

Figure 10.4 depicts an entire congruence development system. The system is

Figure 10.5
The Integration of Congruent Thought and Action

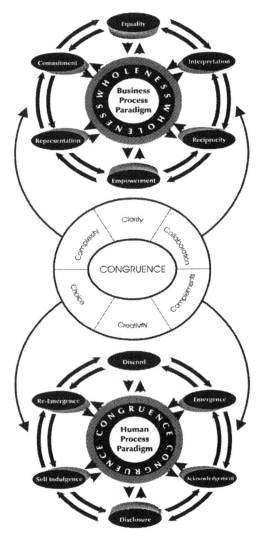

crucial to congruence development as it frames different levels of operational performance. As can be seen in the figure, multiple levels of analysis, planning, intervention, and maintenance comprise the system before you.

Figure 10.5 depicts the integration and balance necessary between congruence thinking and congruence action in the business and human paradigms. Figures 10.6 and 10.7 show both the levels in the operational performance system and the level-system process accompanying that system.

Figure 10.6
Operational Levels of the Congruence Development System

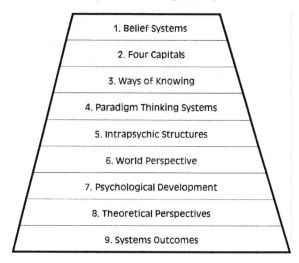

1. Belief Systems
2. Four Capitals
3. Ways of Knowing
4. Paradigm Thinking Systems
5. Intrapsychic Structures
6. World Perspective
7. Psychological Development
8. Theoretical Perspectives
9. Systems Outcomes

Figure 10.7
Level Description of the Congruence Development System

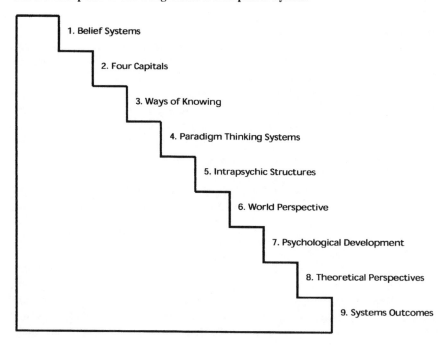

1. Belief Systems
2. Four Capitals
3. Ways of Knowing
4. Paradigm Thinking Systems
5. Intrapsychic Structures
6. World Perspective
7. Psychological Development
8. Theoretical Perspectives
9. Systems Outcomes

THE LEVELS APPROACH TO CHANGE

The first thing to recognize about this congruence development system is the explicit requirement to focus on thinking and acting. Most organizational systems focus on behavioral changes or strategies to frame decision making. In addition, the changes identified are historically structural, environmental, or process (decision making). An earlier chapter described research that has identified five primary leadership strategies that managers and leaders felt would guide their work with organizations and their people. Those areas of focus were *decision making, people behavior, organizational structure, satisfaction parameters, and environment.* The research showed that although each area might impact on the success or deficit effects within organizations, the largest and by far the most critical factor for success was people behavior. Leaders needed to consider people behavior above all else in determining overall strategies for success within organizations. This was an important finding because employers, organizational leaders, and most consultants consider people behavior—that is, people perspectives—a last choice. In fact, the research showed that as quantitative data is most often the deciding force in decision making, phenomenological data—lived experiences—is rarely considered.

This congruence system is therefore explicit in its consideration of people behavior as equal to any other data that can be obtained. In addition, choices are not made without explicit consideration of the human performance factor. In effect, making a structural change without consideration of the persons who will lead that effort is not done with this system. Consider the need for a structural change. In that process, you are cognizant of the degree of ambiguity, flexibility, and the unknown that will impact the success of the change effort. Without this system, you might choose an individual who is a theological/legal and a classical thinker. Most assuredly your efforts will fail. Why? The theological/legal belief structure represents an individual who likes structure, order, and control. The individual usually does not like ambiguity and works diligently to create a chaos-free environment, tight controls, boxes, and rules in order to be comfortable. When they are stressed, they move to their secondary stance, which is legal. In this belief stance, power, control, and authority are the high needs of the Legal Belief Structure to reduce stress and regain harmony within the person. As a classical thinker, thoughts of ambiguity are not present. Remember, the classical thinker is the keeper of the flame. The keeper of the flame avoids conflict at all costs, looking for ways to retain the calm in the organization that he is used to enjoying. This person is likely to fail at the assignment, and it is not his fault. He is likely to be blamed for the unsuccessful change—but the reality is that the wrong person was selected to lead the effort. The choice should have been a psychological/legal person who was an evolutionary or process thinker. A psychological/legal belief structure focuses on the need to ensure that the individual and group are moving effectively through a change process. The process thinker effectively looks for balance and alignment in a change process and is comfortable with issues of the unconscious and the unknown. Feeling excited and comfortable with the unknown is more consonant with their style of being. Does this begin to make more sense to you?

Level One: Data Analysis

Level one focuses on the facts, factors, beliefs, assumptions, experiences, and feelings of all members of the organization around a given issue or set of issues. The analyses allow for integration of multiple data sets to create a realistic picture of the whole that can inform the client in comprehensive and systemic terms.

So we look at the first component of the congruence development system: data analysis is the first component of this system. There are five steps in the data analysis process: (1) understanding the belief systems, (2) assessing the organization's and each individual's orientation to the four capitals, (3) identifying the organization's and the individual or group's way of knowing, (4) assessing the thinking styles of the individual or group and the thought orientation of the organization, and (5) identifying the intrapsychic structure of the organization. These five strategies allow us to understand how both the organization and the people can create effective strategies for growth, development, change, and maintenance.

As can be seen by the figure of analysis (Figure 10.8), the five aforementioned areas represent a cultural competency, people management competency, thematic validation, and belief and thinking audits. Each level of the analysis helps determine the congruity or lack thereof of the values, beliefs, and tenets of the organization and its members. Rarely has there been a system of analysis that allows for in-depth assessment of people and systems, such that decision making, structural development, environmental practices, and satisfaction parameters can be identified through one data-gathering set. This represents the structural analysis critical to effective organizational planning and strategy development.

Belief Systems Audit

The most important assessment is the belief systems audit. It permits an understanding of the individual's world view. When you have determined the individual belief structure of a group, you can then assess the potential of the group to accomplish given work outcomes based on the orientation of their world view. This is essential because no amount of training or development will change the world view of an individual. If the group is theological, assignments that focus on change will not be successful with a group that is primarily comfortable with structure, order, no chaos, and rules. This group does not have a high need for creativity. Getting the tone of the organization is critical to overall systemic success.

Figure 10.8
Phase One: Analysis

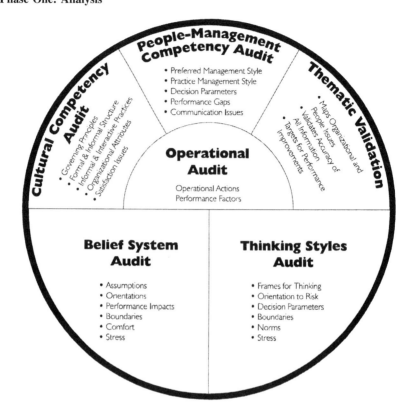

People-Management
Competency Audit
- Preferred Management Style
- Practice Management Style
- Decision Parameters
- Performance Gaps
- Communication Issues

Cultural Competency Audit
- Governing Principles
- Formal & Informal Structure
- Informal & Interactive Practices
- Organizational Attributes
- Satisfaction Issues

Thematic Validation
- Maps Organizational and People Issues
- Validates Accuracy of All Information
- Targets for Performance Improvements

Operational Audit
Operational Actions
Performance Factors

Belief System Audit
- Assumptions
- Orientations
- Performance Impacts
- Boundaries
- Comfort
- Stress

Thinking Styles Audit
- Frames for Thinking
- Orientation to Risk
- Decision Parameters
- Boundaries
- Norms
- Stress

Four-Capital Assessment

The second analysis is both personal and systemic. Based on the world view, discovery of the four-capital system (discussed in a previous chapter) is critical. To accomplish this analysis, a focus group assessment is done with at least a random sampling of 50% of the organization. Appreciative inquiry questions are used to help identify key themes of the organization from a phenomenological point of view. This assessment allows the emergence of hidden or uncovered areas of the organization. The process allows one to identify the issues of balance in the outcomes of the organization. Historically, the organizational themes of money, power authority, human performance, the organizational performance, community value, personal empowerment, group value, and team criticality arise in such a fashion that one can identify the primary themes of the organization. Themes exist only when they are identified at more than one level of the organization (executive, director, manager, supervisor, employee) and represent a central core aspect of the organization's operational performance.

Remember that balance and alignment require a healthy sharing of all four capitals. Without that sharing, imbalance occurs. Consider the number of times you have found your organization paying all of its attention to resource and political capital. You probably would say to yourself that how the company both values and uses *money* is their most important concern. Second, you would say that the *networks of power and authority* are the secondary concerns. In fact, you might even begin to wonder if there is any concern for the human or community capital in the organization. This assessment, together with the belief systems process, begins to give one a picture of the organization. However, making a final decision about what to do or where to go would be precipitous.

Ways of Knowing

Organizations tell you how they gather and use information in the third assessment process. There are six ways of knowing: though *data, information, knowledge, meaning, philosophy, and wisdom. Data* are sets of information that are seemingly unconnected historically, gathered through a quantitative or assumptive process within the organization. *Information* is made up of the collated data sets designed to create a specific picture. *Knowledge* consists of the focused decision points created in the organization that inform a direction for organizational action. These three forms of knowing are *content driven* and focus on specifics as they arise. Meaning, philosophy, and wisdom are *context-driven* forms of facts. Based on the interpretations given to the contextual facts and factors, meaning is extracted that can determine a philosophical or system concern or need. This then is utilized to frame a wisdom strategy that includes history, transition, and transformation approaches for use within the organization.

Thinking Systems

The next area is the thinking style audit process. We have talked a lot about the thinking styles, so repitition here is not critical. What would be helpful, however, is an example of how it works. Take a utility corporation—the Arizona Public Service Corporation. It is a full-service utility, highly regulated through the Department of Energy and the Nuclear Regulatory Commission. It is the parent organization of the Arizona Nuclear Power Project. As a parent organization, regulatory requirements often require very tight, clear boundaries to reduce the potential for mistakes in the development and dissemination of energy. The decision process is long, arduous, and detailed with multiple strategies that focus on absolute accuracy. As a thought style, the Arizona Public Service Corporation is classical. It desires no chaos, clear boundaries, explicit rules, and adherence without question to its authority. Decision making is tiered, hierarchical, and slow—for it takes a long time to make the decisions in an attempt to ensure that all the minds up the chain of command agree with the decision. Conversely, the Arizona Nuclear Power Project is responding to nuclear concerns, requiring fast decisions and innovative actions on a moment's notice. As a relatively new organizational entity, it continually undergoes differing organizational stages, simultaneously participating in start-up activities, transition activities, and systemic maintenance activities for its three reactors. Decision making requires fast, flat action that often cannot be accomplished in the traditional manner of this utility. Its thinking style is field and evolutionary. As an entity, there is recognition that the process of growth and change must be tested quickly to ensure that it has the promise of success. However, the development stage is constantly changing, requiring different decisions from the norm at a moment's notice. There may be errors in the process of construction or an outage; however, change is going to occur, and some evidentiary decision-making process needs to be accomplished.

The struggle begins when the decision-making processes deemed necessary by the two organizations do not gel. The Arizona Nuclear Power Project needs quicker agreements on its decisions from the parent organization than the parent's decision processes allow. The slowdown in the decision process, for example, in an outage, can cost the organization $1.2 million a day. The challenge is building clarity, collaboration, and complements in the executive and managerial tiers of the organization to allow dual paradigmic decision structures to exist. For the Arizona Nuclear Power Project, issues of empowerment, representation, interpretation, and equality are key for the employees at the plant. For the parent—the Arizona Public Service Corporation—reciprocity, commitment, and adherence to the rules is important. Who one chooses to lead, who one chooses to govern, how one builds understanding of the two organizations' needs, how one respects and partners with the other in collaboration, and what the organization has created as effective anchors in the two organizations' ability to achieve results are critical to the success of both organizations. The thinking styles of the organization in many ways dictate the thought styles of the leaders for the two organizations.

Intrapsychic Structures

Organizations and their leaders are often challenged to accept four intrapsychic issues that frame development and strategy: self, others, society, and culture. Each of these issues frames the impact or outcome of the organization's products and services. To be successful and to guarantee organizational sustainability, a balance between the four poles of product and service is necessary to give perspective to the employees and to ward off down cycles in product life cycles for the organization to be sustained. Products and services will impact self, others, society, or culture. When the life cycle of organizational products or services focuses on three of the four, two of the four, or one of the four, the organization, its employees, and the customer base suffer.

Let's take two organizations, Medtronics and Guidant Corporation, both of which produce medical devices as surgical implants. Both operate from a competitive mode in providing service to the society. In their work, each believes strongly that their thought development and the cycles of their products include

Figure 10.9
Phase Two: Planning

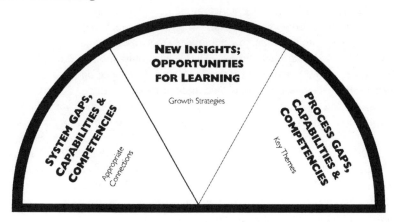

a concern for others, the society, and self. One organization has recently begun to consider the cultural dynamics of how African Americans, Asian Americans, and Latino Americans are different from European Americans in body type and physical development. To that end, Guidant Corporation has begun to research the large body of literature on physical differences and on its impact on rejection theory and retention. Who do you think will have included the necessary strategies to ensure that all four intrapsychic analyses are considered in product and service development?

So we have now looked at all the areas that are essential in a congruence analysis process. Beliefs, four capitals, ways of knowing, thinking styles, and intrapsychic analyses permit full exploration of the people and the organizational system simultaneously. Once the analysis has been accomplished, we are ready to move to Level Two: Planning.

Level Two: Planning

Level two focuses on the planning factors that are necessary to ensure 100% of scope in the work. Key to this area are issues of environmental scanning, gap analysis, functional and implementation planning, and the creation of a detailed work breakdown structure essential for long-term budgeting and sustainability. Each employee or each work team is identified, with specific outcomes being charted for the present and the future.

Figure 10.9 identifies three types of planning efforts: assessment of systems gaps, capabilities, and competencies; assessment of the process gaps, capabilities, and competencies; and opportunities for learning. In effect, the planning process is designed to identify appropriate organizational connections, key themes that undergird success or failure and growth strategies.

Planning for growth, development, and change is best accomplished and enhanced when data, information, and knowledge give meaning to the issues within the organization. Therefore, performance and planning processes focus on the historical and existing practice strategies that are impacting the organization. Attention is given to addressing structure, people behavior, environment, decision making, and satisfaction parameters that often change the real factors necessary for organizational success. The desired outcome is to help the organization develop more successful strategies that will balance operational and employee performance, work scope, and thematic performance. To do this, *the congruence development process looks at the issues of creativity and complexity in the thought process and context, content, and process in the action process.*

Remember: creativity is about "jumping the broom" [moving from one level to another]. It is not about innovation or renovation of what has gone before. It requires original thinking and acting to move beyond what is believed tolerable or possible to a new level of creation of product and service within an organization. Complexity is the exploration of the conscious and unconscious factors of the organization to unleash the creative juices available in people and service.

Planning occurs at three levels. These three models of planning are used to identify gaps in the work and existing plans in relation to the outcomes of the organization. *The strategic planning process, the detailed work breakdown structure, and the thematic analysis* process are created to develop a realistic and comprehensive plan. These steps are also used to create strategies for effective performance of the work and enhancement of the employees. The plans encompass the business, organizational, and emotional intelligence that frames behavior for the long term.

Level Three: The Intervention Process

Level three focuses on the conscious and unconscious issues, practices, procedures, and behaviors that block the potential of the organization and its members to be successful. Interventions are designed to reduce tension, frustration, confusion, and hurt that often get in the way of successful implementation of the work. Business and psychological processes are used here to create contemporary and systemic results.

Level three focuses on the intervening strategies that are used to ensure the congruence of employees in the decision making, people behavior, environmental development, organizational structure and operational implementation, and satisfaction parameters to the desired performance and organization outcomes. Two levels of intervention occur: Systems Connection Strategy and Process Connection Strategy (see Figure 10.10).

The systems connection strategy ensures that the context, content, and process concerns of the organization are integrated in such a way that ambiguity and confusion, creativity instead of innovation, are utilized by the organization and its members in accomplishing the outcomes established. This often means utilizing the analysis section to shift the human and fiscal resources to accomplish

Figure 10.10
Phase Three: Intervention

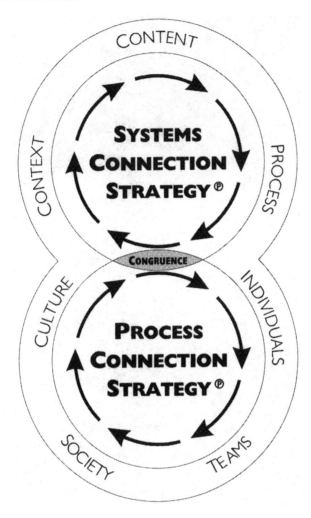

the outcomes. Because the context is critical to this work, the doubters and critics of the strategy are required to participate in the planning and implementation of the strategy, ensuring that the contextual concerns remain the driver of the work, not the content.

The process connection strategy focuses on the conscious and unconscious performance, management, and leadership of the organization and on how those issues impact overall organizational effectiveness. It has been the experience of the congruence development process that the unconscious blocks are the true indicators of organizational success or deficit development.

Figure 10.11
Phase Three: Intervention—Detail

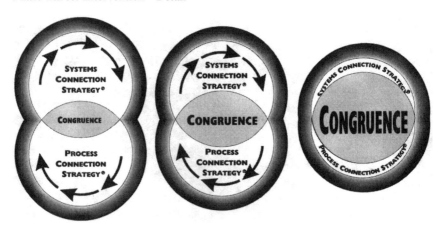

As you can see from Figure 10.11, systems connection focuses on the integration and effective utilization of context, content, and process in framing what needs to be accomplished and according to what critical strategy. The figure also shows the utilization of individual, team, society, and culture to ensure the most effective integration of the critical groups in the intervention process. The more the integrations of the systems connection strategy and the process connection strategy occur, the larger the degree of congruence within the organization and among its members.

Interventions are based on the capacity of the organization. People and systems change and grow at differing paces. Therefore, the congruence development system allows for mirroring the learning and change potential of the organization to build the thought processes and action processes for movement. Whether total system change or incremental strategies are the norm, whether total systems or incremental strategies are pushing the envelope of organizational visioning and implementation—the congruence development system allows the organization to discover what matters so that it can inform planning and performance for the future.

Level Four: The Maintenance Development Process

Level four focuses on the long-term desire of the organization. Change, if it is an option or desire, must be maintained in a fashion that honors the values and beliefs of the organization and the strategy that empowers and frees the employees to continually and congruently create newness for the organization. Therefore, change, development, creation, and growth must be maintained. This process focuses on equal maintenance of these concerns to maintain the organizational system (see Figure 10.12).

Figure 10.12
Phase Four: Sustainability

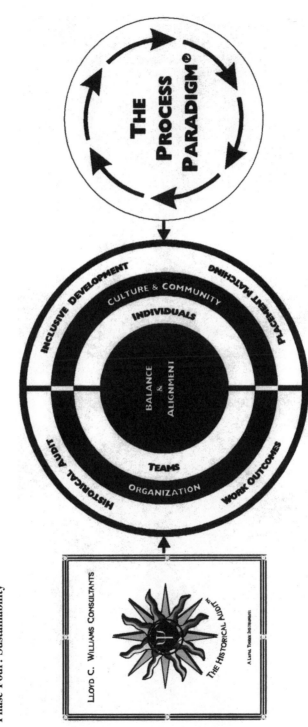

The maintenance system supports the long-term sustainability goals of the organization. Key to this system is the assurance of balance and alignment of employee skill sets to organizational thinking styles. The congruence development system helps organizations reframe the policies, procedures, and practices that guide organizational action. Cultural strategies are redesigned to be more inclusive of behaviors and thinking styles that can enhance overall functioning for the long term. Processes are created to assist the organization in change and maintenance actions necessary for the future. Finally, historical audit is created on existing work to create sufficient meaning for the creation of a maintenance development plan.

This is accomplished through implementating and tracking the detailed work breakdown structure and development strategies beyond training and project management that allow for continual assessment of what works and what doesn't. The process is always balanced by the values and beliefs of the organization, as well as the team accountable for the work. Where there is synergy—congruence—success is more likely. Where there is dissonance, deficits are more likely. The goals are reduction of deficits, advancement of success, and congruence for employees.

We now have a direction for the work of the organization. The next chapter gives you an example of how all of this works together.

Chapter 11

Putting the Process Together: Steps to Energize the Development of Congruence in the Workplace

There is always a challenge for people and organizations when speed, revenue enhancement, downsizing, merger and acquisition, or innovation are the value strategies for product enhancement, growth, and development. Each and every day, organizations seek to improve and enhance their performance through incremental approaches—innovative approaches to product life and organizational performance. And each and every day, organizations consistently make bad decisions and implement ineffective strategies because the purpose of the strategy was to ease the chaos and trauma but not deal with the issues at hand. To create a congruent workplace, one must transform the process of analysis, planning, intervention, and sustainability that often is the hallmark of decision making. What follows is a way to look at that transformation. One needs to get a flavor of the process rather than the process itself because it will be different for each individual or each organization. Therefore, as you read the chapter, focus on how it applies to you and your work, not on the specifics in the case.

THE ANALYSIS PHASE: DISCOVERY

The first issue that organizations must confront is their lack of understanding of the real issues they face. Lacking clarity about the issues is the true challenge, and the primary need of leaders in organizations and other groups is to develop a clear understanding of the factors causing their business strategy to go awry. Clarity is about understanding who you are and what you do. To get there, all organizational leaders must take a deep breath, explain to boards and shareholders that solutions must be time honored, and work toward creating calm among the organizational members to create the space for exploration. If success is to occur, then organizational leaders will need to expand their understanding of knowledge and data. Quantitative data is not the answer; it is only part of the answer. Qualitative data must be obtained honestly to ensure that the underlying themes present in the organization are utilized as equal factors in the development of solutions. Clarity is about taking the risk—up front—to explore the unknown in the organization more than the known. Too often, organizational leaders seek clarity and then make a decision. This is inappropriate because it blocks the other factors that are essential in developing solutions. Therefore, clarity is about the beginning of the process of congruence, not the decision end. Clarity is impacted by your beliefs, your thoughts, and your utilizations and valuing of the four capitals.

Consider one client who stated that changing the culture was essential to replicating healthcare success in the Southwest as it was accomplished in the Midwest. When challenged to seek clarity, he discovered that the business model of a specialty practice that existed in the Midwest was not going to exist in the Southwest. Instead, an HMO practice was the norm and was within the value set of the community capital of the region. This impacted the success of the existing business model. Profit from the existing specialty practice was $15.47 per transaction, and profit from the HMO practice was $1.57 per transaction. Thus, the profit margin desired would never be accomplished using the old business model. What was necessary was increasing the market base by adhering to the beliefs and capital management issues of the region. What did this mean? First, it indicates that how people were valued and how healthcare was viewed were uniquely different. In the Midwest, preventive healthcare was the high value, so specialty practice work was successful. However, the Southwest was more crisis driven in healthcare. Fewer people had health insurance; more pediatric work for children and more obstetric work for newborns were the norm. Families in the area were more concerned with economic sustainability based on racial and ethnic matters, and the traditional Eurocentric medical model was not the same. More midwifery, alternative medicine, and cultural remedies were the drivers, where culture (community capital), people's recommendations based on care (human capital), and historical precedent (political capital) were utilized in the communal decision process than money or appearance (resource capital). The issues for the community were reversed. The challenge for the healthcare organization was "sitting with the data" and integrating its meaning into their thinking rather than making a decision and implementing a program change.

The organization was accustomed to classical thinking—seeking the *what* and *why*—while the community was more communication and field oriented in its thinking—seeking an understanding of the *how* (credibility) and *when* (caution and safety). What the organization said was not important; no Eurocentric organization had, on its face, credibility. The important thing was what persons of influence within the community said about the healthcare organization. This view immediately allowed the organization to recognize that its Eurocentric look from the Midwest did not engender comfort or competence in the community. Instead, it spoke of arrogance and discount of the community. Success, at least at one level, would require changing the appearance of the institution to accurately reflect the community. But here was the real battle: What if those people, those persons of color, those persons who were not trained in the same "specialty practice model," did not fit the culture of the organization that had made the organization great? What would occur?

The challenge for the organization was to move beyond clarity to collaboration. Collaboration is about movement from the one (myopia) to the many (diversity). To be effective, the healthcare organization had to look at other ways of knowing and thinking. It had to move to a systems perspective of working rather than to an individual processing model that was the norm for the organization. It required movement from competition—the normal model of business development (competing with other hospital systems) to collaboration and competence. It had to give up power and control—being the best—to influence (meeting the need). In effect, it had to look at the world differently. You might ask, how?

The next phase of discovery was recognizing that it had moved to a community without any complements (anchors) outside of the healthcare industry. It had established within the community "walls rather than membranes"—traditional models of healthcare management where the doctor is the expert—the decision maker. In its action to be the expert, the organization established its strategy to the discount and partnership of the patient and the community—the family—and the church—the witch doctor, brouhah, or seer. Anchors required a true focus on harmony, bonding, trusting, and honoring of the four capitals. Risking and learning how to embrace resources and people, how to influence communities and communal values, becomes a hallmark of using congruence thinking to develop behavioral strategies. To reach this outcome, the organization first had to accept accountability and ownership for their unintentional arrogance. They had to disclose the arrogance to the community, and they had to acknowledge that, behaviorally, help was needed to be a success and a true partner within the community. These three steps—clarity, collaboration, and complements—represented the discovery stages for the organization. They represented the analysis of thinking that established the dysfunctions of original thought by the organizational leaders.

Behaviorally, these first three stages have consequences in business and human performance. In the business paradigm, systemic empowerment, reciprocity, and representation are the factors that must be addressed. In the case before us, the healthcare organization recognized that its approach of arrogance—its approach of knowing what is best in healthcare and serving the community—was its downfall in its attempts at successful healthcare management. The first recognition was that the experts model did not lend itself very well to issues of empowerment for the employees or the community. Therefore, whatever new strategy was developed, it had to embrace empowerment of all in decision making, organizational and performance structure, service delivery modeling, and people behavior if the model was to meet the communal needs of the client base to be served. Second, the business model would need to embrace the thought issue of collaboration and the behavioral issues embedded in reciprocity—the give and take. Last, medical care and management needed to be a representation of all affected by the healthcare. This would mean that an experts approach might not be as successful as a case conference approach which would involve physicians, mental health professionals (clinical and organizational psychologists, specialty and organizational psychiatrists), social workers, church leaders, family members, and family support system members. Although the process might seem unwieldy, the reality was that differing ways of knowing and differing world views would expand the options and capacities needed to craft strategies that fostered harmony, bonding, trusting, and honoring of the client and the healthcare system.

Yet another area of behavioral awareness comes from the human paradigm. For the clients and the healthcare system, discord, emergence, and disclosure were essential if true discovery was to occur in this analysis phase. Discord represents the chaotic desire in individuals to struggle and expunge whatever is causing discomfort. For some it is the recognition that they are gay; for others it is the recognition that they have participated in their own disempowerment; for still others it is the recognition that a Messianic complex exists in the profession and that their advice is self-serving rather than altruistic. Speaking about the emergence of the feelings and their impacts leads to disclosure—revelations and awareness for all involved. The disclosure also allows everyone to experience the humanity involved, thus giving grace periods (or as my kids call it— tax-free behavior) for the moments and the trauma caused.

We now have the makings of true analysis (quantitative and qualitative data, dialogue, explorations, discoveries, phenomenological inquiries, hermeneutic inquiries) that can give real meaning to the issues before the company and its client base. The building of a congruent workplace began with a discovery— the analysis process—of clarifying the known and unknown, collaborating to move from the one to the many, and assessing and developing complements by risking to learn.

PLANNING: LEARNING TO JUMP THE BROOM AND CREATE, NOT INNOVATE

The second level of building a congruent workplace focuses on planning. Planning is about movement, and in this context movement is about creativity and choices. Creativity is the hallmark of this process. Earlier in chapter 7 innovation was discussed as a process of reawakening the dead. Creativity is about originality and authenticity. Critical to this development process is the recognition that authenticity—a balancing of who you are with your values and belief—is the driver in creating change. The most important aspect of recognizing that authenticity and operating within one's authentic space is learning to operate in calm, not in chaos. Thus, all change planning comes from the inside of the person and the organization—not the external spaces. The person, the organization, the client base, and the community make up internal spaces. The organization is therefore challenged to use passion and emotion to create authenticity and to focus on commitment to transformation, searching within that transformation for the diversity that can drive thought and action.

Choice is about acceptance or abdication of responsibility. People choose to make decisions that honor and propel them to new ways of being, knowing, and doing. Alternatively, people choose to make decisions that mire them in their history and their dysfunctions. Choice therefore becomes the critical space between acting and thinking, establishing the necessary balance in the analysis phase that has gone before. If done well, it focuses on liberation and transformation and becomes the alignment space between what is believed and desired and what is operational.

To elucidate this issue of planning, a different client represented a lighting industry in a small elite California Bay community. The organization was led by individuals steeped in the values and beliefs of the 1960s. Communalism, freedom, love and joy, peace and growth dominated the thoughts and behaviors of the employees. However, their work was in the field of lighting systems for automobiles, and their secondary business was the development of unique home lighting fixtures. The company was discovering that although it had lost 40% of its market share over the past ten years, it was not really changing. The values of the company had allowed it to give 10% of its profit base to community organizations and homeless projects annually—actualizing some of the reasons that the employees chose to work for the organization. In addition the employees had an iron-clad agreement with the company that no one would ever be laid off.

All this sounds great for those of you who go back to 1960s. However, the new CFO was discovering that the company could not be sustained with the existing agreements. He believed that the organization needed to downsize, focus on its core business—headlights for automobiles—and look at the production cycle and the total transaction costs if it was to become profitable. He also believed that the company's consensus model of decision making was the major reason for the company's lack of success. Consensus took too much time, being always focused on compromise, and reduced the overall quality factors he believed essential for the organization.

The analysis processes utilized revealed that adherence to the values and beliefs of the organizational leaders and the employees was more important than the production of headlights. Phenotypically, most consultants would suggest that the CFO and CEO, along with their boards, sell the company, take the profits from the sale, and look for a different type of business for investment purposes. The process of congruence building in the planning process looks at different strategies because planning maximizes congruence—even when that plan radically transforms the business model and business paradigm. What was done instead was a surprise to the CFO, CEO, and the Board.

The analysis revealed that the company was in the wrong line of business. All members of the organization were environmental science graduates who believed in the issue of sustainability. Caught up in the profit issues of the 1980s and 1990s, the organization had gone down a path of production–transaction management rather than green research, management, and development. In addition, the need to continually explore options and possibilities of lighting sources did not fit in with the hustle and bustle of meeting tight deadlines and schedules required of car manufacturers. In effect, the organization's employee and leadership base was not in sync with the mindset necessary for success in production and manufacturing environments.

In initiating the planning, the company determined that true congruence would require that the business shift its focus from manufacturing to research and development. Since environmental science was the employees' real love, focusing on the development of alternative light sources, solar power management systems, compost energy systems, and community partnering activities would be more compatible with their values and beliefs. To make the shift, the CFO bought the manufacturing side of the business, while the CEO and the original employees looked at building a business process that used a nonprofit management business model rather than a profit business model. The planning also showed that the organization still believed in giving to the community, keeping everyone on board, and seeking to expand capacity in creating harmony, trust, human and communal bonds, and faith with the community. Time was spent identifying anchors in the political community, the foundation community, partnerships with other nonprofit and profit organizations that were dedicated or devoted to "green causes," and building an action plan that looked at synergistic movements in the green community.

The organization also began developing relationships with universities such as Antioch University and its whole systems design degree program, the Institute for Transformative Thought and Learning for Think Tank and Research Services, and numerous other organizations for true partnerships. The planning phase generated more operating capital for the company than the manufacturing side of the business had ever achieved. The organization now focuses on consulting to communities, collaboration projects on environmental science and environmental engineering, and development of alternative light sources for community and individual consumption.

On the other side, the CFO's purchase of the manufacturing side of the business has turned out to be a dismal failure. He functioned with business principles, business strategies, performance models, and transaction analyses but still lost his shrinking component of the market to Spectronics Corporation. He is now out of business. This example, might suggest that an incongruent workplace strategy, a strategy that focuses on the resource capital alone and not a balance of all four capitals, ultimately costs organizations their future and their sustainability.

The planning process revealed awareness that took a different path than traditional paths of self-destruction or self-indulgence that are often present in business planning and business modeling. Behaviorally, of equality and acknowledgment were the drivers in the planning process. Equality focused on the potential of each organizational decision and strategy to empower, represent, and allow for reciprocity. It was essential as the values and beliefs were significantly tied to world view beliefs. Continually acknowledging the influence of beliefs on the planned actions was essential to the success of the planning process. From identifying the step-by-step strategies to ensuring that each planning activity somehow aligned with values and beliefs was essential to the success of the planning. Lighting the world with heart and integrity was a mantra that could never be forgotten. What was more important was the recognition that planning and analysis, with heart and head in tow, can yield results and strategies that creatively balance what is desired with what is operational; what is heartfelt with what is actionable; and what is congruent with who one is. The possibilities of success are endless. The reality—analyze and plan in calm, not chaos—and the options are just ends.

THE INTERVENTION PROCESS: CREATING AWARENESSES THAT UNLEASH ORGANIZATIONAL AND PERSONAL POTENTIAL

Intervention is the path to congruent sustainability. Historically, the concept of intervention comes from a clinical psychological framework in which areas of dysfunction are identified, the possibilities are diagnosed, a plan is implemented, and clients move from one space in history to another. Over time, interventions have embraced the concept of a new software program, a new training program, the initiation and implementation of a new fad like the "seven habits of highly effective people," the "five disciplines," the "one-minute manager," the "managerial grid." Interventions have worked in clinical and industrial/organizational psychology in those spaces where thinking and acting have been balanced as a planned strategy. Where interventions have failed has been where the actions of the intervener have myopically focused on one capital rather than all four. Much of my work as a consultant comes from interventions requested by organizations where large consultant firms have focused on an externality—a product, a software package, a new accounting system, a new inventory management system—for the solution to the issues. In effect, corporations, leaders, governments, and nonprofits have been duped into believing that something from outside of who they are and what they do will save the day. It's hogwash because the critical organizational and personal entity necessary for successful movement from one place in history to another has been thwarted or discounted. *People are the critical ingredient in any intervention. It is people who must understand; people who must implement; people who must believe in the new strategy; people who must help in the development of the strategy, AND it is people who must have the revelations and ahas if they are going to expunge the culture of silence.*

So we begin there with the intervention. Intervention is about exploring the unknown and the unconscious—about understanding what is complex without falling prey to the belief that everything and every answer is simplistic. To intervene is to recognize the multileveled factors and impacts of blocks to effective human and organizational performance. First in this process of intervention is speaking what is not spoken—real truths and real secrets that often become sacred cows in the organization and its functioning. These secrets and sacred cows make up the culture of silence, blocking any real potential of organizations to move—transform, if you will—from the historical trappings to new beginnings. As one expunges the sacred cows and secrets and the culture of silence, one discovers that the "pedagogical—banking process—'do it my way and I will scratch your back'—becomes less critical" in the scheme of achieving revelations and ahas. The second step is not accepting on face value any issue raised because people need to experience the anchoring process with interveners. This requires effective building and management of the bonding, harmony, truth telling, and giving grace that is a component of the anchor-building process. Without achieving the anchor, movement to a new space is not possible.

Think of all the times when conflicts in your organization were left unresolved. It is not the strategy that mattered in the long run; it was the healing of the broken space—the broken trust—the broken bond that mattered and liberated the other person to transform him- or herself. It is the same with systemic intervention within an organization. Heal the space of pain and violence, and the possibilities are endless. This becomes an important awareness for all executives and leaders. You cannot skirt the issues of pain that are created by your organizational actions. People are as important to the success equation as any product or service agenda or any business system that you may purchase. Paying PeopleSoft or Oracle $2 million for their Human Resource Information System does no good if you have not planned to meet the real emerging needs of the employees throughout the organization. It is not the business system that will allow one's organization to be successful, but the people who make or break the success. Therefore, any intervention must focus on human thinking and behavior as does any other business dynamic. As discussed earlier in the book, people behavior is the most critical factor in systemic organizational success.

Consider the following. A government social service agency has been led by a dysfunctional executive for ten years. His theoretical background in social service, and his educational and performance would suggest that he could succeed in organizational management and leadership. During the past ten years, nine consulting organizations have provided him with analyses indicating that dysfunction is rampant in his organization in the areas of structure, people behavior, environment, and decision making. The reports have also shown that the impacts of his actions have been increased competition among divisions that must complement one another in the work and charges of racial and gender discrimination for his insensitivity to the community being served and the client needs.

The charges spoken of in the example of the healthcare organization are the same here. Expert strategies discount the client, and the focus has been on political capital—I can do whatever I want as long as I fool the board of commissioners and manage the information—with the culture of silence I will win—rather than on balancing all four capitals in the work. Intervention sometimes requires the removal of the head by bringing to consciousness the thinking and behavior of the leader and how that style has blocked effective human and organizational performance. In this case, the leader was a theological/legal personality with a thinking style of scientific dynamic. In this style, the leader believed that following the rules, having no chaos, adhering to tight boundaries, and bringing no bad news consituted the order of the day and the manner in which directors underneath him should respond to his thoughts and directives. If there was a problem, or if he was threatened, he moved to his legal belief style, which was about gaining more power and control to create comfort for himself. From a thought perspective, his scientific dynamic thought process focused on political skill and aptitude, not competence. He was concerned only with the *Who* and *When*—Blame and Shame. Nothing was ever his responsibility. He was never accountable, and ownership was not an option.

To break that cycle, the intervention focused on uncovering all the thought styles and belief structures of all the leadership, with particular attention to how all the thinking needed to work together. In the process, the leaders and managers revealed their secrets and their culture of silence, explicitly identifying the impediments to growth, change, and development. You have a winner when you can break the history and the sacred cows to liberate potential for transformation. In this case, the leader has moved on, an interim leader has been selected who operates based on a field theory thinking style (credibility is the watchword), and movement is occurring within the organization.

From a business behavioral perspective, the focus was on altering interpretation and enhancing commitment. Because of the need for secrets and the culture of silence, policies, procedures, practices, and strategies were interpreted differently for each employee. Commitment was essential because people make mistakes as they try things, and a new culture of moving toward a just end was necessary, honoring and recognizing that mistakes are a part of growth rather than an indictment of competence.

SUSTAINABILITY: WALKING YOUR TALK

The greatest disappointment that employees experience in the workplace *following* a change effort or an improvement process is the retrenchment by the organization when chaos and crises occur. Phenotypically, organizations revert to old power and control behaviors, inhibiting the potential of employees to continue on creative pathways. Organizations make statements such as "it's only for the short term; new situations cause us to create different strategies; we will return to our planned strategy when the crisis is over" and actually mean the statements made in the face of crisis and ambiguity. Unfortunately, the retrenchment speaks to poor planning and lack of commitment to congruence. When retrenchment occurs, one falls back on history, that is, what worked before can get us through the crunch period. In reality, returning to old strategies rekindles the old issues much more than it resolves them.

Walking your talk, being congruent, is about paying attention to the harmony developing within the organization. It also means that history can be helpful when one considers the successes versus the deficits in the historical auditing process. The sustainability process is about one's commitment to balance and alignment. The balance and alignment must focus on the teams, individuals, processes, and outcomes—and it must be done in concert with the context that one sets for what and how the organization will function. The context is determined not only by the product or service provided but also by the culture and community served. To that end, sustainability is about matching work outcomes with the organizational context, matching people placement to the belief systems and thought styles of the people relative to the work that has to be performed, and expanding the market share by exploring the inclusive issues of diversity, gender, ethnicity, and culture. Sustainability is about staying focused on the whole and not being tripped up by the tangents that arise to thwart progress.

Tangents arise from people, systems, competitors, and partners because not everyone's system is in concert with everyone else's system. Agendas, histories, significant emotional events, and timing spaces all contribute to out-of-sync thinking and behavior. The organizational challenge is to pay attention to "off-center" thoughts and actions and establish strategies that move everyone and all systems toward balance and alignment. Staying focused on the thinking and the action and its relationship to human and organizational performance becomes key to continual and congruent success.

THE OVERVIEW

An overview is important here because the context is so important. The continual challenge in today's business and personal relationships is to focus not on the content, but on the context and processes that permit framing what we see and do. Staying in the context about who we are keeps us focused on the just ends and personal prizes that support honoring, bonding, trusting, giving, perceiving, and belonging. Preserving the context allows us to see the whole of human and organizational performance rather than getting trapped in specific events or incidences that may in fact be tangents that derail a great strategy or plan. We are used to tangents; we are not used to contexts. So that becomes our challenge.

Chapter 12

Where We Go from Here: Risking Being You, All of You

So where do we go from here? What risks can we take to be different in the present and future from what we have been in our past? What reality exists for being oneself rather than a facade and mask that we think the organization and even our families want us to be? The challenge is in the questions, and the answers are there as well. *We must be ourselves if we are to experience congruence in our work, family, and play.*

Table 12.1 details the comprehension of the approach that challenges each leader or manager and each employee to focus on the balance of thinking and acting, the alignment of people and the organization. You might ask, however, where and how can this system be utilized? Here are some areas of discovery.

UTILIZATION OF THE CONGRUENCE DEVELOPMENT PROCESS

Organizational Restructures and Changes

The traditional strategies for restructuring and change are often economically driven rather than systemically driven. The congruence development process requires the utilization of people and system issues, system and process strategies, thought and action. Rarely has a process been developed that demands equity in thought and action, *before* implementation of any plan or course of action. This system therefore challenges each leader or manager to consider the *whole* before addressing any piece of the puzzle.

To be fully congruent and to fully address organizational issues, the challenge is in taking the complex rather than the simple path. Complexity is where the known and unknown, the conscious and unconscious meet. Simplicity and quick

Table 12.1
Creating Congruence in the Workplace

CONGRUENCE PHASES	THOUGHT MOVEMENTS	BEHAVIOR MOVEMENTS		PROCESS TECHNOLOGIES
		Paradigms		
		Business	Human	
Analysis	Clarity Collaboration Complements	Empowerment Reciprocity Representation	Discord Emergence Disclosure	• Belief Systems • Four Capital Analyses • Ways of Knowing • Intrapsychic Structure • Paradigm Thinking Systems
Planning	Creativity Choice	Equality	Acknowledgment	• World Perspective • Strategic Planning • Detailed Work Breakdown Structure • Thematic Analysis
Intervention	Complexity	Interpretation Commitment	Self-Indulgence Reemergence	• System Connection Strategy (Theoretical Perspective) • Process Connection Strategy (Psychological Development)
Sustainability	Congruence	Wholeness	Congruence	• Historical Auditing (Thought Sustainability) • Process Paradigms (Behavior Sustainability)

answers never get one there, and the loss for the organization and the people becomes insurmountable.

Human Resource Management

Human resources represents the soul of an organization (Williams, 1996), accountable for the role prescriptions that drive personal and organizational functioning. Sadly, today's human resource departments have abdicated their accountability and integrity to speak truth for the least of the employees. Policies, rules, practices, and strategies are often the source of organizational violence, and the compliance stance of human resources contributes to the demise of the employee and the organization.

If human resources is to impact the development of organizational systems, then human resources must speak truth in the halls of corporate America. Currently, human resources bears the brunt of organizational jokes and ridicule. The congruence development system allows human resource professionals to effectively explore the full dimensions of employee and organizational pain. Being at the decision table, conducting comprehensive qualitative and quantitative analyses, and planning more comprehensively and intervening with heart and courage form the only path to understanding the complex issues of our day.

Conflict Management

Organizations still see conflict, labor relations, and employee relations as anathema to systemic comfort. To that end, organizations seek the easy path, the control path, and the power stance to ensure sustainability, not recognizing that the power approaches create incongruous competition and strategies to quell the violence received. The congruence development system allows conflicts to be explored in a joint process of discovery, creating options—choices, if you will—for ensuring that the totality of situations and events are uncovered and addressed in appropriate venues.

Administrative Management

Administration—finance, accounting, inventory management, operations management, human resources, and executive management—are all areas of organizational performance that can benefit from an approach that permits the attainment of needed information for effective decision making. Often within organizations, administration is a driver that utilizes inappropriate measures in the decision and action process, creating pain, trauma, sadness, discomfort, and bad actions. The congruence development system can alter that action and the perceptions often created in the minds of employees and stakeholders of the organization.

Creating change and focusing on creation becomes a critical first step in exploring the options of decisions. Remember, the business school process is designed to focus on the compartments, *not the whole*. To create movement, then, requires a fresh look through a new set of lenses that honor the system and all of its parts.

Mergers and Acquisitions

Owners of a consulting organization, Emerge, use a cultural due diligence process to help firms focus on their choices in the merger and acquisition process. Their process system does not mention the necessity to think differently about the whole and the pieces as a performance strategy of operation. The congruence development system focuses on the missing pieces of their system of change. Whether one thinks of governance in the terms used by Senge, structure and process by Schein, Minuchin's systems of interconnectivity, Gibb's system of trust, Covey's systems of habit, or Goldsmith's system of evaluation for change, the challenge for mergers and acquisitions and the leaders who support them is to be thorough—seeking congruity of thought and action between potential mergers and acquisitions.

This system permits effective exploration and discovery of alignments and balances between organizations. Research shows that more than 80% of the attempts fail within eighteen months to three years. It therefore becomes increasingly important that different strategies be employed to create success, not just short-term fiscal gains.

Clinical Therapy

Although this book has not focused on the clinical development of individuals, there is an inherent utilization of this process in healing the dysfunctions of individuals, families, and groups. Succinctly stated, therapeutic options that address only the behavior of individuals end up replicated in some other form of dysfunction. This is critical in the larger scheme of things. Therapists have acquiesced to strategies at the behest of insurance leaders. As a result, the critical therapeutic approaches and needs of the client have been discounted to the detriment of the therapeutic relationship and value. In effect, not having the courage to challenge the insurance industry has meant that the profession has lost.

The true challenge for clinical therapy is to balance the thinking of clients with their behavior. In that approach, clients begin to think through their issues and their participation in their dysfunctions, choosing to alter their actions to match their changed thoughts. The impacts are enormous.

A PERSPECTIVE ON THOUGHT AND ACTION

Where does one get the courage to be fully oneself? Some say that it comes from God, a higher power. Others says it comes from being born into positions of power. Still others say it comes from being oppressed and trying to make a difference. In many ways it could be all of these. However, I sense that real courage comes from an exploration of who you are and what you do with your understanding of self. The challenge for me has come from being a member of many groups and trying to make sense of the interrelationships between all of them. I learned early from my father that everything can be taken away from you except your dreams and your education. Therefore, my father always said to get the best education you can and live your dreams.

My life mentor, Dr. Jack Gibb, always told me that courage comes from one's ability to trust and risk being open to the world. When you listen to what the world offers and you hear it, the world is open to you. His dream for me was to become a serious theorist and writer, and to empower others through the creation of a different voice than what was in the world.

Paulo Freire set the stage for the other component of my sense of me with his dialogues on authenticity. The concepts of being fully human, living with the world—not just in the world—have impacted me more than any other concepts. As he believed, when one embraces their humanity, one sees the real truths of liberation and freedom. I think that is the real challenge for all of us.

So, in the final analysis, we are all challenged to be trust-oriented, risk-taking, authentic beings focused on freedom and liberation—awareness and understanding—as the outcome of being fully human. It was interesting for me as I thought of that process command. The trust and risk components said to me that all the competition, manipulation, abuse, subterfuge, and other actions of destruction that exist in families and groups are about keeping all of us disjointed, apart, separate, and not fully human. Unfortunately, we seem to have transferred all of those human deficits to our world of business and education.

Business should serve as a metaphor for living, instilling courage, passion, honor, integrity, accountability, truth, and human advancement. Too often, it serves as just the opposite, blaming everyone and anything for any deficits that occur. Each time business participates in trying to dominate; each time business demands loyalty and secrecy and then proceeds to dismiss the humanity in all of us; each time we trick, use, manipulate, discount, attack, and shame others and justify our actions as "right for business," everyone loses.

If business is to impact and sustain our society, the business paradigm of the present and future must embrace both humanity and congruence. A friend of mine who had recently returned from Amsterdam was struck by the differences in the people's attitudes versus his experiences in the States. When asked what the difference was, his first comment was that America was young, adolescent, and full of itself much as teenagers often are. He believed that what we thought was power was arrogance and delusion. He felt ashamed of his behavior and the behavior of others who had traversed the waters with him, for in their time in Amsterdam, they acted like Americans—dominating and ordering—controlling and abusing. He asked, "why is our society so dysfunctional, so quick to judge, to abuse, and to take the easy road rather than walk the slow path to understanding and smelling the roses?" As I thought about his question, I was filled with sadness because there was so much truth to his question. We are a nation of domination and control. We exhibit it in our laws, our churches, our businesses, and our families. We respond negatively to the fullness of time and the fullness of information. We do seek the easy, fast path, for most that we do. We are incongruent as a nation and as representatives of humanity, and if we choose not to stop—get off the merry-go-round—and create a different path or strategy, we will continue to lose. Here are some final suggestions for all of us as we consider our role and our responsibility to ourselves.

1. *Take time to understand yourself*—in work, in play, in relationships to others, and in relationships to the family. Give yourself time to explore the values and beliefs that truly shape who you are.

2. *Suspend your personal judgment of others so that they can suspend theirs of you.* In work and in play, we often expect others to see the world as we do, act in the world as we do, criticize the world as we do. Stop the cycle and applaud and explore the diversity of all that we see around us. From small business to conglomerate, from an all-Eurocentric place of business to an extremely diverse society, search for the commonalities, collaborations, and complements in your lives and then build on the discovery.

3. *Keep things and events in perspective.* If I am truly correct as others profess to be that systems exist and govern our lives, then look for the congruence and complexity that surround us. Venture beyond what you can see to what you can't see. Explore what you understand and struggle to sense what you don't understand.

4. *Match what you do to who you are.* The large business is often a coalition of the small ones that used to be. Perhaps it is time to go slow and not go ahead at all.

You hang on to your best people by taking risks, having faith, trusting in their creativity, and challenging your assumptions about self and others. Therefore, I now challenge you. Challenge your assumptions, your realities, and your dreams and truly become. *Create congruence in your workplace, challenging your people and your organization.*

Bibliography

There are numerous purposeful omissions from this bibliography. Throughout the book, there are references to authors and their contributions that are
not cited in the bibliography. The lack of a citation is based on the general
influence of the author, not a specific work that summarizes their contribution. These authors are well known and thus, numerous works could
suggest an appropriate citation. To that end, they are not listed here.

ARTICLES AND REPORTS

Organizational Psychology

Agunis, H., and Kraiger, K. (1997). Industrial and Organizational Psychology Programme
at the University of Colorado at Denver. *International Journal of Selection and
Assessment* 5(1): 69.

Bass, B. M., and Denth, P. J. (Eds.). (1987). Advances in Organizational Psychology:
An International Review. *Books on Demand* 6: 47–54.

Bond, M., Smith, H., and Peter, B. (1996). Cross Cultural Social and Organizational
Psychology. *Annual Review of Psychology* 47: 205.

Cooper, C. L., and Robertson, I. T. (1997). Organizational Studies. *International Review
of Industrial and Organizational Psychology* 10(4): 727.

Cooper, C. L., Robertson, I. T., and Austin, J. T. (1993). Contemporary Psychology.
International Review of Industrial and Organizational Psychology 8(6): 572.

Cropanzano, J. N., and Thornton, G.C.R. III. (1995). Industrial/Organizational Psychology Program. *International Journal of Selection and Assessment* 3(4): 242.

Dipboye, R. L., Smith, C. S., and Howell, W. C. (1995). Understanding Industrial and
Organizational Psychology: An Integrated Approach. *Contemporary Psychology*
40(10).

Dunnette, M. D., Hough, L. M., and Rousseau, D. M. (1995). Contemporary Psychology. *International Review of Industrial and Organizational Psychology* 3(12): 1142.

Grace, W. C., Fernandez, M. I., Battjes, R. J., and Sloboda, Z. (1994). Organizational Psychology Perspectives on Enhancing National HIV Prevention Research among Drug Abusers. *Psychology of Addictive Behaviors* 8(3): 191.

Hantula, D. A. (1998). The Virtual Industrial/Organizational Psychology: Class Learning and Teaching in Cyberspace in Three Iterations. *Behavior Research Methods, Instruments & Computers* 30(2): 205–210.

Katzell, R. A. (1994). Understanding Organizational Psychology. *Contemporary Psychology* 39(1).

Kelley, K. (Ed.). (1993). Issues, Theory and Research in Industrial/Organizational Psychology. *Contemporary Psychology* 38(12).

Koppes, L. L. (1997). American Female Pioneers of Industrial and Organizational Psychology during the Early Years. *Journal of Applied Psychology* 82(4): 500.

Landy, F. J. (1997). Early Influences on the Development of Industrial and Organizational Psychology. *Journal of Applied Psychology* 82(4): 467.

Lyons, D. (1997). The Feminine in the Foundations of Organizational Psychology. *The Journal of Applied Behavioral Science* 33(1): 7.

Sanna, L. J., and Parks, C. D. (1997). Group Research Trends in Social and Organizational Psychology: Whatever Happened to Intragroup Research? *Psychological Science* 8(4): 261.

Tilberg University, The Netherlands. (1996). Research Unit on Work and Organizational Psychology. *International Journal of Selection and Assessment* 4(2): 106.

Triandis, H. C., Dunnette, M. D., Hough, L. M., and Roznowski, M. (1997). Organizational Psychology: Approaches to Organizational Change. *Handbook of Industrial and Organizational Psychology* 4: 834–885.

Venerable, G. (1995). Ven Matrix: A Scientific Assessment of Change and Development. Presentation at the conference on Melanin, San Francisco State University. In L. Williams, *Business Decisions, Human Choices: Restoring the Partnership Between People and Their Organizations*. Westport, CT: Quorum Books, 1996.

Wann, D. L. (1994). Developing Fantasy Organizations in Industrial/ Organizational Psychology Courses. *Teaching Psychology* 21(3): 177.

Business Ethics

Adams, R., and Whyte, W. (1991). Speech to the American Association of Collegiate Schools of Business, Washington, DC.

AGOCS. (1997). Institutionalized Resistance to Organizational Change: Denial, Inaction and Repression. *Journal of Business Ethics* 16(9): 917–931.

Annual Report. (1999). National Bureau of Professional Management Consultants, San Diego, CA.

Astley, W. G. (1983). Central Perspectives and Debates in Organization Theory. *Administrative Science Quarterly* 28(16): 245–273.

Boje, D. M. (1982). A Qualitative Step in OD Interventions: Myth Making. *Journal of Applied Behavioral Science* 24(12): 342–347.

Burke, R. J. (1997). Save the Males: Backlash in Organizations. *Journal of Business Ethics* 16(9): 933–942.

Establishing Community Need. (1998). National Forum of Black Public Administrators and the International City Managers Association. *Journal of Public Administration* 35: 45–53.

Goldberg, B. (1997). Lou Harris to Speak. *Colorado Business Magazine* 24(7): 55.

Gregory, K. (1983). Native View Paradigms: Multiple Cultures and Culture Conflicts in Organizations. *Administrative Science Quarterly* 28(3): 359–376.

Harrison, R. (1972). Understanding Your Organization's Character. *Harvard Business Review* 25(16): 142–148.

———. (1983). Organizational Culture. *Administrative Science Quarterly* 28(3): 122–126.

Jennings, M. (1998). Case Studies in Business Ethics: The Case of Buffalo Pioneering. *The Journal of Consulting Psychology* (August).

Joyce, W. (1979). Climates in Organizations. *Organizational Behavior* 2(4): 317–333.

Maier, M. (1997). Gender Equity: Organizational Transformation and Challenges. *Journal of Business Ethics* 16(9): 943–962.

Mallinger, M. (1997). Decisive Decision Making: An Exercise Using Ethical Frameworks. *Journal of Management Education* 21(3): 411–417.

Martin, J. (1983). The Uniqueness Paradox in Organizational Stories. *Administrative Science Quarterly* 28(3): 438–453.

Merger and Acquisition Study. (2000). *The Economist*, July 22.

1999 Emerging Workforce Study. (1999). *Business Week*, March 1.

Rosengren, W. (1984). Environmental Conditions and Organizational Change: Rational vs. Natural Systems. *Human Organization* 43(1): 54–60.

Social/Cultural Studies

Lordan, E. (1997). The Whole Truth and Nothing But the Truth: Testing the Ethical Standards of Your Employees and Recruits. *Public Relations Quarterly* 42(2): 29–31.

Moorthy, R. S., and DeGeorge, R. T. (1998). Uncompromising Integrity: Motorola's Global Challenge. *Motorola University Press* (January): 28–36.

Wilkins, A., and Ouchi, W. (1983). Efficient Cultures: Exploring the Relationship between Cultures and Organizational Performance. *Administrative Science Quarterly* 28(14): 468–481.

BOOKS

Research

Best, J., and Kahn, J. (1998). *Research in Education* (8th ed.). Boston: Allyn and Bacon.

Denzin, N. (1989). *Interpretive Biography*. Thousand Oaks, CA: Sage Publications.

———. (1994). *Handbook of Qualitative Research*. Thousand Oaks, CA: Sage Publications.

Goleman, D. (1995). *Emotional Intelligence*. New York: Bantam Books.

Harris, M. (1998). *Basic Statistics for Behavioral Science Research* (2nd ed.). Boston: Allyn and Bacon.

Hopkins, K. D. (1998). *Educational and Psychological Measurement and Evaluation* (8th ed.). Boston: Allyn and Bacon.

Leedy, P. D., and Ormrod, J. E. (2001). *Practical Research: Planning and Design* (7th ed.). Upper Saddle River, NJ: Merrill Prentice Hall.

Merleau-Ponty, J. (1962, 1965). *Cosmologie du XXe siècle: Étude épistémologique et historique des théories de la cosmologie contemporaine.* [Paris:] Gallimard.

Moustakas, C. (1990). *Heuristic Research.* Newbury Park, CA: Sage Publications.

———. (1994). *Phenomenological Research Methods.* Newbury Park, CA: Sage Publications.

Patton, M. (1990). *Qualitative Evaluation and Research Methods.* Newbury Park, CA: Sage Publications.

Schultz, A. (1967). *The Phenomenology of the Social World.* Evanston, IL: Northwestern University Press.

Organizational Psychology, Organizational Development, and Organizational Transformation

Badaracco, J., and Ellsworth, R. (1989). *Leadership and the Quest for Integrity.* Boston: Harvard Business School Press.

Beehr, T. A. (1995). *Basic Organizational Psychology.* Boston: Allyn and Bacon.

Birnbaum, M., and Birnbaum, S. (1981). *Organizational Theory: A Structural and Behavioral Analysis* (4th ed.). Homewood, IL: Richard Irwin.

Cassell, C. (Ed.). (1994). *Qualitative Research Methods in Organizational Psychology: A Practical Guide.* Thousand Oaks, CA: Sage Publications.

Checkland, P. (1993). *Systems Thinking, Systems Practice.* New York: John Wiley and Sons.

Gedo, J., and Goldberg, A. (1973). *Models of the Mind.* Chicago: University of Chicago Press.

Gibb, J. (1978). *Trust: A New View of Personal and Organizational Development.* Los Angeles: Guild of Tutors Press.

Hall, R. (1966). *Organizations: Structure, Process and Outcomes.* New York: Delacorte Press.

Hammond, S. (1997). *Organizational Ethics and the Good Life.* New York: Oxford University Press.

Hamner, W. C., and Organ, D. W. (1978). *Organizational Behavior: An Applied Psychological Approach.* Dallas, TX: Business Publications.

Hampden-Turner, C. (1990). *Creating Corporate Culture: From Discord to Harmony.* Reading, MA: Addison-Wesley.

Harman, Hormann. (1990). *Creative Work: The Constructive Role of Business in a Transforming Society.* Indianapolis, IN: Knowledge Systems.

Jackson, J. H., and Morgan, C. (1982). *Organization Theory: A Macro Perspective for Management* (2nd ed.). Englewood Cliffs, NJ: Prentice Hall.

Kanter, R. M. (1983). *The Change Masters: Innovations for Productivity in the American Corporation.* New York: Simon and Schuster.

Kets de Vries, M., and Miller, D. (1984). *The Neurotic Organization.* San Francisco: Jossey-Bass.

Maitlin, M., and Foley, W. (1997). *About Abraham Maslow.* New York: Houghton Mifflin.

McWhinney, W. et al. (1997). *Creating Paths of Change: Managing Issues and Resolving Problems in Organizations* (2nd ed.). Thousand Oaks, CA: Sage Publications.

Muchinsky, P. M. (1993). *Psychology Applied to Work: An Introduction to Industrial and Organizational Psychology* (4th ed.). Pacific Grove, CA: Brooks/Cole.

Robbins, S. P. (1990). *Organization Theory*. Englewood Cliffs, NJ: Prentice Hall.

Rogers, C. (1961). *On Becoming a Person*. Boston: Houghton Mifflin.

Schecter, H. (1995). *Rekindling the Spirit in Work*. Barrytown, NY: Barrytown.

Schein, E. (1979). *Organizational Psychology*. Englewood Cliffs, NJ: Prentice Hall.

———. (1985). *Career Anchors: Discovering Your Real Values*. San Diego, CA: University Associates.

Schultz, D. P., and Schultz, S. E. (1987). *A History of Modern Psychology* (4th ed.). San Diego, CA: Harcourt Brace Jovanovich.

Senge, P. (1990). *The Fifth Discipline: The Art and Practice of the Learning Organization*. New York: Doubleday/Currency.

Siegel, L., and Lane, I. M. (1987). *Personal and Organizational Psychology*. Homewood, IL: Irwin.

Spector, P. E. (1995). *Industrial and Organizational Psychology: Research and Practice*. New York: John Wiley and Sons.

Study of Training Expenditures. (2000). Washington, DC: American Society for Training and Development.

Wheatley, M. (1999). *Leadership and the New Science*. New York: Berrett-Koehler.

Williams, L. C. (1993). *The Congruence of People and Organizations*. Westport, CT: Quorum Books.

———. (1994). *Organizational Violence: Creating a Prescription for Change*. Westport, CT: Quorum Books.

———. (1995). *Human Resources in a Changing Society*. Westport, CT: Quorum Books.

———. (1996). *Business Decisions, Human Choices: Restoring the Partnership Between People and Their Organizations*. Westport, CT: Quorum Books.

Social/Cultural Anthropology

Azumi, K. (1974). *Japanese Society; A Sociological Review: An Introduction to Japanese Civilization*. New York: Columbia University Press.

Bandura, A. (1977). *Social Learning Theory*. Englewood Cliffs, NJ: Prentice Hall.

Blau, P. (1955). *Dynamics of Bureaucracy: A Study of Interpersonal Relations in Two Government Agencies*. Chicago: University of Chicago Press.

Burrell, G. (1982). *Sociological Paradigms and Organizational Analysis*. London: Heinemann.

Deal, T. E., and Kennedy, A. A. (1982). *Corporate Cultures: The Rites and Rituals of Corporate Life*. Reading, MA: Addison-Wesley.

Dennison, D. R. (1990). *Corporate Cultures and Organizational Effectiveness*. New York: John Wiley and Sons.

Freire, P. (1973). *Pedagogy of the Oppressed*. New York: Continuum and Seabury Press.

Hamada, T., and Sibley, W. E. (1994). *Anthropological Perspectives on Organizational Culture*. Lanham, MD: University Press of America.

Taylor, E. B. (1871). *William James on Consciousness beyond the Margin*. Reprint, Princeton, NJ: Princeton University Press, 1996.

Weber, M. (1905). *The Protestant Ethic and the Spirit of Capitalism*. Reprint, Roxbury, MA: Roxbury Publishing Co., 2000.

Business Ethics

Barrett, R. (1998). *Liberating the Corporate Soul: A Values-Driven Approach to Building a Visionary Organization*. Boston: Butterworth-Heinemann.

Barton, L. (1995). *Ethics: The Enemy in the Workplace*. Cincinnati, OH: South-Western.

Bowie, M. E. (1998). *Business Ethics: A Kantian Perspective*. Malden, MA: Blackwell Publishers.

Costa, J. D. (1998). *The Ethical Imperative: Why Moral Leadership Is Good Business*. Reading, MA: Addison-Wesley Longman.

Cowton, C. (Ed.). (1998). *Business Ethics: Perspective on the Practice of Theory*. New York: Oxford University Press.

De George, R. T. (1998). *Business Ethics*. Upper Saddle River, NJ: Prentice Hall.

Getz, D. (1998). *Business, Ethics and Society*. Philadelphia: Ginn Press.

Hartman, E. M. (1996). *Organizational Ethics and the Good Life*. New York: Oxford University Press.

Ingram, L. C. (1995). *The Study of Organizations: Positions, Persons and Patterns*. Westport, CT: Praeger Publishers.

Kumar, B., and Steinmann, H. (1998). *Ethics in International Management*. New York: Walter de Gruyter.

Marx, K. (1859). *Basic Writings on Politics and Philosophy*. Reprint, New York: Anchor Books, 1959.

Newton, L. H., and Ford, M. (1998). *Clashing Views on Controversial Issues in Business Ethics and Society*. New York: McGraw-Hill Higher Education.

O'Connell, C. B. (1991). *A Study of Heinrich Ott's Theological Development: His Hermeneutical and Ontological Programme*. Foreword by Heinrich Ott. New York: Peter Lang.

Rhys-Davis, C. A. (1996). *Buddhist Manual of Psychological Ethics: Creating Ethical Space for Change*. Seoul, Korea: South Asia Press.

Shaw, W. H. (1998). *Business Ethics*. Belmont, CA: Wadsworth Publishing Company.

Werhane, P., and Freeman, R. E. (Eds.). (1998). *The Blackwell Encyclopedic Dictionary of Business Ethics*. Malden, MA: Blackwell Publishers.

Index

About the Author

LLOYD C. WILLIAMS is Professor of Management Leadership in the School of Management, John F. Kennedy University, and an organizational change consultant based in Cave Creek, Arizona. With advanced degrees in the study of organizational psychology, ethics, marriage and family therapy, and personality and culture, he focuses his consulting practice on developmental problems encountered by private, public, and not-for-profit organizations worldwide. His four previous books for Quorum are *The Congruence of People and Organizations* (1993), *Organizational Violence* (1994), *Human Resources in a Changing Society* (1995), and *Business Decisions, Human Choices* (1996).